REFUGEE YOUTH

Migration, Justice and Urban Space

Edited by
Mattias De Backer, Peter Hopkins,
Ilse van Liempt, Robin Finlay,
Elisabeth Kirndörfer, Mieke Kox,
Matthew C. Benwell and Kathrin Hörschelmann

First published in Great Britain in 2024 by

Bristol University Press
University of Bristol
1-9 Old Park Hill
Bristol
BS2 8BB
UK
t: +44 (0)117 374 6645
e: bup-info@bristol.ac.uk

Details of international sales and distribution partners are available at bristoluniversitypress.co.uk

© Bristol University Press 2024

British Library Cataloguing in Publication Data
A catalogue record for this book is available from the British Library

ISBN 978-1-5292-2100-8 hardcover
ISBN 978-1-5292-2101-5 paperback
ISBN 978-1-5292-2102-2 ePub
ISBN 978-1-5292-2103-9 ePdf

The right of Mattias De Backer, Peter Hopkins, Ilse van Liempt, Robin Finlay, Elisabeth Kirndörfer, Mieke Kox, Matthew C. Benwell and Kathrin Hörschelmann to be identified as editors of this work has been asserted by them in accordance with the Copyright, Designs and Patents Act 1988.

All rights reserved: no part of this publication may be reproduced, stored in a retrieval system, or transmitted in any form or by any means, electronic, mechanical, photocopying, recording, or otherwise without the prior permission of Bristol University Press.

Every reasonable effort has been made to obtain permission to reproduce copyrighted material. If, however, anyone knows of an oversight, please contact the publisher.

The statements and opinions contained within this publication are solely those of the editors and contributors and not of the University of Bristol or Bristol University Press. The University of Bristol and Bristol University Press disclaim responsibility for any injury to persons or property resulting from any material published in this publication.

Bristol University Press works to counter discrimination on grounds of gender, race, disability, age and sexuality.

Cover design: blu inc
Front cover image: Stocksy/Rowena Naylor

Contents

List of Figures and Tables		v
Notes on Contributors		vi
Acknowledgements		viii

1	Introducing Refugee Youth: Migration, Justice and Urban Space *Mattias De Backer, Peter Hopkins and Ilse van Liempt*	1
2	Storying Belonging, Enacting Citizenship? (Dis)articulations of Belonging in a Community Theatre Project with Young Refugees and Asylum Seekers in Leipzig, Germany *Elisabeth Kirndörfer*	14
3	Jackets and Jewellery: Racialised Dispossession and Struggles over Public Space in Denmark *Malene H. Jacobsen*	32
4	Venezuelan Refugee Youth and Brazilian Schooling: The Individual between Languages and Spaces *Camila da Silva Lucena and Fabiele Stockmans De Nardi*	48
5	The Inclusionary Potential and Spatial Boundaries of (Semi-)Public Space: Refugee Youth's Everyday Experiences in the Urban Fabric of Amsterdam *Ilse van Liempt and Mieke Kox*	65
6	Navigating 'Purdah' Culture in Urban Space: The Restricted Lives of Young Married Rohingya Refugees in Malaysia *Mohd Al Adib Samuri and Peter Hopkins*	81
7	Inclusive Urban Planning and Public Space for Refugee Youth in Pursuit of a Just City in Amman, Jordan *Rana Aytug*	100
8	Sense of Belonging among Tibetan Refugees in India: A Case Study of the Bylakuppe Settlement in Karnataka, India *Anne Bramwell-Grent and Ajay Bailey*	117
9	Negotiating Identity in Urban Space: Everyday Geographies of Syrian Students in Istanbul *Seyma Karamese*	139

| 10 | 'You're Judged a Lot': Australian Sudanese and South Sudanese Youths' Perspectives on Their Experiences in Public Spaces
Luke Macaulay | 153 |
| 11 | Hair Salons as 'Private-Public Spaces': Exploring the Experiences of Young Migrant Women in an Urban Township in South Africa
Rebecca Walker and Glynis Clacherty | 169 |
| 12 | Emotion and Spatial Belonging: Exploring Young Migrant Men's Emotional Geographies in Cork, Ireland
Mastoureh Fathi | 190 |
| 13 | Homemaking through Music in Urban Africa: Creating Opportunities as a Refugee and a Migrant in Kinshasa and Dar es Salaam
Catherina Wilson | 209 |
| 14 | Planetary Listening
Les Back | 225 |
| 15 | Refugee Youth: Politics, Publicness and Visibility
Mattias De Backer, Peter Hopkins and Ilse van Liempt | 231 |

Index 238

List of Figures and Tables

Figures

8.1	Tashi Lhunpo monastery	123
8.2	Indian autos in Bylakuppe	127
11.1	One of the hair salons where the young women gathered	176
11.2	Inside the hair salon	177
11.3	A cut-out doll used to tell stories	178

Table

9.1	Social functions of spaces	150

Notes on Contributors

Mohd Al Adib Samuri is Associate Professor at the Faculty of Islamic Studies and the Institute of Islam Hadhari, Universiti Kebangsaan Malaysia.

Rana Aytug is Postdoctoral Researcher at the Centre for Trust, Peace and Reconciliation, Coventry University, UK.

Les Back is Professor of Sociology at the University of Glasgow, Scotland.

Ajay Bailey is Professor of Social Urban Transitions in International Development Studies, Department of Human Geography and Spatial Planning at Utrecht University, Netherlands.

Matthew C. Benwell is Senior Lecturer in Geography in the School of Geography, Politics and Sociology, Newcastle University, UK.

Anne Bramwell-Grent is a consultant and former student of International Development Studies, Department of Human Geography and Spatial Planning, Utrecht University, Netherlands.

Glynis Clacherty is Research Associate at the University of the Witwatersrand, South Africa.

Camila da Silva Lucena is a PhD candidate in the Graduate Program in Linguistics at Universidade Federal de Pernambuco, Brazil.

Mattias De Backer is Visiting Professor in Urban Criminology, Vrije Universiteit Brussel, Belgium.

Mastoureh Fathi is Assistant Professor at the School of Sociology, University College Dublin, Ireland.

Robin Finlay is Lecturer in Human Geography, University of Durham, UK.

NOTES ON CONTRIBUTORS

Peter Hopkins is Professor of Social Geography in the School of Geography, Politics and Sociology, Newcastle University, UK.

Kathrin Hörschelmann is Professor of Cultural Geography, University of Bonn, Germany.

Malene H. Jacobsen is a Marie Curie Sklodowska Postdoctoral Fellow in Geography, Newcastle University, UK.

Seyma Karamese is a PhD student in the Department of Sociology, University of Essex, UK.

Elisabeth Kirndörfer is Postdoctoral Researcher in Cultural Geography, University of Bonn, Germany.

Mieke Kox is Assistant Professor in Criminology, Erasmus School of Law, Erasmus University, Rotterdam, Netherlands.

Luke Macaulay is Research Fellow at the Centre for Refugee Employment, Advocacy, Training, and Education, Deakin University, Australia.

Fabiele Stockmans De Nardi is Professor in the Graduate Program in Letters at Universidade Federal de Pernambuco, Brazil.

Ilse van Liempt is Associate Professor in Urban Geography, Department of Human Geography and Spatial Planning, Utrecht University, Netherlands.

Rebecca Walker is Postdoctoral Fellow at the African Centre for Migration and Society, University of Witwatersrand, South Africa.

Catherina Wilson is Postdoctoral Researcher at Radboud University Nijmegen, Netherlands.

Acknowledgements

Many thanks to all the authors in this collection for their contributions, and for their patience as we compiled the collection. Thanks also to the editorial team at Bristol University Press for their support with this collection. The editorial team all contributed equally to the editing of the chapters in this collection. The editors of this collection are all part of a research project about the everyday experiences of young refugees and asylum seekers in public spaces. This project was financially supported by the Humanities in the European Research Area Joint Research Programme (www.heranet.info) which is co-funded by the Arts and Humanities Research Council, BundesMinisterium für Bildung und Forschung via the project management agency DLR-PT, the Foundation for Strategic research – Fonds de la Recherce Scientifique, Nederlandse Wetenschappelijke Organisatie, and the European Commission through Horizon 2020. Many thanks to the QR Enhancing Research Culture fund at Newcastle University for providing support for the proofreading of this text and to Georgina Weaver for her excellent editorial work.

1

Introducing Refugee Youth: Migration, Justice and Urban Space

Mattias De Backer, Peter Hopkins and Ilse van Liempt

Introduction

According to the *Global Trends* report by the Office of the United Nations High Commissioner for Refugees (UNHCR), despite COVID-19-related movement restrictions and pleas from the international community for a ceasefire that would facilitate the COVID-19 response, displacement has continued to occur – and to grow. As a result, above 1 per cent of the world's population – or one in 95 people – is now forcibly displaced. This compares with one in 159 in 2010. At the end of 2020, because of persecution, conflict, violence, human rights violations and events seriously disturbing public order, 82.4 million people were forcibly displaced worldwide, of whom there were 20.7 million refugees under UNHCR's mandate, 5.7 million Palestine refugees under the United Nations Relief and Works Agency (UNRWA)'s mandate, 3.9 million Venezuelans displaced abroad, 4.1 million asylum seekers and 48 million internally displaced people. Meanwhile, during the process of this book being written, the ongoing war that Russia has enacted on Ukraine has led to over six million Ukrainians fleeing to neighbouring countries and beyond to escape the violence and danger of war.

In terms of international displacement situations under UNHCR's mandate alone, Syria topped the list with 6.8 million people, followed by Venezuela with 4.9 million people. Afghanistan and South Sudan came next, with 2.8 and 2.2 million respectively. Turkey continued to host the largest number of refugees with just under four million, most of whom were Syrian refugees (92 per cent). Colombia followed, hosting over 1.7 million displaced Venezuelans. Germany hosted the third largest population – almost 1.5 million, with Syrian refugees and asylum seekers as the largest group (44 per cent). Pakistan and Uganda completed the top-five hosting countries, with approximately 1.4 million each. In comparison, in 2009 there were 43.3 million forcibly displaced persons. Of this number, 27.1 million were internally displaced persons, 983,000 had pending asylum cases and 15.2 million were refugees. Of these refugees, 4.8 million were Palestinian refugees registered with UNRWA (Feldman, 2012).

UNHCR observed that more than half of the 65 million refugees and displaced people identified worldwide are under the age of 18, and a further significant number are in their very late teens or early twenties. Refugee children and youth are therefore an increasingly significant cohort of the global population in many countries across the world, and they are of increasing interest to academic and policy researchers and practitioners working with or for them. This collection of chapters focuses on the experiences of refugee youth in diverse contexts and includes research with children, young people and young adults who are seeking asylum or have secured refugee status in a safe country. We take a broad definition of youth to include younger teenagers and adults in their late twenties and early thirties as we acknowledge that the period of youth has increasingly become elongated and fractured (Hopkins et al, 2015). Coupled with this, the process of migration has sometimes resulted in delays in the transition to the phase of adulthood during the settling-down period. On the other hand, we also observed that, as a result of migration, transitions into adulthood can be speeded up and forced upon some young people.

All the contributions to this book draw on qualitative research with refugee youth, and many utilise participatory research and creative methods to trace the personal geographies and emotions attached to the places under study. First-hand qualitative accounts, ethnographic research and creative methods are key to moving beyond 'crisis-driven' and static representations of refugee youth. We fill a gap in the literature on migrant youth and public space that predominantly tends to start from their precarious situations such as insecure housing, lack of social networks, employment restrictions, mental health issues and lack of money. We do not ignore these structural forms of inequality but, by providing a broader picture that includes refugee youth's own perceptions and their active presence in and around various public spaces, we move beyond traditional, more formal studies of integration and provide space for new stories of citizenship and belonging (see also van Liempt and Staring, 2021).

This book explicitly focuses on refugee youth's negotiations of spatial, social and economic justices and injustices in the public urban spaces in which they arrive after migration. It takes refugee youth as active agents and gives priority to their voices and experiences; the importance of listening to such accounts is emphasised by Les Back in Chapter 14. By putting personal and everyday geographies of refugee youth central, we do not overlook structural forms of exclusion that take place, but we show how young people themselves make sense of their lives in the new places of arrival. By putting their experiences centre stage, we extend scholarship on refugee youth beyond its dominant focus on social work practices and welfare services (for example, Kohli, 2007; Nelson et al, 2016), policy-related responses (for example, Bhabha and Schmidt, 2008; Parusel, 2017; Menjívar and Perreira, 2019), and psychosocial wellbeing (for example, Bean et al, 2007; Derluyn and Broekaert, 2008; Stotz et al, 2015). Thus, some chapters take young refugees' everyday experiences as a starting point to reflect on the infrastructural and organisational context and broader issues of spatial justice. Other chapters, however, work the other way around, by first exploring the legal-political context of migration management, in which, later on, actors within the arrival infrastructure and young refugees' everyday experiences are located. Our focus on public space takes existing scholarship on refugee youth even further because it offers opportunities to explore meaningful spaces for refugee youth in the city that go beyond formal community or organisational settings and include spaces that might be created by refugee youth themselves. It also allows us to explore the notion of visibility along the lines of recognition. In this sense, recognition refers to 'acts of resistance and empowerment by minority groups against the mainstream, for instance, how they claim a space to make themselves visible' (De Backer, 2019, p 309) in the urban landscape.

Introducing refugee youth

The definition of a refugee has historical roots in the Refugee Convention adopted under the auspices of the United Nations in 1951, in the wake of the Second World War and its many displaced victims. The Convention refers to a refugee as any person who experiences:

> a well-founded fear of being persecuted for reasons of race, religion, nationality, membership of a particular social group or political opinion, is outside the country of his nationality and is unable or, owing to such fear, is unwilling to avail himself of the protection of that country; or who, not having a nationality and being outside the country of his former habitual residence as a result of such events, is unable or, owing to such fear, is unwilling to return to it.[1]

Yet, both the definition of the category of 'refugee' and the subsequent development of asylum and migration legislation, are objects of heated debates, because what constitutes a 'refugee' changes over time. As Marshall (2011) points out, there has been a growing consensus in the international arena to include in the definition those people displaced by environmental causes. Recent crises have highlighted failings in international systems for protecting internally displaced persons, based on narrow definitions of the term. The situation in Libya since the Arab Spring, for instance, has called into question the relevance of a refugee definition that focuses on individual persecution by a state, and was devised in a specific historical and geographical context (Moszynski, 2011).

Indeed, as remarked by Rea et al (2019), the stakes of the definition of 'refugee', 'asylum seeker' and other migrant groups are strictly political, in the sense that the choice between one term and the other not only determines people's access to certain rights but also affects the moral dimension of migration policy (p 14). The legal category, 'foreigner', is national legislation, organised according to one of the four major purposes for seeking entry into new territory: economic, familial, humanitarian and study related. A receiving state possesses both the power and the sovereignty to classify foreigners and thus determine who does and who does not have the right to enter into and stay on its territory, and migration policies of individual states determine the categories of 'economic migrants' versus 'refugees', or 'regular migrants' versus 'irregular migrants' (Rea et al, 2019, p 14).

Furthermore, one can also distinguish between a humanitarian and human rights understanding of the 'refugee' category. In the former, a 'refugee' connotes an individual fleeing war, famine and failed states; they are portrayed as victims waiting in a camp until they can return or be resettled. This 'humanitarian' conception of refugees highlights need, vulnerability and passivity, and their agency, the source of their plight and the precise grounds for their claim are absent (Cherem, 2016). Rather than using a humanitarian definition, authors such as Cherem (2016) argue for understanding refugee law in the tradition of human rights. International refugee law and human rights law, although historically developed separately, are severely overlapping. International human rights law has developed since the 1980s to provide protection against refoulement that is 'complementary' to that required by international refugee law (Burson and Cantor, 2016). The non-refoulement principle refers to the right not to be returned to a country where one would be harmed, where one's life is endangered. This rule is even more important for refugee youth as it is against international treaties to deport children under the age of 18.

Interesting are also the national and regional variations of the refugee definition. The 1969 'expanded refugee definition' of the Organisation of African Unity provides that the term 'refugee' also applies to every person who, owing to external aggression, occupation, foreign domination or events seriously disturbing public order in either part or the whole of his country of origin or nationality, is compelled to leave their place of habitual residence in order to seek refuge in another place outside their country of origin or nationality (Wood, 2019, p 291). This expanded refugee definition extends the scope of refugee protection beyond individuals with a well-founded fear of persecution to those fleeing more widespread and indiscriminate forms of harm. UNRWA's definition of a Palestine refugee, similarly, has been adjusted over the years, because, as an operational rather than a legal definition, it identifies those people eligible for UNRWA services (Feldman, 2012). In countries such as China, which has signed the 1951 Refugee Convention and the 1967 Protocol, there are no domestic, legislative or administrative provisions governing the definition of refugees or procedures of refugee status determination. The refugee category has not been incorporated into Chinese law to become fully enforceable domestically (Song, 2014). Turkey is also a good example of how a specific national interpretation of international legislation might result in very different protection opportunities (and we learn more about this in Chapter 11). Turkey has a so-called 'geographical limitation' in its refugee law, which means that it only grants *conditional* refugee status and no refugee status to asylum seekers coming from outside Europe. Although Turkey has been a signatory party to the 1951 Geneva Convention relating to the Status of Refugees, the Refugee Convention is geographically limited in terms of its application, which essentially means that asylum seekers coming to Turkey from outside Europe cannot be recognised as refugees in Turkey. This limitation denies refugees from non-European countries (basically almost everybody) the prospect of long-term integration in Turkey. Until now, Turkey has always resisted demands to lift this geographical ban.

As younger people, refugee youth are worthy of study in their own right (Hopkins 2010, Hopkins and Hill, 2008, 2010). Not only are refugee youth a significant cohort of the overall refugee population, but they are also especially worth paying attention to, given the important role they can play in the future of the society and in politics and the economy. Younger people also offer an important vantage point from which to view broader aspects of social continuity and social change; indeed, it is often among young people that we first start to see the emergence of social changes and transformation, so they have the potential to offer valuable insights into the future. In this book, numerous examples are given of how refugee youth – despite strong and strict politics of belonging – claim space and recognition in the cities where they have settled and how new places and encounters are shaping up as a result of these interventions by young people.

Migration

A key issue that sits across the chapters is migration; this includes accounts of migration and also experiences of, and challenges associated with, having a migration background. Connected to this are the negotiations of the often-complex processes, services and organisations that operate to support the arrival and integration of refugees – or what has been termed 'arrival infrastructures' (Meeus et al, 2019) – and how these present themselves in new places. Some chapters give more attention to migration issues than others, yet this remains a consistent focus throughout the book. For example, in Chapters 4 and 7, we learn about the experiences of Venezuelan refugee youth in Brazil and Syrian youth in Jordan respectively. In Chapter 8, the authors explore the situation for Tibetan refugees seeking sanctuary in India, and in Chapter 10 we find out about South Sudanese refugees in Australia.

Some research on refugee youth tends to focus on their experiences with war and violence, their life in refugee camps and/or closed institutions, and their mental health outcomes (Ajdukovic and Ajdukovic, 1998; Harrell-Bond, 2000; Betancourt et al, 2015; Stotz et al, 2015; Zijlstra et al, 2020). A substantial part of the literature also focuses on the status of refugee children, especially when it is about unaccompanied minors and undocumented children and the hardship that comes with their precarious position (Clayton et al, 2019) including from a social work perspective (Kohli, 2007). In the current refugee reception crisis in Europe, the unaccompanied minor has come to be constructed as a 'crisis figure' (Lems et al, 2020).

Appreciating the arrival infrastructures negotiated by refugee youth allows us to study the experiences and realities of arrival through a mobile perspective, and refers to 'those parts of the urban fabric within which newcomers become entangled on arrival, and where their future local or translocal social mobilities are produced as much as negotiated' (Meeus et al, 2019, p 1). The arrival infrastructures concept refers to the infrastructures with which migrants interact on arrival (Boost and Oosterlynck, 2019; Kreichauf, 2019; Swyngedouw, 2019). One of the central assumptions of the 'arrival infrastructures' concept is that it 'allows for a critical as well as transformative engagement with the position of the state in the management of migration' (Meeus et al, 2019, p 2). This state, in the words of the authors, 'has produced new layers of supportive and exclusionary governmental infrastructures' (Meeus et al, 2019, p 2) on the one hand, and 'a considerable amount of labour from diverse actors ... to continuously maintain, repair and update state infrastructures' (Meeus et al, 2019, p 2), on the other. This perspective draws attention to the division of tasks and responsibilities among actors in the arrival infrastructure and to the often-overlooked role of informal actors. A useful example of one part of the arrival infrastructure in Amsterdam is provided in Chapter 5, where Ilse van Liempt and Mieke Kox reflect on the semi-private spaces of a community centre that provides lunch and informal learning opportunities for newcomers to the city.

This 'infrastructural turn' is motivated by several factors. Firstly, rather than focusing on a migrant's rights and citizenship status, the study of processes of arrival draws attention to 'how and where people find some stability in order to move on' (Meeus et al, 2019, p 1). Secondly, an infrastructural perspective on processes of arrival allows for a critical as well as transformative engagement with the position of the state in the management of migration (Meeus et al, 2019, p 2). Thirdly, an infrastructural approach emphasises interlinked social and spatial dynamics, 'thereby revealing how city dwellers access shared resources in the context of growing inequality' (Hall et al, 2017, p 1411). Fourthly, an infrastructural approach allows for a simultaneous analysis of commerical, technological, humanitarian, social and legal aspects of the phenomenon of arrival (see also Xiang and Lindquist, 2014). Finally, this framework includes translocalism, which refers to 'the processes by which immigrants forge and sustain multi-stranded social relations that link together their societies of origin and settlement' (Basch et al, 1994, p 6). This indicates that migrants are simultaneously linked to a multitude of places, through history, emotional attachment, family ties, legal status and technology, across geographic, cultural and political borders.

The contexts in which new migrants find themselves not only include relevant formal community or organisational settings; there also exist relatively informal contexts in which refugees socialise and spend their time, some of which are created by refugees themselves. Examples in the book include refugees participating in community theatre groups, other forms of artistic and creative practice, and the spaces of friendship and creativity found in hair salons. For example, in Chapter 2, Elisabeth Kirndörfer considers how belonging and citizenship are enacted by refugees in a community theatre group in Leipzig, Germany. In Chapter 11, the focus moves to Johannesburg, South Africa where Rebecca Walker and Glynis Clacherty draw attention to young women's use of hair salons to form friendships, build networks and establish trust. We learn about Catherina Wilson's research, in Chapter 13, on the process of homemaking in new places through the narratives of two artists in Kinshasa and Dar es Salaam and how these young artists are using their artistic skills in creating a better future. The ways in which making music in public space is a central component in understanding emergent public spaces and citizenship practices in Africa's present and future are illustrated in this chapter.

Justice

Intersecting with migration, a key theme of this book is justice and in particular spatial justice, which is 'an intentional and focused emphasis on the spatial or geographical aspects of justice and injustice' (Soja, 2009, p 2). This concept allows us to explore the lived experiences of refugee youth, not only through appreciating their migration experiences and accounts of arrival and integration, but also the injustices that shape these. We foreground justice in the processes of migration and arrival, and, more specifically, Soja's (2009, 2010) notion of spatial justice, which argues that justice has a geography *and* that space produces (in)justice. Spatial (in)justice can be seen as both outcome and process, as geographies or distributional patterns that are, in themselves, just/unjust and as the processes that produce these outcomes (Soja, 2009, p 3). An example of the latter is locational discrimination, which is created through the biases imposed on certain populations because of their geographical location.

Spatial justice is not a substitute for, or alternative to, social, economic or other forms of justice, but rather a way of looking at justice from a critical spatial perspective (Soja, 2010, p 60). It refers both to the equitable distribution of resources and services and to the procedural justice of access to basic human rights, which speaks about how cities and communities are negotiated, planned, designed and managed. Spatial justice describes justice struggles that attend to concerns over how space is used and how decisions about the use and design of particular spaces are determined (Nordquist, 2013). Soja argues that the pursuit of justice requires gaining control over the processes producing unjust urban geographies. He does not identify specific programmes to reduce spatial injustice but rather looks to coalitions of groups demanding the right to the city as the vehicles for achieving both greater material equity and greater respect for marginalised populations (Fainstein, 2014, p 12).

The perspective of spatial justice is tightly interwoven with the right-to-the-city debate (Lefebvre, 1996), I.M. Young's (1990) discussion of justice, oppression and difference, and the notion of the 'just city' elaborated by Fainstein (2014). The first, defined by Lefebvre as a 'demand ... [for] a transformed and renewed access to urban life' (Lefebvre, 1996, p 158), criticises modern cities as places for consumers rather than citizens, and as places where individuals' needs in urban areas have been prioritised over society's needs. Young (2011), in her book *Justice and the Politics of Difference*, identifies injustice as a type of oppression and justice as the absence of forms of domination. Fainstein considers the problem of justice as the clash between the logics of development and redistribution. The just city is democratic in the sense that people have control over their living environments, it allows diversity of various kinds, and features equity (Uitermark, 2012). Of these three values, equity takes primacy.

With the focus on spatial justice in this volume, we wish to emphasise how young refugees and asylum seekers, in their negotiations of the urban everyday, unsettle and challenge bordering regimes that work with racialisation and othering. Issues of injustice are perhaps most obvious in Chapter 3 by Malene Jacobsen. The attention in this chapter is focused on Denmark, where the Danish government introduced new legislation that enabled the state to carry out search-and-seize orders on refugees, taking their cash and other personal belongings. Jacobsen argues that attention should be paid to issues of dispossession and the gendered and racialised othering involved in this. The justice framework also enables us to think about potential ways to overcome specific forms of exclusion. Rana Aytug, for example, draws attention in Chapter 7 to the potential for inclusive urban planning and intercultural place-making to generate just cities for refugee youth in Amman, Jordan.

Urban space

In concert with discussions about, and reflections on, migration and justice, the final key theme of this collection is urban space. Research on migration, globalisation and identity has noted the need for more grounded, contextualised accounts that specify how differently positioned social agents experience and coproduce translocal geographies and social relations (Hörschelmann and El Refaie, 2014; Mitchell and Kallio, 2017). Cities have been identified as particularly important places for such negotiations (Isin, 2007; Bauder, 2017) that may afford power to the marginalised and help them articulate claims to political participation and citizen rights. As Sassen (2013, p 70) notes, '[t]he last two decades have seen an increasingly urban articulation of global logics and struggles, and an escalating use of urban space to make political claims not only by the citizens of a country but also by foreigners.' There is a real need to examine the daily realities of urban life at the local level, where migrant rights and claims to citizenship are articulated.

By investigating the relationships between refugee youth and urban space, we offer insights into the role that public space plays in providing for encounters that could contribute to integration and participation in society. We believe that refugee youth contribute to the development of convivial public space by bringing their own histories and voices, and by actively using and claiming public space. As such, they do not only blend in in already existing landscapes and infrastructures, but also actively produce new layers of urbanity. As such, the book also challenges the still dominant one-way-process way of thinking about integration as 'fitting in', rather than 'creating something new'. In this volume, new insights are presented into how refugee youth's place-making practices can contribute to the transformation of urban public spaces. A useful example here is the efforts of Syrian students in relation to place-making and identity construction in Istanbul, which is explored in Chapter 9 by Seyma Karamese.

By focusing on urban public spaces, we also move away from the context of refugee camps, reception centres and shelters, which are spaces most often associated with refugee youth and spaces that are forced on refugees instead of being actively chosen by them. This allows us to identify visibly claimed, but also more hidden, spaces for urban citizenship, such as, for example, hair salons, that have emerged in the city of Johannesburg and act as safe spaces for young women, as demonstrated in Chapter 11. Spaces like this can play important roles in refugee youth's daily lives and contribute to the process of finding their way into a new society that goes beyond formal arrival infrastructures.

Conclusion

This collection explores the lived experiences of refugee youth in urban public space in a highly diverse range of international contexts. Pritchard et al (2019) conclude that most articles on refugee youth tend to focus on countries that resettle high numbers of refugees and focus on Africa and the Middle East as countries of origin. They also find that most studies on refugee youth do not explicitly mention gender. In this volume, we take a broad social and geographical perspective and include research from many parts of the world to capture diverse experiences from refugee youth in different settings. We pay explicit attention to gender (for example, in the contributions by Rebecca Walker and Glynis Clacherty in Chapter 11 and by Mastoureh Fathi in Chapter 12). And in Chapter 6, we learn from Mohd Al Adib Samuri and Peter Hopkins about the deeply problematic ways in which Rohingya refugee young women are forced to be invisible in Malaysia by being prevented from entering urban public spaces through the patriarchal and sexist reinforcement of discourses of 'purdah', which essentially limit many of them to living a life in which they have no access to urban public spaces. By emphasising the broad variety of refugee youth's personal geographies and everyday use and experiences in public space in various cities across the world, we illustrate how urban public space is actively produced in many different ways.

Note
[1] www.unhcr.org/4ae57b489.pdf

References

Ajdukovic, M. and Ajdukovic, D. (1998) 'Impact of displacement on the psychological well-being of refugee youth', *International Review of Psychiatry*, 10(3): 186–195.

Basch, L., Glick Schiller, N. and Szanton Blanc, C. (1994) *Nations Unbound: Transnational Projects, Postcolonial Predicaments and Deterritorialized Nation-States*, Basel: Gordon & Breach.

Bauder, H. (2017) 'Sanctuary cities: policies and practices in international perspective', *International Migration*, 55(2): 174–187.

Bean, T., Derluyn, I., Eurelings-Bontekoe, E., Broekaert, E. and Spinhoven, P. (2007) 'Comparing psychological distress, traumatic stress reactions, and experiences of unaccompanied refugee minors with experiences of adolescents accompanied by parents', *The Journal of Nervous and Mental Disease*, 195(4): 288–297.

Betancourt, T., Abdi, S., Ito, B., Lilienthal, G., Agalab, N. and Ellis, H. (2015) 'We left one war and came to another: resource loss, acculturative stress, and caregiver-child relationships in Somali refugee families', *Cultural Diversity and Ethnic Minority Psychology*, 21(1): 114–125.

Bhaba, J. and Schmidt, S. (2008) 'Seeking asylum alone: unaccompanied and separated children and refugee protection in the US', *The Journal of the History of Childhood and Youth*, 1(1): 126–138.

Boost, D. and Oosterlynck, S. (2019) '"Soft" urban arrival infrastructures in the periphery of metropolitan areas: the role of social networks for sub-Saharan newcomers in Aalst, Belgium', in B. Meeus, K. Arnaut and B. van Heur (eds) *Arrival Infrastructures*, Cham: Palgrave Macmillan, pp 153–177.

Burson, B. and Cantor, D.J. (2016) *Human Rights and the Refugee Definition: Comparative Legal Practice and Theory*, Leiden: Brill Nijhoff.

Cherem, M. (2016) 'Refugee rights: against expanding the definition of a "refugee" and unilateral protection elsewhere', *Journal of Political Philosophy*, 24(2): 183–205.

Clayton, S., Gupta, A. and Willis, K. (eds) (2019) *Unaccompanied Young Migrants: Identity, Care and Justice*, Bristol: Policy Press.

De Backer, M. (2019) 'Regimes of visibility: hanging out in Brussels' public spaces', *Space and Culture*, 22(3): 1–22.

Derluyn, I. and Broekaert, E. (2008) 'Unaccompanied refugee children and adolescents: the glaring contrast between a legal and a psychological perspective', *International Journal of Law and Psychiatry*, 31(4): 319–330.

Fainstein, S. (2014) 'The just city', *International Journal of Urban Sciences*, 18(1): 1–18.

Feldman, I. (2012) 'The refugee in the postwar world, 1945–1960', *Journal of Refugee Studies*, 25(3): 387–406.

Hall, S., King, J. and Finlay, R. (2017) 'Migrant infrastructure: transaction economies in Birmingham and Leicester, UK', *Urban Studies*, 54(6): 1311–1327.

Harrell-Bond, B. (2000) 'Are refugee camps good for children?', *Working paper no 29*, Geneva: UN Refugee Agency.

Hopkins, P. (2010) *Young People, Place and Identity*, London: Routledge.

Hopkins, P. and Hill, M. (2008) 'Pre-flight experiences and migration stories: the accounts of unaccompanied asylum-seeking children', *Children's Geographies*, 6(3): 257–268.

Hopkins, P. and Hill, M. (2010) 'The needs and strengths of unaccompanied asylum-seeking children and young people in Scotland', *Child & Family Social Work*, 15(4): 399–408.

Hopkins, P., Olson, E., Baillie Smith, M. and Laurie, N. (2015) 'Transitions to religious adulthood: relational geographies of youth, religion and international volunteering', *Transactions of the Institute of British Geographers*, 40(3): 387–398.

Hörschelmann, K. and El Refaie, E. (2014) 'Transnational citizenship, dissent and the political geographies of youth', *Transactions*, 39(3): 444–456.

Isin, E.F. (2007) 'City state: critique of scalar thought', *Citizenship Studies*, 11(2): 211–228.

Kohli, R. (2007) *Social Work with Unaccompanied Asylum Seeking Children*, London: Bloomsbury.

Kreichauf, R. (2019) 'From forced migration to forced arrival: the campization of refugee accommodation in European cities', in B. Meeus, K. Arnaut and B. van Heur (eds) *Arrival Infrastructures*, Cham: Palgrave Macmillan, pp 249–279.

Lefebvre, H. (1996) *Writings on Cities*, edited by E. Kofman and E. Lebas, Cambridge, MA: Wiley-Blackwell.

Lems, A., Oester, K. and Strasser, S. (2020) 'Children of the crisis: ethnographic perspectives on unaccompanied refugee youth in and en route to Europe', *Journal of Ethnic and Migration Studies*, 46(2): 315–335.

Marshall, L.W. (2011) 'Toward a new definition of "refugee": is the 1951 convention out of date?', *European Journal of Trauma and Emergency Surgery*, 37(1): 61–66.

Meeus, B., van Heur, B. and Arnaut, K. (2019) 'Migration and the infrastructural politics of urban arrival', in B. Meeus, K. Arnaut and B. van Heur (eds) *Arrival Infrastructures: Migration and Urban Social Mobilities*, Cham: Springer International Publishing, pp 1–32.

Menjívar, C. and Perreira, K. (2019) 'Undocumented and unaccompanied: children of migration in the European Union and the United States', *Journal of Ethnic and Migration Studies*, 45(2): 197–217.

Mitchell, K. and Kallio, K.P. (2017) 'Spaces of the geosocial: exploring transnational topologies', *Geopolitics*, 22(1): 1–14

Moszynski, P. (2011) 'Definition of refugee is inadequate for current patterns of migration in armed conflicts, report says', *British Medical Journal*, 343(November): d7390.

Nelson, D., Price, E. and Zubrzycki, J. (2017) 'Critical social work with unaccompanied asylum-seeking young people: restoring hope, agency and meaning for the client and worker', *International Social Work*, 60(3): 601–613.

Nordquist, M. (2013) 'Seeking spatial justice by Edward W. Soja', *Contemporary Political Theory*, 12(1): e16–18.

Parusel, B. (2017) 'Unaccompanied minors in the European Union: definitions, trends and policy overview', *Social Work and Society*, 15(1): np (online).

Pritchard, P., Maehler, D., Pötzschke, S. and Ramos, H. (2019) 'Integrating refugee children and youth: a scoping review of English and German literature', *Journal of Refugee Studies*, 32(1): 194–208.

Rea, A., Martiniello, M., Mazzola, A. and Meuleman, B. (2019) 'The refugee reception crisis in Europe: polarized opinions and mobilizations', in A. Rea, M. Martiniello, A. Mazzola and B. Meuleman (eds) *The Refugee Reception Crisis in Europe: Polarized Opinions and Mobilizations*, Brussels: Éditions de l'Université de Bruxelles, pp 11–30.

Sassen, S. (2013) 'When the center no longer holds: cities as frontier zones', *Cities*, 34: 67–70.

Soja, E. (2009) 'The city and spatial justice', *Justice Spatiale/Spatial Justice*, 1(1): 1–5.

Soja, E. (2010) *Seeking Spatial Justice*, Minneapolis: University of Minnesota Press.

Song, L. (2014) 'Who shall we help? The refugee definition in a Chinese context', *Refugee Survey Quarterly*, 33(1): 44–58.

Stotz, S., Elbert, T., Müller, V. and Schauer, M. (2015) 'The relationship between trauma, shame, and guilt: findings from a community-based study of refugee minors in Germany', *European Journal of Psychotraumatology*, 6(1): 25863.

Swyngedouw, E. (2019) 'Governing newcomers' conduct in the arrival infrastructures of Brussels', in B. Meeus, K. Arnaut and B. van Heur (eds) *Arrival Infrastructures*, Cham: Palgrave Macmillan, pp 81–101.

Uitermark, J. (2012) 'Review of *The Just City*, by S. Fainstein', *Journal of Housing and the Built Environment*, 27(1): 107–109.

van Liempt, I. and Staring, R. (2021) 'Homemaking and places of restoration: belonging within and beyond places assigned to Syrian refugees in the Netherlands', *Geographical Review*, 111(2): 308–326.

Wood, T. (2019) 'Who is a refugee in Africa? A principled framework for interpreting and applying Africa's expanded refugee definition', *International Journal of Refugee Law*, 31(2–3): 290–320.

Xiang, B. and Lindquist, J. (2014) 'Migration infrastructure', *International Migration Review*, 48(1): 122–148.

Young, I.M. (1990) *Justice and the Politics of Difference*, Princeton, NJ: Princeton University Press.

Young, I.M. (2011) *Responsibility for Justice*, Oxford: Oxford University Press.

Zijlstra, E., Menninga, M., van Os, C. and Kalverboer, M. (2020) 'They ask for protection: an exploratory study into experiences with violence among unaccompanied refugee children in Dutch reception facilities', *Child Abuse & Neglect*, 103. https://doi.org/10.1016/j.chiabu.2020.104442

2

Storying Belonging, Enacting Citizenship? (Dis)articulations of Belonging in a Community Theatre Project with Young Refugees and Asylum Seekers in Leipzig, Germany

Elisabeth Kirndörfer

Introduction

Participatory theatre has, in a wide body of work, been discussed as an artistic format that bears the potential to enhance processes of participation, empowerment and resistance – especially when involving participants who experience marginalisation and racialisation in their societies (Butterwick and Selman, 2012, 2020; Chou et al, 2015; Sonn et al, 2015; Erel et al, 2017; Stam, 2020). The articulation of marginalised knowledges is considered to be an enactment of citizenship insofar as it uncovers oppressive structures and interrupts hegemonic regimes of belonging and citizenship that, ultimately, exert violence on racialised subjects (Butterwick and Selman, 2012, p 62; Stam, 2020, p 290). Participatory theatre can, in this sense, even serve as a decolonising practice (Perry, 2012; Erel and Reynolds, 2014; Sonn et al, 2015), especially in a societal climate that is increasingly marked by 'divisive politics and racism' (Butterwick and Selman, 2020, p 35). For newcomers such as young refugees and asylum seekers, participatory theatre provides a valuable resource in the process of negotiating arrival, engaging in and with a new place and connecting with other newcomers and longer-term residents in the city.

Personal stories and the practice of storytelling play a decisive role within participatory theatre (Kaptani and Yuval-Davis, 2008; Chou et al 2015; Sonn et al, 2015; Erel et al, 2017; Stam, 2020). They appear to be the basic tool for acting against racialisation and othering, for challenging disenfranchising citizenship regimes and for enhancing transformative processes from below. Working with story-based theatre can, however, 'be risky, even harmful' insofar as it can 'trigger unremembered and unprocessed stories and memories' (Butterwick and Selman, 2012, p 62). Despite this acknowledgement by Butterwick and Selman (2012), there has to date been little discussion in the literature on the complicated nature of 'storying', sharing emotional, close-up and personal narrative in the context of participatory theatre. Hence, what is largely missing is a critical focus on the (im)possibilities of speech, on moments of silence and disarticulation.

In this chapter, I will investigate the ambiguities and ambivalences that accompany the key practice of storytelling, of sharing personal stories in participatory theatre, especially when involving 'mixed groups' such as, in our case, young refugees and asylum seekers as well as other newcomers to the city. My aim is to provide a detailed analysis of a participatory theatre process in which I engaged as participant observer. The process brought to the fore various moments of silence, of refusal to speak, of withdrawal and closure that I wish to reflect on in depth. In my analysis, I take a closer look at these moments of rupture, ask what they articulated, how these articulations were re-translated into the theatre process and how, in the end, 'not-telling' personal stories, the possibility to remain silent, turned into a significant message and political act in the final performance. I understand these moments of (dis)articulation as active statements and enactments of citizenship (Isin and Nielsen, 2013) rather than as moments of failure or suppression that, supposedly, conceal traumatic experiences. From my perspective, these moments bear an underestimated potential to learn how processes of arrival are negotiated and crafted and, ultimately, how justice is claimed in a socio-political landscape of exclusion and 'everyday bordering' (Yuval-Davis et al, 2018).

In this chapter, I ask: What does the sharing of 'your story' mean in the context of forced migration? How does the racialisation of young people as 'refugees' or 'asylum seekers' impact on the act of storytelling? (How) can the implicit correspondence between 'your story' and 'your journey' be ruptured – or not – in the process of participatory theatre? In sum, I investigate silence, rupture, diversion and withdrawal as political articulations that enact citizenship in the same way that stories and shared experiences do. Beyond this, I ask which kinds of 'risks and ethics' (Barnes, 2009) narrative-based and corporeal theatre work with young refugees and asylum seekers involves.

In the first section, I will discuss the interrelation between participatory theatre, storytelling/articulation and citizenship from a theoretical perspective. After giving an overview of the methodological approach followed, I will offer an empirical analysis that follows the chronology of the events and discuss two key themes: (1) silence as disarticulation/the withdrawal of stories; and (2) silence as articulation/the return of stories. The reflection of my positionality within the research process, then, will lead me towards my conclusion, in which I will discuss the need for an intersectional sensibility within story-based theatre with young refugees and asylum seekers in the city.

Theoretical discussion: stories/storying in participatory theatre's negotiation of citizenship and belonging

What can storytelling through participatory theatre contribute to citizenship and belonging? This is the question that I wish to address first by discussing current analytical work on participatory theatre, citizenship and the role of storytelling. For this purpose, it matters little whether participatory theatre is used and reflected on as a tool in research (Kaptani and Yuval-Davis, 2008; Erel et al, 2017; Stam, 2020) or, for example, as an educational method (Butterwick and Selman, 2012, 2020). Rather, what I am interested in here is to lay the theoretical grounds for a critical reflection on the role of storying/storytelling within participatory theatre that involves racialised subjects: in our case, young refugees and asylum seekers.

Erel and colleagues (2017) reflect on participatory theatre as a technique that allows marginalised people – in the case of their project, migrant mothers – to explore and challenge oppressive social structures and, in doing so, enact citizenship (p 306). The creation of their own narrative is highlighted as a powerful way to 'make visible the subjugated knowledges of participants' (p 310). Butterwick and Selman (2020) refer to the latter as the 'stories missing' (p 35) from public discourse and emphasise that 'the arts, specifically community-based theatre, offer spaces for changing the public narrative so that stories from the missing and disenfranchised are spoken and heard' (p 37). New futures and 'other possibilities of belonging' (Stam, 2020, p 291) can become imaginable as a result of this 'practice of citizenship' (Stam, 2020, p 289).

The sharing of stories, according to Stam, plays a decisive role within these processes: 'Through theatre, participants can tell the stories that matter to them and share their knowledge with a wider audience. Stories help us make sense of the world' (Stam, 2020, p 290). Addressing sensitive topics, hence, is at the heart of participatory theatre. Here, however, I argue for a more nuanced and detailed analysis. For, while Butterwick and Selman (2020) refer to the 'unequally shared' 'risks of storytelling' (p 39) and Erel et al (2017, p 307) and Stam (2020, p 294) thematise issues of privilege and power *within* the theatre space, the concrete practice of telling stories, sharing intimate experiences and becoming emotionally close up in a setting of differing vulnerabilities has received too little attention in my view. As Razack noted as early as 1998, in her book *Looking White People in the Eye: Gender, Race, Culture in Courtrooms and Classrooms*, an 'unreasonably high demand for storytelling' tends to be placed on marginalised people by 'those in dominant positions' (Razack, 1998, p 48).

Razack formulated a poignant critique of the use of storytelling in workshop contexts. She shares several incidents that occurred in her human rights training workshops, that all disclose versions of 'difficulties with a critical use of storytelling' (Razack, 1998, p 47). When, for instance, a Black participant from South Africa was repeatedly prompted to share her story, until she 'left the room in tears' (p 48), the author reflects on this incident in a conversation with her colleague, saying 'that we (people of colour) are always being asked to tell our stories for your (white) people's edification, which you cannot hear because of the benefit you derive from hearing them'. Her critique touches a very sensitive aspect of 'mixed group' interactions: the practices of telling and hearing (stories) are deeply embedded in (post-)colonial power relations in which feelings of comfort and safety are unevenly distributed and the 'legibility' of the knowledge shared is not to be taken for granted. The 'inscription of difference' (Minh-ha, 1989) is, indeed, no straightforward process, 'serving' both tellers and listeners in the same way. On the contrary, Razack concludes that 'storytelling serves various groups differently and that it should never be employed uncritically in mixed-race groups' (Razack, 1998, p 50).

> The problems of voice and identity are packed with internal dilemmas not only for the listeners but also the tellers of the tale. Often women of colour are asked to tell their stories while others will do the theorizing and the writing up. ... What kind of tale will I choose to tell, and in what voice? (Razack, 1998, p 53)

Razack ends up claiming a 'right to silence' (Razack, 1998, p 53), as defended by the Black participant referred to earlier. She quotes Minh-ha, who in her work *Woman, Native, Other: Writing Postcoloniality and Feminism* (1989) states that 'silence as a will not to say or a will to unsay and as a language of its own has barely been explored' (Minh-ha quoted in Razack, 1998, p 53). 'Silence as a refusal to partake in the story does sometimes provide us with a means to gain a hearing. It is voice, a mode of uttering, and a response in its own right' (Minh-ha, 1989, p 83).

Bringing these postcolonial and feminist perspectives on voice, difference and encounter into dialogue with the perspectives on participatory theatre quoted earlier, I would conclude the following: participatory theatre opens a space for 'outsiders' of official citizenship regimes to enact themselves as political and creative subjects. This is especially so in the context of arrival, for example by young refugees and asylum seekers, where participatory theatre carries the potential to create an affective space for sharing, for encounters and, hence, for homemaking and belonging. It is at the same time a highly political arena that newcomers can use in order to assert their right to create, (re)imagine, but also critically interact with the (urban) society that they have come to live in. The centrality of stories and storytelling in this process is not unproblematic, however, especially when this practice is shared between differently positioned subjects. As Butterwick and Selman (2020, p 68) conclude: 'A decolonizing approach to embodied theatre pedagogy is all about being safe enough to be dangerous.' There remains a need to reflect on 'disclosure consequences ... before inviting others to tell their stories or telling our own' (Butterwick and Selman, 2020, p 68). This cautionary conclusion is echoed by Sonn et al's (2015, p 244) calls for 'decentring whiteness' in storytelling. In the analysis that follows, I will trace the process of 'silence' as, indeed, a 'language of its own' (Minh-ha, quoted in Razack, 1998, p 53) and a 'response in its own right' (Minh-ha, 1989, p 83). I seek to uncover how (dis)articulation, paradoxically perhaps, opens spaces for voices and stories to reappear from the sidelines. The impact and entanglement of my own position as a white female researcher within the social fabric that emerged will also be highlighted in the analysis and then explicitly addressed in a subsection before the conclusion.

Methodological approach and empirical material

The material I discuss in this contribution stems from research conducted as part of the Humanities European Research Area (HERA)-funded project, 'The everyday experiences of young refugees and asylum seekers in public space'. This international project realised in parallel at the Leibniz Institute for Regional Geography, Leipzig and the Universities of Amsterdam, Brussels and Newcastle (2019–2021) works in close connection with local partners and is strongly anchored in creative qualitative methodologies. The aim of this project was to explore refugee youth's stories of homemaking, their interaction with arrival infrastructures and their negotiations of inclusion and exclusion in public spaces. We focused particularly on the role of arts and culture during the process of arrival, asking how the latter can support young refugees' and asylum seekers' senses of belonging to the city. It is with this emphasis in mind that we decided to include participant observation of a theatre project in our research that involved a 'mixed' group of young newcomers in the city, with and without migration histories. The project was run by a community centre in the east of Leipzig (Germany). It was evolving from a series of workshops that a theatre coach had conducted with the aim of empowering participants to speak (up), to get in touch with their new living environment and to engage with the new place. The interactive, theatre-based workshop exercises culminated in the collective preparation of a performance at a big sociocultural festival themed 'It's enough. For everyone' that was held in October 2020 in one of the city's central public spaces. I took part in four of five workshops and in 16 of 17 rehearsal meetings at the community centre, in the park and, immediately prior to the final performance, on stage at the festival location, Wilhelm-Leuschner-Platz. At the beginning of every meeting, and especially when there were new participants, I introduced myself and explained the purpose of my research and my presence as a participant observer. I also regularly engaged in conversations about my role, my focus and my presence in the group during the course of the theatre project. After every meeting, I wrote fieldnotes from memory (19 entries in total). In these protocols, I noted who had attended the meetings and what had happened as well as any doubts and discomforts I perceived. I also reflected in greater depth on the social dynamics that evolved around a corporeal and story-based play that I participated in. A recorded interview with the director of the theatre production equally forms part of the ethnographic material.

The composition of the group was subject to constant fluctuation: while nearly one-half to two-thirds of participants in the initial workshops were young people with migration histories (most of them refugees/asylum seekers), at one point during the summer, only two women who had recently migrated to the city attended the rehearsals for the final production. At this point, I began to develop doubts about the project that coincided with concerns that I started to have about the relationship between gender and social engagement. However, I decided to continue my participation and to add observations on the dynamics of 'dropping out' and 'getting in' to the research agenda. New entries followed in early autumn and early 'dropouts' of the project returned – not always as actors on stage, but as faithful supporters, or associated artists. Taking part and dropping out, I observed, were closely tied to content-related dynamics in the project, as I will demonstrate in the empirical section. In total, around 30 young people engaged with the project and its different workshops and activities. In the end, a group of nine people, including myself, performed on stage. Two of us had a history of forced migration, three a family history of migration, and four were German-born white women. We were guided by our white, male theatre coach and supported by a make-up artist from Iran. Of this whole group, four identified as men, seven as women. The youngest participant was in her early twenties, while the oldest member of the group – the make-up artist – was around 70 years old. The age group that is in the focus of this contribution, hence, are young adults, aged between 20 and 30, with histories of forced migration.

My own stance on the degree to which I should engage with the project changed over time. While I had initially intended to act more as an observer and less as a participant (such as not to disrupt and influence the project unduly), after some reflection, I decided to take part fully in the process, including exercises, the sharing of personal stories, the shaping of the piece. The reflective process had strengthened my conviction that 'taking part' in a process that involved sensitive topics and exposed the vulnerability of participants without 'really' taking part would have been in conflict with my ethical commitment to the participants – and to the principles of participative research itself. I analysed the protocols with the help of the qualitative data analysis software MAXQDA, adopting a Grounded Theory-inspired (Glaser and Strauss, 1967) coding process that combined inductive and deductive approaches. Codes were developed from the notes themselves and supplemented by literature-based terms that allowed me to focus more specifically on varied forms and expressions of (dis)articulation.

Empirical analysis: bringing our personal stories on stage?

Silence as disarticulation/the withdrawal of stories
In this first empirical section, I will sound moments of rupture, silence and withdrawal that accompanied the theatre process from the start. As I have mentioned in the methodological section, this project has evolved out of a series of theatre-based communication workshops held in a sociocultural centre in the city during summer 2020. These workshops had been attended by a wide range of young newcomers and longer-term residents, with and without migration histories. I will start with a rather detailed description of the kick-off of the project, constituting one of the key moments I identified in my data.

At the kick-off meeting of the subsequent theatre project, we are eight people in the room: three young female students who, at that point, are still quite new to the city (Lisa, Johanna and Nina),[1] two young men who have migrated to Leipzig as refugees from Syria and find themselves in a legally stable but economically rather unstable position (Saad and Mahmoud), one young woman from Mexico who returned to Leipzig after her studies (Ela), me (Elisabeth) and the male theatre coach (Erik). After some warm-up exercises and a small round of introductions, the theatre coach, Erik, presents his general idea for the performance: to bring our personal stories on stage. The project is to culminate in a performance at a major sociocultural festival in one of the city's public spaces, in autumn 2020. This biennial community project is organised by the working group 'Socioculture' in Leipzig and culminates in the public presentation of a 'theatre collage' at the square of Wilhelm-Leuschner-Platz, one of the city's central public spaces.

In 2020, its overarching theme was 'It's enough. For everyone'. There will be no script, no guidelines – everything will evolve from a joint process (fieldnotes, 16 July 2020). With this in mind, we are asked to put our chairs aside and adopt a 'crazy' movement like carrying our leg behind us and moving across the room, as our coach demonstrates. I perform this with an uneasy feeling, thinking of how people with physical impairments might perceive this task, and I become particularly attentive to the opera song that our coach is playing in the background. The words 'One World' are sung repeatedly, first softly, then swelling and diminishing again, embedded in electronic tunes that, in the middle of the song, build up in an increasing frenzy. Then, we find ourselves in a circle again and, approaching the end of our meeting, Erik asks us to meditate for ten minutes. In our meditations, we are to reflect on whether there is a story from our lives that we want to tell, a story that is important to us, that the world should hear, and that we could transform into a message, in public. After thinking in silence, Erik asks us whether we would be ready to tell this story in groups of two. There is hesitation in the room and, as nobody answers, I decide to speak up and declare that this would be a very intimate practice – not impossible, but that I, at least, would have to think about it. Most of the group members agree. Erik expresses his satisfaction: our hesitation, in his understanding, shows that we had something serious and personal in mind. Wounds, ruptures, he says, speculating that this would be our concern, forming part of our lives, making us the person we are. It would not be easy, but sometimes helpful to tell these stories. As nobody speaks, Erik starts telling *his* story – a story that he decided to come out with in a blog several years before. Between the age of ten and 18, he experienced sexualised violence in the context of a youth group at the Catholic church he attended at that time. Regarding their 'gravity', he locates his experiences 'in the middle': neither were they minor, irregular happenings, nor did he experience direct physical violence. It took him until adulthood to partially digest this and to make his story public. Eric tells us his story to encourage us to come out with our own experiences, while by no means wanting us to feel pushed to tell something as intimate and grievous. The reaction to his story, again, is silence. Nobody speaks (fieldnotes, 16 July 2020). As I have a care commitment at home, I have to leave the room, very awkwardly, a bit earlier than the others, but I am told later that no discussion took place after Erik's intervention – the meeting closed, and people went home.

What can we deduce from this first meeting? First, Erik decides to 'open the stage' with a story that exposes the highest possible vulnerability: experiencing sexualised violence at a young age. Storying traumatic experiences, like this, is jotted as a possible script for our joint process. Although it has not been planned like this, the particular 'set-up' of the stage, as described earlier, almost inevitably casts those project participants who have experienced forced migration as bearers of wounds and ruptures related to their migration journeys. A dimension of debordering is added to this script by the opera song, 'One World'. We become 'tuned' to the vision of being one of building a community that overcomes fractures and differences so that it can tell 'its' stories. But are we really 'all one', in our stories/as bearers of stories? What kind of space does the story-based theatre project produce and, importantly, which means are used to appropriate the stories, for whom?

In the weeks that follow, I observe several dropouts and withdrawals that I interpret as being directly related to the way in which Erik had 'opened the stage' at our first meeting: Saad and Mahmoud do not return. In several meetings in July and August, we find ourselves in a smaller group of three or four women, none of us with a history of forced migration, working with Erik on our performance. Erik shares with us the doubts and struggles he went through after his 'coming out' (fieldnotes, 23 July 2020), questioning his 'rushing ahead' and wondering whether, in our view, the two young men's non-return was related to his story. And indeed, Ela tells us that Mahmoud, her friend, explained to her that he would not feel comfortable speaking personally about himself. "He doesn't like that," she says. Two months later, Mahmoud attends our first public performance on stage. I ask him how he looks back at the first meeting. How did it make him feel? "No", he replies, "This did not work for me, this storytelling." He shakes his head, puts his hands on his chest. He could not and would not retell his story over and over again. He also expresses that his main interest lies in encounter and exchange and not in theatre work. Here, I can only speculate whether class-related boundaries might also have played a role in his withdrawal from the project. Theatre spaces, and these concern also community theatre, are constitutively classed spaces that presume forms of knowledge and practice – condensed within cultural capital – that reproduce feelings of (dis)comfort.

Saad, whom I already knew before the project, equally explains to me via WhatsApp that he would not like to enact his personal story on stage. What he was mostly interested in were the theatre-based communication workshops in which he had taken part in May and June. These did not involve his personality 'as a whole' quite so strongly. "I am an iceberg," he replies to his friend, Johanna, when she asks him why he would not participate any longer. With this metaphor he emphasises his *right* to keep locked up and confined and to stay protected, not to 'dissolve' through emotional and personal close-up and disclosure.

My final reflection concerns a moment in which Fajid, a young refugee from Iraq, expresses his reservations about the sharing of stories. Fajid struggles with securing his legal position in Germany with the help of an apprenticeship and, as I learn later, with family reunification. Our encounter is mostly marked by his dream of establishing himself as a photographer. He had participated with a lot of motivation in the summer workshops. On his return to the theatre project at a later stage, Erik proposes a scenario in which Fajid would 'tell his story', and we as a group would comment on and co-narrate while Fajid's photographs were presented in the background. Fajid makes his opposition to this idea demonstrably clear by positioning his hand on his upper chest, saying that he would neither want nor be able to tell his story. With a low voice and a slight shaking of his head, he is rejecting this possible script. He is expressing, very physically, his right to remain closed, covered, concealed – a gesture-based renunciation that I had already observed several weeks earlier, when I had asked Fajid whether I could interview him for our research project. He agreed to a photo-walk but declined to speak of himself, tell his story, with a clear "No, rather not."

Erik's intervention, we can conclude, has provoked a rupture in participation. His attempt to create an atmosphere that allows the *sharing* of intimate and sensitive topics and the *opening* of a space of trust has rather had a counter-effect: closure and withdrawal. With reference to Butterwick and Selman, his spontaneous impulse to invest in high 'risk-taking' (2020, p 39) in order to decrease the risk of self-exposure for other participants in the room has not proven successful. Story-spaces here reveal themselves as highly fractured and power-laden discursive spaces in which 'high risks' might be shared, while the stories at play might involve very different realms of social experience and, hence, vulnerabilities with regards to the body, affect, gender, status and sexuality. The means of articulation, within these spaces, are unevenly distributed: story-spaces are intersectionally rifted. Furthermore, the described process raises questions about the taken-for-granted nature of narrative disclosure and exposure as supposedly liberating practices that enhance homemaking processes: we can transfer Sanchez's critical analysis of queer coming out as a practice that is grounded in whiteness (2017), to the story-based space described earlier, and ask: 'Which kind of space is it, that different participants are encouraged to "come out" in with their story?' First, does it feel safe enough? And second, which benefit can they expect from acceding to it through their story-sharing? While interculturality was clearly set as one central component of the theatre process, newcomers' everyday experiences of being racialised or excluded, for instance, were not prefigured in the narrative set-up. Sanchez writes: 'This vision of coming out implies access to a cultural space where identity is well-defined and validated' (Sanchez, 2017). The young refugees' dropping out, I come to learn, performs a response to a setting in which the story-space they could unfold in was limited: the combination of an intercultural invocation with the invitation to story violence and trauma worked as an equivalent to pinning young newcomers down to an identity that is confined by the racial category of 'refugee' – an un-homed victim of violence. And finally, while Erik's intervention laid out strings one could possibly attach to, with regards to experiences of (sexualised) violence, it also pre-assumed a particular *access* to and conscious work on bodily experiences and sensations and violence-related memory.

In sum, the whole process reveals how privilege and oppression can intersect in a highly ambivalent manner and simultaneously empower and hamper the articulation and, subsequently, the spatial unfolding of differently positioned subjects. While stories, in participatory theatre and beyond, bear the power to subvert power structures and enhance processes of empowerment, the centrality of storytelling within participatory theatre can, at the same time, reproduce discursive orders that privilege realms of experience tied to particular subjectivities, while muting or silencing others. 'Race, context and subjectivity' (Hopkins, 2017, p 942) interact in such a way here that young people with histories of forced migration withdraw from the process. In the context of the theatre project, it was first assumed that they would feel safe enough to speak out. Yet, in this space, whiteness posed a 'silent norm' (Dietze, 2014. Second, community theatres, too, reproduce class-related boundaries that bestow a privilege on participants who, through their personal or familial biographies, gained knowledge and habits within cultural social spaces. And third, the project addressed them as deliverers of a story already known: their migration journey.

Silence as articulation/the return of stories

In this second empirical section, I trace how silence and not-speaking, the absence of stories, were eventually put very centrally on the agenda of the performance work and became transformed into the piece's central message. I argue that it was through this, the absence of certain subjectivities, that paradoxically a transformative and constitutive presence could unfold. This change in direction equally re-directs our attention back to the potentiality of participatory theatre as a space that is, while being prefigured, not scripted.

It is our fourth meeting when Lisa, whom we had just updated on the preceding week's thematic brainstorming, declares that she feels increasingly bothered by the fact that silence and the practice of remaining silent are always associated with such negative connotations. According to her, remaining silent is a decision that results from the awareness that speaking out/telling our stories would not always heal the wound. Silence, she explains, has been central to the project from the start: at the beginning, when we were asked to share our stories, then, when Erik's story was responded to with silence, and, finally, when participants dropped out due to their reluctance to tell their stories (fieldnotes, 6 August 2020). Lisa conceives of silence, non-disclosure, the right to keep things to oneself, as a response in its own right. Erik directly picks up on this idea and re-imagines Saad's, Mahmoud's and Fajid's return to the project – "They could join us on stage while remaining silent." With their resistance to the telling of stories, they are put centre stage. Their absence has unleashed an agenda-setting dynamic. The focus has switched: from stories to concealed presences and absences on stage.

In the weeks that follow, we prepare a performance built around very concise 'topics' that we are 'fed up with' – in response to the motto that frames the sociocultural festival we will become part of: 'It's enough. For everyone'. Interpreting 'It's enough' in the sense of 'Enough!' ('Stop!'), we assemble personal statements – as, for instance, 'violence against women', or 'pollution of the woods', without, however, further exploring them. We equally work on how to stage silence. Saad and Mahmoud, in the meantime, have not returned and other participants drop out shortly before our performance, such as Fajid, who has to study for his language exam. However, the project has also won new participants: Lucius, who migrated from Nigeria to Leipzig one and a half years before and still lives in an initial reception centre at the outskirts of the city; Katarina, born in Spain, who has returned to Leipzig and found the project while searching for new people and spaces to connect with; and Ammer who favours music over words as language and joins the group as a guitarist. At the beginning of September, I mark a 'turning point' in my fieldnotes. The room is crowded during rehearsals, and the group starts to be caught in a constructive dynamic of progression. The performance takes shape. At its beginning, we stand in rows, keeping a distance. One by one, we first shout our messages towards the public: "All lives matter." "Food waste." "Discrimination." Then, our voices, different languages and topics increasingly overlap, intermingle and end up in an ear-piercing, incomprehensible cacophony. Erik's idea to interrupt this noise with a loud "Stop" in order to let it drop into silence is critically debated as a 'muting'. Finally, we decide to let silence speak out of a particular person and story: Raheel, who was born in Iran and joined the group one month before the presentation.

Raheel's dropping-in happens rather accidentally. Originally, she was present only as a language support for an elderly make-up artist who only spoke Farsi and who was supposed to paint our faces for the presentation. After being quickly introduced to our project, Raheel literally jumps in, spontaneously entering the stage where we are already lined up, ready to rehearse. Erik asks us to close our eyes, to take deep breaths, to meditate on our topic, to sense the feelings that we relate to it and to localise them in our bodies. He asks us to open our eyes when being called up and to shout out our topic loudly, increase the speed of our shouts until we reach the aforementioned overlapping noise. Erik calls up Raheel first. She keeps silent. We wait. There is tension in the room. We were tuned to expecting a moment of discharge that does not materialise. Erik takes a step closer to Raheel, asks her if everything is OK. She nods, and we start again. This time, we agree, Raheel will not be appointed first. We shout our words and when, by the end, Raheel is appointed: silence, again. She does not get the words out. Again, we wait – all moved by this very special and tense moment. Raheel starts to cry and leaves the room. Nina follows her. When they come back, Raheel smiles again. Erik asks her how she feels. Would she like to tell us what her topic will be? Raheel struggles for a minute. Then it bursts out of her: suppression. "Not being able to speak, not being able to express what you feel, the suppression of words and thoughts – it's enough!" She is very moved, as we all are in the room. Lucius asks me, whispering, whether what she means is 'freedom of speech'. I partly confirm this, describing it as "not being able to say what you think and feel". Erik explains to Raheel that what has just happened has accompanied our rehearsals from the start: moments of silence, of not-speaking, of disarticulation. He mentions his story that nobody had reacted to and the general topic of silence. "It's okay", he says. "It's enough. Silence is enough" (fieldnotes, 17 September 2020). After this second key moment in the process of developing the theatre performance, Raheel forms part of the group. She expresses her topic in Dutch, her second mother-tongue: "underdrykking". It will be her role, we all agree, to articulate silence. After more dialogical rounds, in which we explore our topics a bit further, calling each other in, we end up asking, first with stronger, then with softer voices: "Raheel? … Raheel?" And Raheel keeps silent. Her silence speaks violence and pain. After a 'utopian part' – a dancing scene accompanied by the opera song 'One World' – we, again, stand in rows, silently. Lisa then, after a minute, reads a poem that she has written on the topic of silence. The poem relates to her grandmother's memory of violence and is accompanied by Ammer's soft guitar sounds.

We can conclude that the young newcomers' 'refusal to partake in the story' (Minh-ha, 1989, p 83) has ultimately provoked a 'hearing' (Minh-ha, 1989, p 83), a moment of awareness and insight within the group that has inspired the participants to sound silence as a 'response in its own right' (Minh-ha, 1989, p 83). I would go as far as to say that silence, the right not to speak within the performance, was exactly one of these 'stories missing' (Butterwick and Selman, 2020, p 35) within public discourses that tend to stage stories of migration (journeys) as spectacles. Their (dis)articulation continually ruptured the process. It can hence be understood as a moment of self-assertion in the sense meant by Razack (1998, p 50), who asks critically whom 'storytelling serves', and how. Silence, literally, made the story.

When I interview him about the process, Erik reflects on the conversion from sharing stories to staging silence. He describes the moment of his "coming-out story" as a "neuralgic point" (fieldnotes, 10 September 2020) that has triggered a learning process in him on the nature of storytelling: "Namely, that not everyone feels the urge, like me, to make a particular story public." Retrospectively, Erik acknowledges that he "projected his own character on others" (fieldnotes, 10 September 2020), and that recognising "that this is not the case, that people simply do not want to tell their stories" has "worked in him" and "entered the further process" (fieldnotes, 10 September 2020). While the decision to lay the focus on "topics that infuriate us", without further exploring the "stories behind" (fieldnotes, 10 September 2020), has not provoked the immediate return of former members of the group (with migration histories), it has created a space that allows articulation within concealment. I could witness how this very particular story-space on stage could be appropriated almost without bridging work: only a few minutes after Lucius' first presence in the group, he exclaims, "All lives matter", and later "racism" across the room, expanding, in the second and more dialogical round, on his claim "to stop racism – in the tram, in the supermarket, in the streets" (fieldnotes, 28 September 2020).

What I equally observed was a 'return' of stories, not on stage but aside from the project. When Mahmoud, on the day of our first public performance, shares with me why silence is better for him, he evokes the violence that he went through during the war in Syria and the dreadful experiences related to his journey. I get to learn more and more details about his story as I try to communicate to him my respect for his decision not to tell his story, to remain silent and to withdraw from the process. Hence, it does not seem to be the mere action of telling stories that is refuted, but the invocation to do so in a space that is, first, opened from a position of (relative) power and, second, lined by a story template that promotes not only narrative disclosure but does not explicitly rupture with the public desire for (dramatic) 'refugee stories'. What I can also observe, however, is that young newcomers to the project, such as Lucius, can build connections: I notice him telling different participants about the political and economic situation in his home country, about everyday racism he encounters in the city, his complicated legal situation and his passion for theatre. It seems as if our familiarisation with one another has indeed been enhanced by the vulnerabilities we have disclosed, without exposing ourselves, on stage. In the end, participatory theatre has created, in its unpredictability, a space of mutual care, trust and, paradoxically, articulation.

Reflection of my presence and positionality within the project

Witnessing the drop-outs and withdrawals, I noticed, very awkwardly, an increasing impulse to legitimise my presence as a researcher on 'everyday experiences of young refugees and asylum seekers in public space' in the group. How could I continue my participative engagement in this setting without young people with histories of forced migration attending? Repeatedly, I caught myself 'lurking' for stories, *their* stories as well. 'I am a bit disappointed', I note, when for one story-based exercise I find myself in the group with Katha and Alina, 'because I know them already and because I'm indeed more interested in the group members with histories of forced migration'. In a reflection on my positionality within the research process, I write:

> I orient my ears and my perception on *their* stories, want to hear something from *them*. Again and again, then, I re-orient my focus on the group, the interactions, the whole. But this 'checking out' (who might 'fit' into our research) is by itself such a practice of differentiation, contradictory to all research ethical approaches. (Fieldnotes, November 2020)

So, while critically reflecting my contribution to the 'fetishising' migrant narratives, I am enmeshed in the focalising on personal narratives and narrative disclosures that is characteristic of the social sciences. I thus contribute to the 'migrantising' of young newcomers' negotiations of arrival and emplacement in the city. The virtue of ethnographic approaches (patience, attentiveness, openness to the field) has, however, worked as a corrective here: the dynamics of the field re-oriented my focus – from the *stories* of newcomers to the power dynamics that constitute relations of speech, encounter, disclosure and emplacement. The process has equally exemplified how academic and non-academic spaces can fruitfully intersect within knowledge production. Here, it was an arts-based process that stimulated conceptual reflection and led me to the insight of 'silence as articulation', an insight that I, as researcher, can now further explore theoretically and empirically. My participative presence sensitised me to the spatialities of theatre-based storytelling, in which, more than anything else, what matters is from which position a stage-space is opened and awareness of 'intersectional vulnerabilities' (Ho and Maddrell, 2020) constitute it. This reflection involves, very centrally, the reflection of privilege. 'Whose vision is "one world"?', I noted in my research diary. 'Is it a white phantasy?' In certain moments, I perceived this performed dream of 'one world without suppression, without racism, where there is enough for everyone' (fieldnotes, 24 September 2020) as 'cynical'. My reflection was prompted, for instance, by a moment in which Erik encouraged us to radiate boundless joy through dancing, in relation to the opera song, in the 'utopian part' of the project. This happened shortly after Lucius had shared with me that he had not seen his daughter for more than a year. Similarly, when in one theatre exercise I found myself in a small group with two other white, German-born women and we narrated to each other where we had travelled to and stayed abroad, across the globe, I noted, 'Our stories are stories of privilege, of the luxury to be mobile, of education backgrounds that allow developing international professional biographies' (fieldnotes, 22 June 2020). To sum up: my self-reflexive observations call for a more nuanced exploration of the 'whiteness' of stories and storytelling within participatory theatre.

Conclusion

The first conclusion I would like to draw with regards to the complicated relationship between story-based theatre and the living situation of newcomers in the city directly follows up on the concluding statement made earlier: the articulation of subjugated knowledges through stories in participatory theatre calls for *intersectional story-work* in the sense of creating a space that makes it possible to recognise and deliberate the gendered, race- and status-related orders that enable and disable us in different ways. Participatory theatre does not, per se, imply equal participation. The way we are called into being by discursive structures that continually reproduce what is centred, normal, inside, impacts on the distribution of speech among members of a group and on the unfolding of affective (im)possibilities. These invocations and embodied 'responses' to unequally distributed means of articulation, however, are not static. They depend very strongly on the particular social context, which, in the case of the theatre project, was a space dedicated to the empowerment of newcomers, but which nonetheless remained primarily a 'white' space. They also depend on how the relational mesh of identifiers (Collins and Bilge, 2016), in terms of body, language, gender, status or religion, are displayed. Butterwick and Selman's reflection on 'risk-taking' within story-based theatre (2020, p 39) gives this argument a further twist. 'Risks' that involve intersecting experiences related to body, sexuality and emotions, and that tell stories of violence, equally unfold in imbalanced fields of power that are shaped by global histories of domination. Here is where 'race' is at play. It wouldn't suffice, however, to apply a categorial understanding of story-spaces as crossed by race, gender, age and status in order to create a 'safe space' for everyone. The relationship between the affective and body-related experience of comfort and safety to differences in positionality is a very unpredictable and complex one. It demands high investment in shared consciousness and active sensibility in order to anticipate the following questions: For whom is storytelling a relief? For whom is it a burden? And what can the audience to whom the storytelling is directed hear at all in the end? 'A decolonising approach to embodied theatre pedagogy is all about being safe enough to be dangerous', Butterwick and Selman (2020, p 68) remind us. Providing this safety, in my view, not only involves the collective reflection on 'disclosure consequences' (Butterwick and Selman, 2020, p 68) but also addresses participants, not as potentially vulnerable story-bearers, but rather as agents of knowledge and expertise who have learned to negotiate a position within urban societies marked by spatial borderings that are discursive as well as material.

The second conclusion I would like to draw departs from this emphasis on the *agency* of young refugees and asylum seekers. Experiences of crafting arrival has bestowed young refugees and asylum seekers with the capacity to make use of community spaces as 'toolkits', as spaces with resources that they can draw on and decide to invest in or receive something from, or not. Practices of taking part and dropping out, hence, should not be interpreted from the angle of potential trauma and its concealment alone but most centrally as strategic evaluations of community spaces. Projects are used here as resources for finding one's way in the new urban society, for building networks, knotting ties to stabilise one's position and secure a future. Speaking from, and further exploring, this knowledge and affective expertise can, then, turn related storytelling processes within participatory theatre into a highly valuable resource for young newcomers in the city and in the respective sociocultural spaces. In sum, the process described in this chapter demonstrates how micro-interactions can provoke the re-setting of agendas and, hence, unleash a dynamic of change that challenges bordering regimes that do not come to a halt in front of arts-based spaces of participation.

Note
[1] These names have been anonymised.

References
Barnes, S. (2009) 'Drawing a line: a discussion of ethics in participatory arts with young refugees', in *Participatory Arts with Young Refugees: Six Essays*, London: Arts in Education, Oval House Theatre, pp 34–40.

Butterwick, S. and Selman, J. (2012) 'Embodied knowledge and decolonization: walking with theater's powerful and risky pedagogy', *New Directions for Adult and Continuing Education*, 134: 61–69.

Butterwick, S. and Selman, J. (2020) 'Community-based art making: creating spaces for changing the story', *New Directions for Adult and Continuing Education*, 165: 35–47.

Chou, M., Gagon, J.-P. and Pruitt, L. (2015) 'Putting participation on stage: examining participatory theatre as an alternative site for political participation', *Policy Studies*, 36(6): 607–622.

Collins, P. and Bilge, S. (2016) *Intersectionality*, Cambridge: Polity Press.

Dietze, G. (2014) 'Race, gender and whiteness', *Einige Überlegungen zu Intersektionalität. FKW// Zeitschrift für Geschlechterforschung und Visuelle Kultur*, 56.

Erel, U. and Reynolds, T. (2014) 'Black feminist theory for participatory theatre with migrant mothers', *Feminist Review*, 108: 106–111.

Erel, U., Reynolds, T. and Kaptani, E. (2017) 'Participatory theatre for transformative social research', *Qualitative Research*, 17(3): 302–312.

Glaser, B.G. and Strauss, A.L. (1967) *The Discovery of Grounded Theory: Strategies for Qualitative Research*, Aldine Publishing Company.

Ho, E. and Maddrell, A. (2020) 'Intolerable intersectional burdens: a COVID-19 research agenda for social and cultural geographies', *Social & Cultural Geography*, 22(1): 1–10.

Hopkins, P. (2017) 'Social geography I: intersectionality', *Progress in Human Geography*, 43(5): 937–947.

Isin, E.F. and Nielsen, G.M. (eds) (2013) *Acts of Citizenship*, London: Zed Books.

Kaptani, E. and Yuval-Davis, N. (2008) 'Participatory theatre as research methodology: identity, performance and social action among refugees', *Sociological Research Online*, 13(5).

Minh-Ha, T.T. (1989) *Woman, Native, Other: Writing Postcoloniality and Feminism*, Bloomington, IN: Indiana University Press.

Perry, A. (2012) 'A silent revolution: "image theatre" as a system of decolonisation', *Research in Drama Education*, 17(1): 103–119.

Razack, S. (1998) 'Race, space, and prostitution', *Canadian Journal of Women and the Law*, 19(2): 338–376.

Sanchez, A. (2017) 'The whiteness of "coming out": culture and identity in the disclosure narrative', *Archer Magazine*, available from: http://archermagazine.com.au/2017/07/culture-coming-out/

Sonn, C., Quayle, A., Belanji, B. and Baker, A. (2015) 'Responding to racialization through arts practice: the case of participatory theatre', *Journal of Community Psychology*, 43(2): 244–259.

Stam, V. (2020) 'The possibilities and limits of participatory theatre: exploring belonging and resistance with second-generation Black and Muslim Dutch youth in the Netherlands', *Migration Letters*, 17(2): 289–297.

Yuval-Davis, N., Wemyss G. and Cassidy, K. (2018) 'Everyday bordering, belonging and the reorientation of British Immigration legislation', *Sociology*, 53(2): 228–244.

3

Jackets and Jewellery: Racialised Dispossession and Struggles over Public Space in Denmark

Malene H. Jacobsen

Introduction

During the late summer and fall of 2020, the Danish Prime Minister, Mette Frederiksen, repeatedly claimed that groups of so-called '*indvandrerdrenge*' (immigrant boys) were creating public insecurity. According to Frederiksen, '*indvandrerdrenge*' were hanging out in groups along sidewalks, on public transportation and in neighbourhood parking lots and public squares, where their (supposedly) inappropriate behaviour was making others feel unsafe. In response, Frederiksen and her government proposed to provide the police with a new authority to break up these groups of '*indvandrerdrenge*', fine them and confiscate their 'expensive jackets, watches and mobile phones' (Frederiksen, 2020, translation by author).

In this chapter, I examine this imperative to remove so-called '*indvandrerdrenge*' from public spaces and confiscate their personal belongings. The literal translation of the term '*indvandrerdrenge*' in English is 'immigrant boys'. Yet, within the contemporary Danish context, this term is far from neutral. As a compound term of 'immigrant' and 'boy', '*indvandrerdrenge*' conjures a specific racialised demographic of male youth or young adults. Referring to this group as 'boys' relies on an unsubtle paternalism, framing this group as lacking adult characteristics. Furthermore, rather than immigrants per se, '*indvandrerdrenge*' refers to young 'non-western' immigrants or young men whose parents or grandparents have immigrated from so-called 'non-western' countries. These associations are tied to growing attempts by the Danish state to collect data testifying to the existence of this new social category. Since 2002, the national statistical agency, Statistics Denmark, has recorded statistical information about *indvandrer* (immigrants) and *efterkommer* (their descendants) living in Denmark. Statistics Denmark classifies immigrants and their descendants according to two categories: 'western' and 'non-western'. Western countries include the member states of the EU (including the UK), Andorra, Iceland, Liechtenstein, Monaco, Norway, San Marino, Switzerland, Vatican City, Canada, the United States, Australia and New Zealand. The rest of the world's 156 countries are defined as 'non-western' countries.

This categorisation enables politicians, journalists and social scientists to refer to 'non-western' immigrants and their descendants – people from over 150 different countries – as 'a somewhat monolithic object of governmental intervention and social scientific inquiry' (Zhang, 2020). For instance, the government has described 'non-western' immigrants and their descendants living in socially marginalised areas as 'a group of people who do not take on Danish norms and values' (Regeringen, 2018, p 5, translation by author), and it has instituted a range of punitive policies, such as the 2018 ban on wearing the burqa and niqab in public (Folketinget, 2018). Moreover, the terminology of 'non-western immigrants' as well as '*indvandrerdrenge*' functions as a euphemism for Muslims (Yilmaz, 2016; Zhang, 2020). Thus, when Frederiksen and others used the seemingly neutral expression, '*indvandrerdrenge*', it crucially worked as a dog whistle, in the sense of categorising Muslim male youth in Denmark as designated Others, unruly and menacing to public order and safety, without the use of explicit racial signifiers. I here use the Danish word '*indvandrerdrenge*' to highlight its specific contextual meaning, yet in quotation marks to problematise it.

Frederiksen's attack on '*indvandrerdrenge*' and proposal to confiscate their belongings is illustrative of a broader trend within western states' reception of refugees (Ziadah, 2016) and treatment of racialised migrants more broadly (Bhandar, 2016; Cahill et al, 2016; Farris, 2016). In this chapter, I situate Frederiksen's attack within the Danish state's ongoing use of dispossessive practices to manage, control and eliminate racialised groups. Through a close reading of the government's initiative to combat '*indvandrerdrenge*', I demonstrate the ways that moments of dispossession work to classify and differentiate '*indvandrerdrenge*' as a social category of undesirables and police their behaviour and presence in public accordingly. It does so through colonial, racial and gendered grammars, which effectively regulate and criminalise the visibility of Muslims in Danish public space. Furthermore, refugee/migrant youth's refusal to engage with dominant discourses of criminalisation and standard liberal terms of the model minority offers important insights into the ways in which youth reclaim public space and political belonging, suggesting a need for geographers and others to pay greater attention to youth's counter-politics, framings and expressions.

This chapter is based on an analysis of political documents, policy proposals, officials' speeches and press releases pertaining to the prime minister's call as well as public advocacy campaigns, which have emerged in response. Through a feminist intersectional reading (Fluri, 2014) of these texts and the context in which they emerge, I trace the emergence of particular state-led discourses and practices of 'casting out' (Razack, 2008) and the ways in which the individuals and communities affected by such measures have attempted to push back. Here I unpack a range of responses, from more traditional liberal critiques of racialised statecraft to alternative forms, characterised by a commitment to an ethics and politics of refusal.

In what follows, I first provide a brief overview of dispossession as an analytic lens and how this concept has been taken up by scholars working on issues of migration and migrant subjectivity. Second, I unpack the prime minister's call to confiscate down jackets, watches and mobile phones, and the following proposal to enhance police power. I then examine how racialised youth (including refugees and migrants) have sought to counteract the idea of '*indvandrerdrenge*' as a security 'threat' to the Danish public. I conclude this chapter by discussing what the analytic of dispossession offers research on the racialisation of youth and struggles for spatial justice.

Politics of dispossession

Critical scholars, including geographers, have examined various forms of dispossession and their entanglements. These include the appropriation of Indigenous lands (Coulthard, 2014; Byrd, 2018; Launius and Boyce, 2020), labour (Harvey, 2003; Chakravartty and Ferreira da Silva, 2012), bodies and personhood (Hartman, 2008; Butler and Athanasiou, 2013; Fuentes, 2016; Roy, 2017; Threadcraft, 2018). In relation to migration and migrant/refugee communities specifically, scholars have long framed forced migration and displacement as a form of dispossession because displaced people often lose their homes and their access to land and territories (Chatty, 2010; Ziadah, 2016; Canefe, 2018). Yet, dispossession is more than the practice of *taking* materials such as land, resources, homes and personal belongings. It also refers to a broad yet specific set of (historical) processes that work to systematically exclude, eliminate and alienate particular groups of people from others (Nichols, 2019). Indeed, as Bhandar and Bhandar (2016) have argued, we need to conceptualise territorial dispossession and displacement *in relation* to other forms of dispossession such as cultural, psychic and affective dispossession, which (forced) migrants and other racialised communities are subject to.

A few scholars have already taken up this call. Cahill et al (2016), for example, have drawn attention to the ways that the immigration policies and everyday practices of racialised exclusions work in concert to (re)produce a 'school-to-sweatshop pipeline', through which young people of colour, including young (undocumented) immigrants, are forced into exploitative and precarious labour conditions. As a result, undocumented students are dispossessed of potential futures. These findings resonate with Bhandar's (2016) work on legal status as central to the politics of dispossession of liberal-democratic nation states. Drawing together the experiences of both Indigenous peoples and migrants, Bhandar illustrates how regimes of legal status and political membership are 'formed out of the multiple layers of exclusion, dispossession and displacement' (p 2) and establish 'differential and contingent forms of belonging to the state' (p 2). Bhandar argues that processes of ethnicisation and racialisation are central to the ways in which status-making operates as a form of bordering and dispossession.

More broadly, processes of dispossession operate through and (re)produce social formations, such as race, gender, age, sexuality and class (Bhandar and Bhandar, 2016; Nichols, 2019; Gazzotti and Hagan, 2021). Through her research on civic integration programmes in France and the Netherlands, Farris (2016, p 1) demonstrates how European governments target migrant Muslim families, particularly migrant Muslim mothers, seeking to extract these women 'from the backward worlds in which they are deemed to live, that is, to "emancipate" them'. Through educational materials, mandatory exams, so-called 'integration' contracts and introductory meetings, these civic integration programmes emphasise themes such as gender equality, sexuality and women's rights, and the rights and duties of parents, (re)producing 'derogatory images of non-western, Muslim immigrants' cultural practices' (Farris, 2016, p 7). In doing so, they work through the private sphere to dispossess migrants' identities and values. Furthermore, Farris' research importantly highlights how these programmes are animated by colonial logics and anxieties (see also Bhandar, 2016). This challenges us to more actively guard against exceptionalising contemporary moments or events of dispossession by situating them within long and ongoing histories of dispossession and drawing attention to the continuities in the outcomes they produce, even if shifting in their specific 'techniques, methods and justifications' (Nichols, 2019, p 90).

Indeed, while critics called Frederiksen's proposal to confiscate valuables from '*indvandrerdrenge*' as highly unusual, even unprecedented, it was anything but. The practice of *taking* – expropriating, confiscating and appropriating – possessions (land, status, money, labour, family members and personal belongings) from people has a long history in Denmark. During its colonial and imperial era, Denmark stole land, resources and people as it established colonies on the east coast of India and the coast of contemporary Ghana, colonised the Virgin Islands, Iceland, Greenland and the Faroe Islands, and actively participated in the Atlantic slave trade (Jensen, 2015). Over time, Denmark's practices of dispossession have changed form and been rationalised in the name of modernisation, development and security. For instance, in 1951, the Danish state forcibly removed 22 Indigenous children from their families and communities in Greenland and sent them to Denmark as part of an effort to 'modernise' Indigenous people. Most of these children never saw their families again and lost their language, culture and identities (Jensen et al, 2022).

More recently, in January 2016, the Danish government instituted Bill 87 (*Lovforslag nr: L 87*), also known as the Jewellery Bill (*Smykkeloven*) (Bilefsky, 2016). The bill was rushed through the legislative procedure and passed by a majority of the parliament on 26 January 2016. This bill enabled the Danish police to search newly arrived asylum seekers' bodies and luggage in order to seize their cash and other assets of 'considerable value', including rings, necklaces, watches, mobile phones and computers. An item is defined as being of 'considerable' value if the police deem it to be worth more than 10,000 DKK (€1,345). The government first proposed to make this threshold 3,000 DKK (€403). The ostensible rationale of the bill was to defray the cost of asylum seekers' stays in an asylum centre (Folketinget, 2015), reinforcing myths of refugees and asylum seekers as 'bogus' and 'freeloaders'. Yet, the idea that asylum seekers' possessions would raise significant funds is plainly absurd. Reports have shown that, within the first three years of this law being in place, the police have seized one car and approximately 186,800 DKK (€24,893) in cash, but no jewellery (*Politiken*, 2019).

Although seized possessions such as jackets, jewellery, computers and cars have little economic value to the Danish state, I suggest that this practice is nevertheless highly significant. More specifically, I argue, the act of taking asylum seekers' valuables should be seen as a form of dispossession working to sunder 'humanity into categories' (Nichols, 2019, p 115) and thereby reinscribe boundaries between saviour and refugee, host and guest, and Dane and foreigner. It is in this moment of seizing and taking asylum seekers' valuables – a practice instituted and legitimised through law – through which the categories of 'asylum seeker' and 'refugee' are (re)produced as a constitutively different group of people that is a 'threat' to the (White) Danish welfare state. It serves as a tool of domination through which the Danish state can subject asylum seekers and refugees to practices that would otherwise be deemed unacceptable.

However, as Black feminists, Indigenous scholars and other critical scholars have shown, 'dispossession is partially constitutive of the modes of subjectivity and forms of group identification ... it engenders, but it is not determinate' (Nichols, 2019, p 108). People subject to dispossessive processes actively negotiate, challenge and resist dispossession and the relations produced and manifested through acts of dispossession. More specifically, refusal has been central to the ways in which marginalised groups contest practices of dispossession (Bhandar, 2016). Simpson's (2014) account of a 'politics of refusal' importantly highlights a politics that does not necessarily involve direct opposition. Rather, it denounces the normalised order of things and may offer radical alternatives and political possibilities (also see McGranahan, 2016; Newhouse, 2021). A politics of refusal is a useful lens for interpreting the multiple ways in which racialised youth contest and push back against structures of dispossession, contributing to the existing literature on youth politics (Skelton, 2010; Kallio and Häkli, 2013; Hopkins et al, 2019).

Building on these insights, I draw on dispossession as an analytic to examine how racialised youth are policed as threats to public security and subject to practices of removal and confiscation. While I am concerned with the actual (material) *taking* of possessions (down jackets, watches and mobile phones) from racialised male youth, my focus is on how such actions work to inscribe and consolidate particular geographies of public exclusion by criminalising certain kinds of bodies, behaviours, comportment and sociality. It is to this that I now turn.

'Jackets, watches and mobile phones'

The attack on the presence and behaviour of '*indvandrerdrenge*' in public first began at a press conference held in front of Benniksgaard Hotel in Gråsten on a sunny afternoon in late August of 2020. Lined up in front of reporters from major Danish news agencies and TV channels, Mette Frederiksen and the Minister of Justice, Nick Hækkerup, used the pretext of dealing with '*indvandrerdrenge*' as a justification for the government's new police reform to be presented the following week. As Frederiksen explained: 'This [policy] concerns the fact that when people use the S-trains in Greater Copenhagen then they should not be afraid to travel home at night because there are 15–17 *indvandrerdrenge* who do not know how to behave properly' (cited in Holm, 2020, emphasis and translation by author).

At the annual opening of the Danish Parliament on 6 October 2020, Frederiksen expanded her claims against '*indvandrerdrenge*' as she spent much of her speech asserting that this group is creating insecurity across the country. Frederiksen referenced crime statistics suggesting that one in five men in Denmark of 'non-western' origin born in 1997 had broken the law before turning 21, arguing that: 'It is not everyone, certainly not everyone. But it is patently too many. Young men, who take the freedom of others, steal children's futures, intimidate prison guards – and leave behind a long trail of insecurity' (Frederiksen, 2020, translation by author). Frederiksen further claimed that these boys and young men often gather in parking lots of residential areas and at train stations, where they create insecurity. In order to deal with this issue of public (in)security, Frederiksen proposed that the police should be able to ban groups of '*indvandrerdrenge*' from certain areas at certain times of the day. If a group refused to observe such a ban, the police should issue a fine of 10,000 DKK (€1,343) to each person. Furthermore, a person was to pay this fine on the spot if they had state debt (this could include unpaid fines for other minor offences, such as traffic tickets); otherwise, the police should confiscate their personal belongings such as 'expensive jackets, watches and mobile phones' (Frederiksen, 2020, translation by author). For second offences, Frederiksen stated that suspects would be punished with imprisonment for up to 30 days.

In the policy document, 'Security for all Danes' (*Tryghed for alle danskere*) published the following day, the government repeated Frederiksen's arguments about *'indvandrerdrenge'*. Throughout the document, the government claimed that young men's behaviour and appearance create insecurity. The government stated that groups of young men 'exercise unacceptable behaviour. ... They are dominating areas in public spaces and create an everyday that is marked by fear and insecurity for other people', thereby 'limiting *normal people's* freedom' (Regeringen, 2020, p 2, translation by author). In an attempt to define so-called 'behaviour that creates insecurity' (*utryghedsskabende adfærd*), the government stated that it was to be defined through a concrete assessment on a case-by-case basis. One has to 'consider the number of people in the group, nuisance noise, and whether the group is exercising harassing and/or threatening behaviour that can create insecurity among other people within the particular public space' (Regeringen, 2020, p 4, translation by author). Finally, the government outlined a 'safety and security package', which included four new initiatives to combat insecurities created by criminals and groups of youth hanging out in public spaces, initiatives promised to be instituted by law in 2021 (Regeringen, 2020).

The prime minister's attack on *'indvandrerdrenge'* and the government's initiatives to criminalise their presence and behaviour in public is just one of many examples of xenophobic anti-immigration discourses and policies in Denmark. In debates about migrants and other racialised communities in Denmark, 'non-western' immigrants and their descendants as a 'unified' group are often a euphemism for Muslims (Zhang, 2020). While politicians have managed to eliminate the burka and niqab from public display, they have also insisted on the need to serve pork in public daycare centres and argued that people observing the Ramadan should be forced to take vacation during this time because they are not able to carry out their jobs in a productive and safe manner. In all these respects, Danish politicians' attempts to demonise Muslims' ways of life and cultural practices are far from unique and resonate closely with a range of xenophobic policies in Europe and elsewhere, such as the 2004 ban on religious symbols in public institutions in France and the increase in everyday Islamophobic attacks that followed (Najib and Hopkins, 2019), integration programmes targeting Muslims' way of life (Farris, 2016), the increased surveillance and monitoring of Arab and Muslim communities in the US and UK post-9/11 (Staeheli and Nagel, 2008), and President Donald Trump's attempt to implement a 'Muslim ban' (Gökariksel, 2017).

These policy interventions work through manoeuvres that cultivate a sense of fear and insecurity under the spectre of 'new' threats facing the (White) nation (Pain, 2009; Fluri, 2014).

Yet, the government's invention of the category of '*indvandrerdrenge*' and subsequent efforts to mobilise it to stoke fear around urban (in)security worked to direct state resources to eliminate racialised male youth's 'bad behaviour' and 'threatening appearance' in public spaces. Working through inherently gendered and racialised language and grammar (that is, dangerous *male* youth of colour), this spectre of '*indvandrerdrenge*' criminalises certain male youth, whose mere presence, appearance and behaviour in public are deemed to create insecurity for those described as 'normal' people by Frederiksen – White Danes. In turn, it authorises new police powers to regulate their presence in public spaces and the seizure of their personal possessions. This policy is punitive in nature and remains rationalised in terms of protecting the 'common good', both in the sense of protecting public safety and enabling the police to compel the '*indvandrerdrenge*' to pay debts owed to the state. In this sense, racialisation through criminalisation focuses on rendering some groups as out of place (Wolfe, 2016).

While it is important to highlight how the Danish government's recent interventions were legitimised through the criminalisation and racialisation of a radical Other, the lens of dispossession further illustrates how these initiatives serve to produce and anchor particular proprietary relations, rights and power. Analytically, it is crucial to grasp how these acts of banning people and taking possessions for the sake of punishment enable the Danish state to provide 'security' to those defined as 'normal' Danes through its negation of others, reflecting the relational character of dispossession (Harris, 1993; Nichols, 2019). What is taking place through the confiscation of trivial personal objects and the banning of some groups' presence is an assertion of a proprietary claim to public space in Denmark – a form of possession that is afforded to some *through* its denial to others. In doing so, these relations of dispossession work to naturalise and reify '*indvandrerdrenge*' as a specific racialised group and *the* principal source of threat to 'normal' Danes.

In the following section, I examine the reactions to Frederiksen's statement about '*indvandrerdrenge*' and the government's attempt to criminalise racialised youth's presence and behaviour in public. I focus particularly on a campaign produced by the Danish grassroots organisation, Mino Danmark, released just a few weeks after Frederiksen first invoked '*indvandredrenge*'. I show how this campaign offers an alternative reading of young men hanging out in public spaces, challenging the government's representation of racialised youth as dangerous. Moreover, it provides insights into the ways that racialised youth (including refugees and migrants) reclaim their right to be in public spaces as fellow residents through performances and other forms of media engagement.

'Do you see me as ...?'

The government's xenophobic attempts to combat 'insecurity' in public spaces received a lot of attention from Danish mainstream media, which largely replicated the terms of the government's pronouncements on *'indvandrerdrenge'*. For instance, the Danish newsagency, *Ritzau*, published an article under the headline, 'Mette F: immigrant boys should not make it unsafe to ride the S-train' (translated by author). Likewise, the Danish newspaper, *Politiken*, published an article with the headline, 'When Bente rides the train home after zumba, she should not be afraid of the immigrant boy' (translated by author), and the online newspaper, *Altinget*, published an article under the headline, 'See and read Mette Frederiksen's opening speech: "You are not allowed to take our freedom"' (translated by author).

At the same time, human rights and anti-racism non-governmental organisations (NGOs) as well as left-wing politicians and other Danish residents pushed back against the government's plan through demonstrations, political campaigns and petitions. For instance, ActionAid Denmark (2020) started the campaign 'All are equal and should be treated equally' (*Alle er lige og bliver behandlet lige*), and Afro Danish Collective (2020) began collecting signatures for a protest petition to the prime minister, calling out Frederiksen's misuse of statistical data and her key role in the criminalisation, racialisation and stigmatisation of Brown and Black young people. Several other organisations, including ActionAid Denmark, Centre for Danish-Muslim Relations, Common Resistance (Almen Modstand), Afro Danish Collective, SOS Racism, BLM Denmark, Tal Ud and Nok er Nok, organised a demonstration under the slogan, 'Mette Frederiksen makes *us* feel unsafe', while others turned to social media. The radio host and writer, Nima Zamani (2020), for example, posted on Facebook a photo of himself at Copenhagen Central Station wearing a t-shirt with the text, 'I do not create insecurity. I am just riding the train' (*Jeg skaber ikke utryghed. Jeg er bare med toget*). These protests are all examples of how certain people and organisations in Denmark used standard liberal motifs of equal rights, anti-discrimination and an imperative of inclusion to call out the government's racist politics and rhetoric as unwarranted and harmful. By defaulting to liberal politics of inclusion and recognition to challenge the Danish government's attempt to 'cast out' (Razack, 2008) *'indvandrerdrenge'*, these actors reproduced the state as the arbiter of recognition and self-determination (Coulthard, 2014; Singh, 2014). In keeping with such liberal premises, these groups and individuals expressed a desire for political recognition in the sense of a desire 'to be seen by another *as one wants to be seen*' (Simpson, 2014, p 23; original emphasis).

In this section, however, I turn to the response from Mino Danmark – a grassroots NGO working for a more inclusive and just society for all minorities in Denmark. Mino Danmark's response, I argue, offers an alternative to this liberal demand for recognition and inclusion as minorities within (White) Danish society. As I show, its work offers insights into the ways that racialised youth can use performance art and social media to counteract xenophobic statements and racist policies, and thereby claim their right to public space *on their terms*. On 14 September 2020, Mino Danmark launched the campaign, 'Do you see me as an "*indvandrerdreng*"?' (*Ser du mig som en 'indvandrerdreng'?*) and posted the following statement (in Danish) on their Facebook page and Instagram profile:

> Language and choice of words shape the reality that we are part of. Exclusionary rhetoric reproduces and legitimates the discourses that take part in painting a misleading image of our fellow citizens. If we are interested in equality, then we have to speak to and with ethnic minority Danes in a way that does not discriminate. This principle has to be the starting point for our approach to each other – politically as well as in everyday speech. If we do not comply with this, we will actively contribute to increased stigmatisation of parts of the Danish population. Mino Danmark encourages all to take responsibility for the power of language and the consequences that discriminatory rhetoric gives rise to. (Mino Danmark, 2020, translation by author)

This statement was accompanied by a one-minute video. Filmed in the midst of the COVID-19 pandemic, the video shows a young man wearing a facemask entering a red S-train (an urban-suburban rail service) at Copenhagen Central Station, where he meets up with a group of young teenagers – all persons of colour. The young men greet each other before they start taking turns breakdancing to the song 'Samurai' by the Danish rap artist, Stepz, featuring the Iranian-born Danish rapper, S!vas. This short video ends with a series of questions moving across the screen one by one:

> Do you see me as a friend?
> Or do you see me as a brother, a colleague, a teacher, a student, a son, a cousin, a hairdresser, a professional, a break dancer, a social worker, an artist, a passenger, a doctor, a bus driver, a dad?
> Or do you see me as *part of Denmark*? (Mino Danmark, 2020, translation by author; original emphasis)

This video has been viewed more than 80,000 times on Instagram and became part of Mino Danmark's broader campaign, 'Do you see me?' (*Ser du mig?*) launched a few weeks later.

What is notable about this text and video is the way that this group of youth mobilises performance art to reclaim their right to be in public space. Dressed in tracksuits, hanging out in a group, and taking turns breakdancing on the S-train floor while listening to urban Danish rap music, this group repossesses its right to act playfully as *youth* in public space. In doing so, they are not only reclaiming their right to be in public and use public infrastructure but also reclaiming identities and ways of being. Furthermore, Mino Danmark's campaign is distinct from the other responses to Frederiksen mentioned earlier because it refused paradigms of (in)security and criminalisation altogether. Rather than making the claim that racialised youth are *not* creating insecurity, as on Nima Zamani's t-shirt (and thereby implying that this could be the case), Mino Danmark's response refused the premise that the mere presence, appearance and behaviour of a certain 'kind' of male youth *could* be threatening and that some youth behaving 'badly' on the S-train might indeed require a police response.

Finally, the campaign asks, 'Do you see me as "*indvandrerdrenge*"?' without taking the category at face value as meaningful or accurate. Rather than conceding a kind of outsider status, the campaign speaks as Danes in Danish to fellow Danes, asking them to reflect on what is keeping *them* from being able to see racialised male youth as members of a common society. The campaign also asks other Danes to consider whether '*indvandrerdrenge*' actually captures the actors' behaviours and identities. It does so by inviting the viewer to consider whether these young men might alternatively be seen as 'a brother, a colleague, a teacher, a student, a son, a cousin …' – the identities that are precluded by '*indvandrerdrenge*'.

This campaign signals the ways that racialised youth (refugees, migrants and others) can reclaim their right to public spaces and redress ongoing racialised dispossession of their identities, cultures and ways of life through performances characterised by a self-conscious *politics of refusal* (Simpson, 2014). Indeed, rather than articulating an explicit opposition to power, their refusal 'reconfigures the relationship of domination and subordination altogether' (Bhungalia, 2020, p 388). In other words, rather than saying, 'I oppose you', a politics of refusal says, 'Your power has no authority over me' (Bhungalia, 2020, p 389). Refusal, I suggest, also crucially locates the horizons of life for racialised Danes beyond bourgeois horizons of the so-called 'model minorities' or 'good Muslims'. Instead of conceding that minorities should strive to become more 'Danish', gain higher education, accumulate more wealth and thereby earn their place as members of society, Mino Danmark's campaign instructively locates Othered ways of being as already part and parcel of contemporary Denmark. As such, this video represents a way through which racialised youth can mobilise (performance) art to maintain their sovereignty, destabilise the normative script of inclusion, and 'imagine alternatives, new worlds' (Phạm and Tường Đỗ, 2019).

Conclusion

Through a focus on Denmark's increasingly xenophobic policing of migrants, asylum seekers, refugees and racialised youth, this chapter has argued that we need to critically examine these political interventions and moments of dispossession – as they unfold and are contested across material, social, psychic and juridical fields. Doing so helps us to better understand the contemporary struggles over public space and political belonging, which asylum seekers and refugees often become subject to and part of on their arrival in a country of supposed refuge. The analytic of dispossession usefully apprehends the intersections between the discursive and material dimensions of these practices and strategies, while foregrounding their racial and gendered underpinnings, prerogatives and logics of criminalisation. Through a close reading of these discourses and practices and their racialising imperatives, I extend the recent efforts to write against ongoing forgetting, elision and disavowal of race and racism in Danish institutions, politics and wider public culture (Ahmed, 2020; Sen, 2020). Indeed, while my focus has been on very recent phenomena, the frame of dispossession not only challenges their authority and legitimacy but also their pretences to being 'new' and 'exceptional' responses to external crises, whether that of the 2015 'European refugee crisis' or the spectre of the '*indvandrerdrenge*'.

Importantly, the frame of dispossession situates these processes as a 'scene' of active contestation, whereby challenges to the rationalisations of dispossession are central rather than peripheral or incidental to the sovereign politics of dispossession. By examining how these processes of dispossession are contested by youth and advocacy organisations, moreover, I have reflected on what ethics and repertoires of refusal might offer us in writing, thinking and struggling against public dispossession in scholarly and activist communities. In doing so, this chapter is written in the spirit of thinking about race and racism in Denmark and Europe beyond prevailing liberal paradigms of inclusion and integration, challenging other scholar-activists to rethink our own assumptions about the norms governing contemporary societies and whom or what they serve.

Acknowledgements

This work was supported by the Irish Research Council under Grant: GOIPD/2019/773. Any opinions, findings and conclusions expressed in this material are those of the author and do not necessarily reflect the views of the Irish Research Council.

References

ActionAid Denmark (2020) 'Lad os skabe et Denmark, hvor alle er lige', available from: www.ms.dk/alle-er-lige?fbclid=IwAR2itv3fKPlef1w7NEH5ByqA1FNbBTRG3bDlpqMDysyTd-RsgIHAodJ8iU0#krav

Afro Danish Collective (2020) 'Protest: et åbent brev til vores Statsminister Mette Frederiksen', available from: www.change.org/p/statsminister-mette-frederiksen-protest-et-%C3%A5bent-brev-til-vores-statsminister-mette-frederiksen?utm_content=cl_sharecopy_25151222_en-US%3A0&recruiter=185851656&utm_source=share_petition&utm_medium=copylink&utm_campaign=share_petition&fbclid=IwAR3RIpT_MppRzfxMPVREbAYcNN1mxA6tuQzh3iJTSx7VLnbj1jD8lEXzz_0

Ahmed, M. (2020) 'Danish innocence, Muslim guilt', *The Disorder of Things* (blog), 2 October, available from: https://thedisorderofthings.com/2020/10/02/danishinnocence

Bhandar, B. and Bhandar, D. (2016) 'Cultures of dispossession: rights, status and identities', *Darkmatter*, 14.

Bhandar, D. (2016) 'Decolonising the politics of status: when the border crosses us', *Darkmatter*, 14.

Bhungalia, L. (2020) 'Laughing at power: humor, transgression, and the politics of refusal in Palestine', *Environment and Planning C: Politics and Space*, 38(3): 387–404.

Bilefsky, D. (2016) 'Danish law requires asylum seekers to hand over valuables', *The New York Times*, 25 January, available from: www.nytimes.com/2016/01/27/world/europe/denmark-asks-refugees-for-valuables.html

Butler, J. and Athanasiou, A. (2013) *Dispossession: The Performative in the Political*, Malden, MA: Polity.

Byrd, J.A. (2018) '"Variations under domestication": indigeneity and the subject of dispossession', *Social Text*, 36(2): 123–141.

Cahill, C., Alvarez Gutiérrez, L. and Quijada Cerecer, D.A. (2016) 'A dialectic of dreams and dispossession: the school-to-sweatshop pipeline', *Cultural Geographies*, 23(1): 121–137.

Canefe, N. (2018) 'Invisible lives: gender, dispossession, and precarity amongst Syrian refugee women in the Middle East', *Refuge: Canada's Journal on Refugees / Refuge: Revue Canadienne Sur Les Réfugiés*, 34(1): 39–49.

Chakravartty, P. and Ferreira da Silva, D. (2012) 'Accumulation, dispossession, and debt: the racial logic of global capitalism – an introduction', *American Quarterly*, 64(3): 361–385.

Chatty, D. (2010) *Displacement and Dispossession in the Modern Middle East*, Cambridge: Cambridge University Press.

Coulthard, G.S. (2014) *Red Skin, White Masks: Rejecting the Colonial Politics of Recognition*, Minneapolis, MI: University of Minnesota Press.

Farris, S. (2016) 'Dispossessing the private sphere? Civic integration policies and colonial legacies', *Darkmatter*, 14.

Fluri, J.L. (2014) 'States of (in)security: corporeal geographies and the elsewhere war', *Environment and Planning D: Society and Space*, 32(5): 795–814.

Folketinget (2015) *Bemærkninger til lovforslaget L 87* [the explanatory memorandum of Bill 87], available from: www.ft.dk/ripdf/samling/20151/lovforslag/l87/20151_l87_som_fremsat.pdf

Folketinget (2018) *Loven som vedtaget af Folketinget (Tildækningsforbud)* [Bill 219 as passed in the Parliament (Ban on face covering)], available from: www.ft.dk/ripdf/samling/20171/lovforslag/l219/20171_l219_s om_vedtaget.pdf

Frederiksen, M. (2020) *Statsminister Mette Frederiksens tale ved Folketingets åbning den 6. oktober 2020*, Statsministeriet, 6 October, available from: www.stm.dk/statsministeren/taler/statsminister-mette-frederiksens-tale-ved-folketingets-aabning-den-6-oktober-2020/

Fuentes, M.J. (2016) *Dispossessed Lives: Enslaved Women, Violence, and the Archive* (illustrated edn), Philadelphia, PA: University of Pennsylvania Press.

Gazzotti, L. and Hagan, M. (2021) 'Dispersal and dispossession as bordering: exploring migration governance through mobility in post-2013 Morocco', *The Journal of North African Studies*, 26(5): 912–931.

Gökariksel, B. (2017) 'The body politics of Trump's "Muslim ban"', *Journal of Middle East Women's Studies*, 13(3): 469–471.

Harris, C.I. (1993) 'Whiteness as property', *Harvard Law Review*, 106(8): 1707–1791.

Hartman, S. (2008) *Lose Your Mother: A Journey Along the Atlantic Slave Route* (1st edn), New York: Farrar, Straus and Giroux.

Harvey, D. (2003) *The New Imperialism*, Oxford: Oxford University Press.

Holm, J.M. (2020) 'Se hele pressemødet: Regeringen er på trapperne med oplæg til nyt politiforlig', *Altinget*, 19 August, available from: www.altinget.dk/artikel/se-hele-pressemoedet-regeringen-er-paa-trapperne-med-nyt-politiudspil

Hopkins, P., Hörschelmann, P., Benwell, M.C. and Studemeyer, C. (2019) 'Young people's everyday landscapes of security and insecurity', *Social & Cultural Geography*, 20(4): 435–444.

Jensen, E.L., Nexø, S.A. and Thorleifsen, D. (2020) 'Historisk udredning om de 22 grønlandske børn, der blev sendt til Danmark i 1951' [A historical inquiry about the 22 Greenlandic children who were sent to Denmark in 1951], 15 November.

Jensen, L. (2015) 'Postcolonial Denmark: beyond the rot of colonialism?', *Postcolonial Studies*, 18(4): 440–452.

Kallio, K.P. and Häkli, J. (2013) 'Children and young people's politics in everyday life', *Space and Polity*, 17(1): 1–16.

Launius, S. and Boyce, G.A. (2020) 'More than metaphor: settler colonialism, frontier logic, and the continuities of racialized dispossession in a southwest U.S. city', *Annals of the American Association of Geographers*, 111(1): 157–174.

McGranahan, C. (2016) 'Theorizing refusal: an introduction', *Cultural Anthropology*, 31(3): 319–325.

Mino Danmark (2020) 'Ser du migh som en Indvandrerdreng?', Facebook, 14 September, available from: www.facebook.com/watch/?v=3222502677840819

Najib, K. and Hopkins, P. (2019) 'Veiled Muslim women's strategies in response to Islamophobia in Paris', *Political Geography*, 73: 103–111.

Newhouse, L.S. (2021) 'On not seeking asylum: migrant masculinities and the politics of refusal', *Geoforum*, 120: 176–185.

Nichols, R. (2019) *Theft Is Property!: Dispossession and Critical Theory*, Durham, NC: Duke University Press.

Pain, R. (2009) 'Globalized fear? Towards an emotional geopolitics', *Progress in Human Geography*, 33(4): 466–486.

Phạm, Q.N. and Tường Đỗ, L. (2019) 'A conversation on art, epistemic violence, and refusal', *International Feminist Journal of Politics*, 21(3): 499–511.

Politiken (2019) 'Smykkelov har på tre år ikke ført til et eneste smukky', 24 January, available from: https://politiken.dk/indland/politik/art6997666/Smykkelov-har-p%C3%A5-tre-%C3%A5r-ikke-f%C3%B8rt-til-et-eneste-smykke

Razack, S. (2008) *Casting Out: The Eviction of Muslims from Western Law and Politics*, Toronto: University of Toronto Press.

Regeringen (2018) 'Et Danmark uden parallelsamfund', Økonomi- og Indenrigsministeriet, Copenhagen, March.

Regeringen (2020) 'Tryghed for alle danskere', Justitsministeriet, Copenhagen, October.

Roy, A. (2017) 'Dis/possessive collectivism: property and personhood at City's End', *Geoforum*, 80: A1–11.

Sen, S. (2020) 'Race, racism and academia: a view from Denmark', *The Disorder of Things* (blog), 29 September, available from: https://thedisorderofthings.com/2020/09/29/race-racism-and-academia-a-view-from-denmark/

Simpson, A. (2014) *Mohawk Interruptus: Political Life Across the Borders of Settler States* (illustrated edn), Durham, NC: Duke University Press.

Singh, J. (2014) 'Recognition and self-determination: approaches from above and below', in A. Eisenberg, J. Webber, G. Coulthard and A. Boisselle (eds) *Recognition versus Self-Determination: Dilemmas of Emancipatory Politics*, Vancouver: UBC Press, pp 47–75.

Skelton, T. (2010) 'Taking young people as political actors seriously: opening the borders of political geography', *Area*, 42(2): 145–151.

Staeheli, L.A. and Nagel, C.R. (2008) 'Rethinking security: perspectives from Arab-American and British Arab activists', *Antipode*, 40(5): 780–801.

Threadcraft, S. (2018) *Intimate Justice: The Black Female Body and the Body Politic* (reprint edn), New York: Oxford University Press.

Wolfe, P. (2016) *Traces of History: Elementary Structures of Race*, London: Verso.

Yilmaz, F. (2016) *How the Workers Became Muslims: Immigration, Culture, and Hegemonic Transformation in Europe*, Ann Arbor, MI: University of Michigan Press.

Zamani, N. (2020) 'Kære 15–17 indvandrerdrenge I S-togene', 26 August, available from: www.facebook.com/photo?fbid=10158495703042 207&set=pcb.10158495700532207

Zhang, C. (2020) 'The epistemic production of "non-Western immigrants" in Denmark', *The Disorder of Things* (blog), 30 September, available from: https://thedisorderofthings.com/2020/09/30/the-epistemic-pro duction-of-non-western-immigrants-in-denmark/

Ziadah, R. (2016) 'Journeys of dispossession: Palestinian refugees from Syria confronting fortress Europe', *Darkmatter*, 14.

4

Venezuelan Refugee Youth and Brazilian Schooling: The Individual between Languages and Spaces

Camila da Silva Lucena and Fabiele Stockmans De Nardi

Introduction

In 2018, Brazil began to experience what was popularly and discursively framed as a 'migration crisis', due to its geographical situation as a border country with Venezuela, from where a significant number of immigrants came to the country (UNHCR, 2020). Although immigration was an important part of the formation of Brazil itself, accentuated at specific periods in its history, immigration from Venezuela began to attract national attention when thousands of Venezuelans started crossing the border, after a long journey in search of food and healthcare (UNHCR, 2020). According to data from the Brazilian Federal Police, in March 2018, almost a thousand Venezuelans entered Brazil[1] every day, through the city of Pacaraima, in the state of Roraima. This phenomenon subsequently became known as the Venezuelan migratory crisis in Brazil,[2] which led to a wave of xenophobia that marked the arrival and reception of Venezuelans, not only in Roraima but throughout the country.

The situation of Venezuelan refugees and migrants is relevant for us, especially the arrival of groups in the state of Pernambuco (Northeastern Brazil), through the programme for the nationalisation of refugees, in particular in the city of Igarassu, metropolitan region of Recife (capital of the state of Pernambuco), which in 2019 had more than 120 migrant families under the coordination of the youth-focused non-governmental organisation (NGO), Aldeias Infantis SOS. We understand that the designations 'refugees' and 'migrants' determine different meanings. The group we are working with is made up of refugees and migrants with temporary residence. For standardisation purposes, we will call them 'migrants'.

According to information from the United Nations Children's Fund (UNICEF), 10,000 Venezuelan children entered Brazil between 2018 and 2019. The children who arrived needed to be taken to public schools in the country, which had different implications for those schools. By law, every refugee and migrant is entitled to a place in public education. In order to enforce the law, the state, through the public education system, must guarantee each school the means of communication to integrate these new students into different school practices. Not only students, but their parents and the entire school community should have the possibility of integration, which could be mediated/promoted by the school. However, the fact that there is a law that guarantees migrants the right to access public school in Brazil does not mean that access is possible without significant difficulties or that access itself results in integration and reception of these individuals.

In these conditions, the Venezuelans arrived, modifying the situation of some schools in the state. Until then, the number of foreign students in public education was not significant. Teachers, then, are faced with students who bring another language to their classes, mainly Spanish. Some of the Venezuelan migrants who enter Brazil are of Indigenous descent and, therefore, speak Indigenous languages as their mother tongue. However, more than that, they are also new students who bring experiences of pain and discrimination that they cannot articulate due to language barriers. How do teachers deal with it? What does it mean to host in this context? What is the role of language/cultures in building hosting?

On the methodological paths of research

This work emerges as a first observation of field analysis, where we as researchers were able to follow the initial process of integration of Venezuelan children and adolescents into the Brazilian municipality of Igarassu. Several people participated in this research: the field researcher (Camila) and the supervisor (Fabiele), in field observation and interviews. The subjects who took part were 22 in total: the school headmaster, the school's Portuguese teacher and 20 Venezuelan students aged 4–12. These students were selected because they were all in a single class with refugee students, so the class was chosen for observation. They represent our interest, since our focus is to follow the difficulties of school-aged refugee youth. The work was guided in methodology by the ethnographic work of Medvedovski and colleagues (2015) and Rockwell (2009). Initially, we wrote the field diary by hand, but then we started to build a digitally written journal. We followed the integration process of Venezuelan refugees from their moment of arrival, until their installation in temporary homes and their initial access to classroom education.

In the first section of this chapter, we present a quantitative sample of the context of arrival of migrant families, revealing the reasons for displacement, their reception in the country and some other data that help us understand the profile of these migrants. We draw on the 'Quick Urban Diagnosis' (Medvedovski et al, 2015), a methodological tool that allows us to understand the context in numbers, in order to move forward to a qualitative and practical analysis. In the second empirical section, we present an analysis stemming from participant observation in education settings (Rockwell, 2009) – in the classroom and the wider school – with the objective of analysing the main difficulties faced by the Venezuelan refugee youth in these contexts.

Many progressive educators have sought a relationship between ethnography and transformative processes in education. But Rockwell (2009) advises caution. In fact, the most important transformation that ethnography achieves occurs in the people who practise it. Field experience and analytical work must change the researcher's consciousness and change the way he or she views educational and social processes. Social transformation originates in political processes and collective actions of a different order, which have their own logic.

Ethnographic research (Rockwell, 2009) allows the understanding of educational processes 'from the inside out' by seeking to explain reality based on perception, attribution of meaning and opinion of the social actors involved. Thus, ethnography focusing on research in education contributes to the discovery of the complexity of educational phenomena and enables a real and deep knowledge of them, from which possibilities for intervention, innovations, curricular changes, dialogue with student and teaching knowledge can be considered.

Within the qualitative method of participant observation (Rockwell, 2009), the participant is the protagonist of the research. This can be reached through an immersion in the local culture for a prolonged period of time and the search for typical and atypical cultural 'events', and the analysis by inductive processes. According to Rockwell (2009), participant observation in a pedagogical environment, such as the classroom and the teaching staff meetings, for example, simultaneously requires an expanded and focused attention from the researcher. This participation can be challenging especially if the researcher is an 'outsider' and there is some suspicion or resistance to their presence. Participation also limits the focus of attention due to the researcher's cultural filter, and this will set the tone for research, analysis and interpretation of the data. The researcher inevitably gives more attention to what is familiar and of greater interest; hence, there is a need for critical reflection on the researcher's positionality throughout the research process.

Based on this sensitive methodology, this chapter contributes to the theorisation of the relations between migration and education, focusing on Brazil in its relationship with Venezuela. To consider this aspect, we draw from international experiences such as the work of Bhabha (2014), who considers the arrival of refugee children in the context of the United States, and Bartlett (2015), who analyses the access and performance of refugee and migrant students, also in the United States, as well as Revuz (1998), who analyses the linguistic aspects of the integration of migrants in France. The conclusion outlines future research areas and important issues for the studies of migration and education, which can set off from this initial qualitative study.

Within this chapter, we want to contribute to debates about how schools can be increasingly welcoming spaces, recognising their positive aspects, but also pointing out their flaws, so that we can engage with them. Thus, in a transversal way, we also aim to draw attention to the need to think about relevant issues for the training/qualification of teachers, as well as education and language policies that could facilitate the integration of the school community and these new student profiles, an issue of relevance for the state of Pernambuco, since until recently there were no significant numbers of foreign students in their schools.

The displacement and the context of arrival in Brazil and Pernambucco

The aim of this section is to present the initial context of arrival of Venezuelan refugees in Brazil and later in Igarassu/Pernambuco. To this end, we will address some general issues from the moment of arrival, the organisation of the Brazilian federal government and, in a quantitative way, we will also expose the sociodemographic profile of refugees. As a second step, we will address the initial observations of the integration of children and adolescents into school, from an ethnographic approach that sets out to understand the main challenges facing migrant youth.

The increase in the flow of Venezuelans into the country began to attract attention in 2016, when Brazil's neighbour experienced an acute political and economic crisis, heightened by international economic blockades. Yet, at that time, the migrations were round trips, since the objective was to buy food and medicines and return, because cities, especially in the Venezuelan countryside, faced shortages. This movement took place more intensely in Pacaraima, a Brazilian city that borders Venezuela, a path facilitated by the 'dry border', that is one without great natural obstacles such as rivers or seas (Bergamo, 2019). There are borders with other natural obstacles, such as rivers or a dense forest, but the border previously mentioned is especially favourable because it is flat and dry. According to news sources,[3] at that time some traders in Pacaraima started to open their establishments seven days a week to increase food sales, because there were more potential customers about as a result of the movement of migrants.

A year later, in 2017, a state of social emergency was decreed in the state of Roraima. The presence of Venezuelans, which used to be considered as something positive, in the sense that these individuals were stimulating local trade, became, in less than a year, a 'problem' associated with the so-called migratory crisis (Bergamo, 2019). In early 2018, the flow of Venezuelans crossing the border was already high. Roraima, then, received a visit from representatives of the federal government with a plan to transfer Venezuelan refugees to other states in Brazil, a proposal known as the 'hosting operation'.[4] Before proceeding, we would like to clarify the difference between reception and integration, terms that are part of this work, and the process of refugee mobility. Drawing on previous work (Lucena, 2017) that analyses the meanings of these terms, integration is considered to be the primary outcome of the welcoming process. In this way, we conceive of reception as something that plays a key role in determining integration, in the sense of creating paths for refugees to integrate into a new society. In this way, integration is the goal that must be reached and, from a political and public point of view, it is about tools that enable the refugee to be present in a dignified way in all social spheres, such as school. This is the meaning of integration: to feel belonging and be able to act and be recognised as a citizen with rights.

The hosting operation, according to information from the Brazilian federal government, is based on three pillars: hosting, sheltering and national internalisation of Venezuelan refugees who arrive in the country in a vulnerable situation. This sees initial border planning activities carried out, such as vaccination, asylum requests and obtaining documents necessary for staying in the country (UNHCR, 2020). Then, they are directed to shelters and, later, displaced to Brazilian cities in the interior of the country. This project is developed in partnership with UN agencies, such as United Nations High Commissioner for Refugees (UNHCR) and UNICEF, as well as with the support of different civil society entities, such as Caritas and the NGO, Aldeias Infantis in Pernambuco. Until the beginning of 2020, Brazil was in fifth place in the ranking of countries where Venezuelans would seek refuge, with around 260,000 Venezuelans in Brazilian territory, behind Colombia, Peru, Chile and Argentina (UNHCR, 2020).

The internalisation project, which aims, among other concerns, to reduce the pressure caused by the migratory wave in the state of Roraima, has already displaced more than 35,000 Venezuelans to more than 300 cities throughout Brazil (UNHCR, 2020). The choice of cities that should receive immigrants is made by considering, in particular, the economic development of the place and its absorption capacity of working immigrants, aiming to facilitate the socioeconomic integration of Venezuelans. The promotion of this internalisation and the desired socioeconomic integration of groups of immigrants, however, have been heavily dependent on the activities of civil society entities, which have received groups of refugees, helping to direct them to financial help offered by UNHCR agencies, federal government and armed forces (UNHCR, 2020).

In Pernambuco, the first Venezuelans arrived in July 2018. Through the 'Quick Urban Diagnosis' (*Diagnóstico rápido urbano*) (Medvedovski et al, 2015), a survey carried out in Pernambuco, in partnership with the Caritas organisation, we were able to gain a better understanding of the profile of Venezuelans in the state. Through this survey, it was possible to find out that the number of women (61 per cent) was greater than the number of men, and that the majority of them have children. This fact points to the understanding that internalisation is prioritising vulnerable groups, such as women with children. More than half of the interviewees (56 per cent) were 30 years old and younger, which highlights the prevalence of young people who are part of families, since less than half (44 per cent) the respondents declared themselves to be single.

In terms of level of school education, the great majority of adult respondents had secondary-level education (equivalent to high school), and only 22 per cent of respondents had university-level education. This group faces another difficulty: that of proving university studies and the school documents of the children. Most migrants do not carry documents proving their school education, which remained in their country of origin, and those who have the documentation face difficulties in revalidating their titles; revalidation is one of the main demands of this group before children can continue with their education. In relation to the children's documents, many schools were closed and/or refused to give the families the necessary proof of their children's educational level. Further, some families left without gathering the necessary documents, due to the urgency of leaving Venezuela.

Through conversations with parents, it was clear that the education of children was the priority at this initial moment of integration. In Brazil, according to the refugee law (N° 9,474/1997), no child or adolescent can be denied the right to education due to lack of documents. However, in some cities, this law was not followed and, thus, many children were rejected from the school system. Nevertheless, after the first months of arrival of a large number of refugees, the hosting operation began to regularise them, by giving them the necessary documents for access to basic services in Brazil, such as health and education (UNHCR, 2018). Thus, regularisation policies also have a significant impact on school outcomes. This experience differs somewhat from that of other countries, where access to education is not universally guaranteed, especially for children with irregular status. According to Bartlett (2015), it is not uncommon for children to be denied access to schools or charged tuition beyond their means. In situations that lack clear and timely pathways for legal entry and residence or legalisation, people remain in an unauthorised status for longer periods, and educational inequalities persist. A survey on migration policies in 28 countries (Bartlett, 2015), including 14 'developed' countries with high rates of human development and 14 'developing' countries with a lower rate of human development, found that 40 per cent of the former and more than 50 per cent of the latter denied access to schooling for children with irregular status. Moreover, according to Bartlett (2015), an analysis of Mexican migration to the United States concluded that legal status negatively affects the academic success of the children of unauthorised immigrant parents. This holds particularly true for mothers who, according to Oliveira (2018), constitute an even more subalternised group, for reasons of gender-related inequalities that materialise through, for instance, having to care for their children in the hosting country as well as family left behind in their country of origin.

The laws on refuge and migration in Brazil put the country in a leading position in the protection of migrant rights (Novo, 2018). In fact, the new legislation goes against what has been done by other countries, especially the United States and Europe (UNHCR, 2018). It is a humanitarian and human response to a world that is moving towards criminalising the other and criminalising a social phenomenon that has shaped societies on the planet since the dawn of civilisation (UNHCR, 2018). However, in the next section we will see how many challenges still need to be faced, especially when we think of education and refugee/migrant youth.

Refugee/migrant youth and the right to education

In our decision to study the relationship between migration and school education, we want to draw attention, first of all, to the issue of migrant youth. Most of the time, this group migrates accompanied by parents or guardians. Teenagers and children who were already attending school are faced, in this process, with the need to interrupt their studies – an abandonment or pause, the effects of which are aggravated by the uncertainty concerning when they will study again.

In this migratory journey, children and teenagers experience the horror of uncertainty, discrimination and accompanying fear on the faces of their parents or guardians, who are equally affected by the conditions of this migration (Oliveira, 2018). However, the consequences for a child and for a young person undergoing psychosocial formation can be even worse (Bhabha, 2014; Oliveira, 2018). In addition, there is another more tragic scenario for young people who arrive unaccompanied and who suffer violence, such as human trafficking. These issues, which we have mentioned very briefly, point to the fact that children and adolescents represent a group of extreme vulnerability in migratory contexts. This perception is what makes authors such as Jacqueline Bhabha (2014) argue that infant/juvenile migration should be treated as a social phenomenon that requires a different perspective, since we are discussing individuals in formation in a vulnerable state. She points out how laws and legal instruments, for the most part, assume that children arrive accompanied. However, this is not always the case due to the unpredictability of the migratory path. Bhabha (2014) seeks to listen to this group and to think about their specific needs, which allows her to define three axes of child migration: (1) migration in relation to the family; (2) migration due to exploitation, such as human trafficking and recruitment of child soldiers; and (3) migration for survival. In this paper, the group of children we follow belongs to groups 1 and 3.

Bhabha (2014) points out that when a young person arrives unaccompanied in a country, the first movement of the authorities is to look for the means for a possible repatriation, without even listening and considering the wishes and fears of that underage person. Thus, the punitive will of the state prevails at the expense of the rights of minors. By deporting children, the state puts them at greater risk, since, on returning to their country of origin, the probability of encountering further situations that involve violence is heightened.

According to a survey by Instituto Unibanco (2018), the enrolment of foreign students in Brazil has doubled in recent years, and most of them are placed in public schools. This represents a major change in classrooms in the cities where migrants are concentrated and a major challenge for Brazilian public education. With this background given, access to formal school education emerges as a right of migrants and an elementary process in view of integration. Nevertheless, how does this arrival and related integration process take place? Is the Brazilian school prepared to receive these new individuals in its classrooms?

According to Candau (2011), the school culture of education institutions prioritises the common and the homogeneous, and this is an inheritance of the political-social and epistemological matrix of modernity, from a Eurocentric base. 'In this light, differences are ignored or considered a "problem" to be solved' (Candau, 2011, p 2). The construction of Latin American national states was based on a process of cultural homogenisation, with the school being one of the instruments through which this was realised. Thus, children from Black and Indigenous communities are often the 'victims' to this predominantly Eurocentric curriculum and, many times, do not have their identity recognised or represented.

Therefore, a common culture was created, and imposed, that denied the different voices, colours and values apparent in the classroom. Candau (2011) argues that this problem within schools in Latin America in the 21st century is a consequence of the previous century, determined by the historic attempt to create a single people. Equality was read in the light of homogeneity, so that if the laws said that citizens were equal, schools should train these citizens accordingly. An example of denying the differences was the valorisation of a single and official language and the exclusion of Indigenous and migrants' languages.

However, for Candau (2011), it is possible to observe some dynamics that counter this movement as well – milestones that would contribute to the viability of differences in Brazilian education. Since the first half of the 20th century, indeed, prominent strands of psychological research highlight the differences between people, focusing on physical, sensory, cognitive and emotional characteristics on the level of the individual. A pedagogy that focused on learning particularities emerged at this time: 'The focus was on the individual and his or her specificities. This perspective is still very present in the imagination of teachers, especially those who work in the first years of elementary school' (Candau, 2011, p 243).

These perspectives brought significant contributions to the development of school education. However, this focus on the individual level entailed a very limited conception of learning processes, insofar as it did not account for broader social, historical and cultural contexts.

From the 1970s onwards, the sociology of education began to emerge and influence thinking in Brazil. This branch of educational sociology analysed socioeconomic variables and educational processes with regards to school failure. As a result, social discussions entered into debates about the student's school development. But, for Candau (2011), psychological and sociological theories still worked to overcome differences, hoping to obtain the same results for all students. 'In this sense, differences must be overcome and homogenisation is what we want to achieve' (Candau, 2011, p 244).

In opposition to this movement of homogeneity, in Brazil, one can highlight the contributions of Paulo Freire (1997) that will break with the vision of the common, for the valorisation of the cultural and the different as fundamental in education. Freire valued culture in the processes of social transformation, considering it fundamental in education. According to Candau (2011), we could consider Paulo Freire (1997) as a precursor to the intercultural perspective in education because he believed that it is indispensable to recognise didactically that schools should work with diversity. Freire (1997) highlights even more the cultural dimension in the processes of social transformation and the role of culture in the educational act. In addition to reinforcing his arguments in defence of a liberating education that respects the culture and previous experience of the students, he also highlights the importance of ethics and a culture of diversity. The theme of cultural identity gains relevance in Freire's work, as well as interculturality.

Through these brief indications, we aimed to show that the question of differences has been present in pedagogical theories, especially with contributions from the field of psychology, in which the theme of individual differences is privileged, and also from the field of sociology, in which differences in social class and other socioeconomic determinants, and their impact on school processes, are analysed. These developments, however, did not have a significant impact on pedagogical practices in schools. As for Paulo Freire's contributions, they developed and informed the field of non-formal education more significantly. In general, school culture and pedagogical strategies remain strongly marked by the logics of homogenisation and uniformity. Thus, we will discuss in the next section the main difficulties faced by Venezuelan refugee youth in this educational context and whether they correspond to the problems that come along with the characteristic of homogenisation presented by Candau (2011) and Freire (1997).

Migrant youth and the paths of school integration

In this section, we present our observations regarding the beginning of the integration process of Venezuelan refugee youth in local schools in the city of Igarassu/Pernambuco. These insights were possible as a result of ethnographic fieldwork, undertaken as a volunteer and assistant teacher (participant observation according to Rockwell, 2009) at the school in which the children were received.

Our observations were made from the accompaniment of Venezuelan children in the schools, and the majority of the children were received in the city of Igarassu/Pernambuco. We have observed that the issue of language is a fundamental element in the process of insertion of subjects in school. According to Bartlett (2015), language education policies also make a significant difference in immigrant youth education. Proficiency in the teaching language profoundly affects educational outcomes.

The group we have followed from an ethnographic perspective (Rockwell, 2009) is composed of Spanish speakers. One might think that the use of the Spanish language is strong in Brazil, since the country is surrounded by Spanish-speaking neighbours, but this is not the case. Besides, nowadays, the country is experiencing a strong debate regarding the offer of foreign languages by the public formal education system. The Spanish language is at the centre of this discussion, since the Spanish law (11.161) of 2005, which determined the compulsory offer of Spanish language education by high schools in Brazil, was revoked in 2017, meaning that Spanish did not end up in the Brazilian basic education curriculum.

On their arrival in the city of Igarassu, Venezuelans of school age were divided into groups within the schools: one composed of children aged 4–12, gathered in a single classroom, intended only for Venezuelan children; and another juvenile group, children aged over 12 years old, with Venezuelan students allocated to school grades that roughly corresponded to their age group. So, at first, the youngest stayed in classrooms only with Venezuelan classmates, based on the conviction of the education department that, this way, they would experience more comfort within their integration efforts. There was little contact with Brazilian students during breaks, aside from short visits of a curious Brazilian child to the 'Venezuelan students' room'. The objective was to teach this group basic principles of mathematics and Portuguese, so that they would not be so 'intimidated' in regular classes.

This strategy adopted in the initial stage, which lasted one semester, proved, however, to be ineffective. From the monitoring of the children, it was observed that integration was not actually occurring, since the Venezuelan students were separated from the other children. We must highlight that, at this point, the mother tongue of these children, the Spanish language, was still banned at that school. There was a kind of prohibition of the use of Spanish by the children, under the justification that the purpose of their stay at school was to learn Portuguese. One of the teachers I spoke with told us, "They arrived thinking that nobody would speak Spanish with them. Then I arrived saying 'Buenos días' and smiles opened up. But I always value communication in Portuguese, because it is the language they need to learn." During my stay in the classroom with the children and the teacher, several of these moments of the interdiction of Spanish language were observed, under the justification that Portuguese was the language they had to learn. The ban was also put on Brazilian students who came to interact with the Venezuelans. Brazilian students, with whom Venezuelans only had contact at break-time, showed interest in Spanish and learning words in a different language, but teachers always said, "In Portuguese. In Portuguese."

In Brazil, there is considerable resistance to the teaching of Spanish, which is justified first by the idea that Portuguese and Spanish are similar languages: a discourse that can be easily rejected when one has actual experience of attempting to communicate across these linguistic boundaries. The illusion of the spontaneous command of the language breaks down in the face of contact with Venezuelan individuals and shows itself cruelly at school; it is here where the effects of the language and culture ban (Bennett, 2001) are felt. The latter materialises not only in the ignorance of the Spanish language of those responsible for hosting, but also in the absence of knowledge (or of a desire to acquire the knowledge) about others – beyond the stereotypes or the reductionist view of who they are or where they live.

Our research suggests that the school should have a fundamental role in the integration of the migrant, since it is through children and adolescents that adults would also be affected by a new process of learning. Thus, in addition to adaptations in teaching practices, it would be essential that schools create a welcoming environment for families and stimulate sensitivity and respect for the language and culture of the other (Bennett, 2001).

Ignorance of the language, then, intersects with cultural-historical ignorance (Bennett, 2001), as previously mentioned. These types of obstacles for mutual discovery and recognition favour xenophobia and racism, especially when we consider people who come from situations and countries that are not socially privileged and recognised. According to Revuz (1998, p 217), 'It is precisely because the language is not in principle, and never, just an "instrument", that the encounter with another language is so problematic, and that it provokes such lively, diverse and enigmatic reactions.' That is why, with the Portuguese and Spanish languages, which have a historical similarity, their teaching and learning processes cannot be underestimated. Indeed, language is not a simple communication tool, but rather one of the principal elements of interaction with others, from which an individual assumes him or herself as the subject of his or her sayings and desires (Revuz, 1998; Bennett, 2001).

After one semester, the group we were accompanying was sent to regular education grades with Brazilian students. It was only at this point that the interaction between the children realised what was longed for: integration. However, integration is not only realised through contact but by respect and appreciation of the other, for example respect for their culture and languages, and our research shows how some schools continue to find it difficult to recognise this.

According to Bartlett (2015), this is because bilingual and multicultural education is not really prioritised. According to the author, bilingual education brings many cognitive, academic and social benefits, but it remains expensive and difficult to implement, and, in many places, there is little political will to provide such services. Support for language learning is essential to ensure the education of migrant children. Early childhood education greatly improves the language learning of migrant children, and (if well designed) can improve their reading readiness. What remains a complex question is how to teach the target language in broader communication. What is clear, however, is that attention to language learning is essential; successful language learning programmes should provide high standards and educate teachers about the benefits of second language learning. This point entails another urgent debate on the fact that the provision of quality education for migrant children depends on the recruitment and retention of qualified teachers. The quality of education has a huge influence on student outcomes, regardless of the socioeconomic and demographic factors of the students.

The juvenile group (the ones who were over 12 years old) were, from the beginning, present in regular grades with Brazilian students, as previously mentioned. In this age group, we could observe the same problems with the mother tongue ban, with the excuse, "They must learn Portuguese." In addition, a small group of Venezuelan students showed signs of isolation and difficulty in integrating with older Brazilian students. According to their schoolteachers, however, a good number of them managed to integrate well: "They are well accepted by the school, classmates and teachers." However, when we talked to this group of older students, they complained about the way that some Brazilian students, and even teachers, talked about Venezuela and the problems their country faces. They reported that there is a tone of discrimination and generalisation and that they, Venezuelans, do not have the opportunity to explain the reasons for the crisis in their country: "Any difficulty in learning or behaviour we hear, 'It's because they are Venezuelans'." Thus, Venezuelan students feel that they are not heard in the classroom. Listening only happens when they are asked about something related to their culture, in answering curious questions, or for school presentations.

One of the practices considered to facilitate the integration process was the promotion, by schools, of cultural festivals, in which Venezuelans were invited to present their culture. These moments, in which the entire school community participated, presented themselves as positive hosting strategies since, as explained, until then the state of Pernambuco and, more specifically, the city of Igarassu, had no tradition of receiving large migratory groups. It was, therefore, still necessary to raise awareness with regards to the social diversity of the school community. However, these presentations are at the level of spectacle and attraction, and do not promote an effective reflection on integration and respect for cultural traditions and the migrant's language.

These festivals, although small spaces, appear as an opening for the Venezuelans to talk about themselves, in their language, based on what they want the others to know about their culture, giving them the opportunity to build an open space for dialogue. The hosting process needs, in some way, to go through the process of recognition of this individual as someone who not only 'receives' favours from the community, someone who needs to be helped, but also as someone who brings a story, who has knowledge to share and who has a language to teach.

For Bartlett (2015), the receptivity of curricula and pedagogies to migrants, and the openness to diversity, are important characteristics of effective schooling. While there have been widespread efforts to make curricula more sensitive to culture, more work needs to be done in this direction (Bennett, 2001). Regarding pedagogy, there is clear evidence of the importance of teachers' expectations for students' aspirations and achievements. Pre-service and in-service training on inter/multicultural education, social inequality and equity is essential. In addition, teachers must learn to use formative assessments and differentiated instruction to meet individual learning needs. Bartlett (2015) refers to an example that highlights the lack of unity in laws that consider the education of refugees/migrants, namely, the United States: it is a decentralised education system that is in place here, which means that individual states make many of the decisions that affect the education of migrant children. Thus, there is not a national consensus on how to act on the formal education of these children.

Conclusion

In general, we observed that interventions in the Venezuelan students' language space occur through the interdiction of the Spanish language and the moulding of behaviour that interferes with the individuality of the foreign students. This integration proves to be determined by discursive practices built on the imaginary representations about what Venezuela and the Venezuelans are and how Brazil should deal with this situation.

As a consequence, we could observe that the place the Spanish language occupies in the city of Igarassu is a place of exclusion, that is, its use is forbidden or discouraged within educational spaces. It is neither present in the range of disciplines, nor are its use and learning allowed through contact with Venezuelans and Brazilians. The ban on Spanish, under the assumption that it could disrupt the development of learning Portuguese, since "they have to learn" and "they're in Brazil", is illustrative of how the search for homogeneity is still present in Brazilian public education (Candau, 2011). Hence, in the school space, there is an understanding that these new individuals in the classroom are different, with different experiences; however, they are expected to overcome this difference in order to integrate with the local public. Although not explicitly stated, these policies geared towards engendering integration are, in fact, oriented towards assimilation. Culture, language and even behaviour are rated as inappropriate – an experience that deeply interferes with the migrant's schooling process. However, there are still signs of resistance from the migrants and their families at home, with the preservation of language and culture through cooking, for example (Bennett, 2001), and, also, through the actions of others, such as Brazilian children, who are curious about the Venezuelan students, and go to talk to them, invite them to play and ask them questions about the Spanish language. The broader integration policies in the city are, however, non-existent. The school makes choices with the objective of reducing the negative impact on the ingress process, but the lack of government guidance results in a fragile and improvised response. Due to the lack of experience in the school and city, attempts to welcome and integrate migrants are overlooked in favour of expectations of assimilation. Considering the current scenario, welcoming means, above all, offering migrants and refugees wider possibilities of safe and legal entry into their countries of destination. Integrating is based on the opportunities for intercultural enrichment generated by the presence of migrants and refugees.

Thus, when we talk about respect for the cultural traditions of migrants, we are defending the right to cultural expression, through the language and its rituals, as well as the right to education and the new possibilities of speaking in another language (Bennett, 2001; Bartlett, 2015). We advocate an education based on intercultural precepts (Freire, 1997; Candau, 2011), an education that is based on the realisation of difference and the coexistence with interaction and self-knowledge for all involved. And, indeed, knowing another language and another culture by integrating with migrants also represents a possibility of rich learning for Brazilians. So, an education based on interculturality, which promotes a dialogue between cultures, promotes not only this knowledge, but also the tools to fight structural prejudice, one of the great problems faced by migrants and refugees.

The aim of this chapter was to give an overview of the challenges of migrant childhood and youth when trying to establish themselves in Brazil, with data and exemplification of the reality found, more specifically, in the state of Pernambuco. We identified as one of the major obstacles the lack of a broader understanding of the hosting process, especially with regard to the relation between languages, whether in terms of policies and practices for teaching Portuguese to immigrant students, or in terms of provision for learning foreign languages, including Spanish, in public schools.

Consequently, we advocate an educational practice that values dialogue and experiences between Venezuelan immigrant individuals and Brazilian locals, so that prejudices are overcome in order to encourage integration within schools in ways that encompass students, education professionals and family. Finally, we believe that this chapter can both be fruitful for the implementation of public policies and for the formulation of strategies by civil society organisations, most especially those that aim to contribute to humanitarian assistance and create a more just set of responses to hosting and integrating migrants in Brazil.

Notes

[1] Almost 455,000 Venezuelans entered Brazil from 2017 to 2019, according to the government. Available from: www1.folha.uol.com.br/colunas/monicabergamo/2019/10/quase-455-mil-venezuelanos-entraram-no-brasil-de-2017-a-2019-aponta-government.shtml

[2] Venezuelan migratory crisis in Brazil. UNICEF's work to guarantee the rights of Venezuelan migrant children. Available from: www.unicef.org/brazil/crise-migratoria-venezuelana-no-brasil

[3] The Venezuelan exodus that changes the face of South America. Available from: https://brasil.elpais.com/brasil/2019/11/08/internacional/1573170768_919898.htm

[4] Operação Acolhida. Available from: www.gov.br/acolhida/historico/

References

Bartlett, L. (2015) Paper commissioned for the EFA Global Monitoring Report 2015, 'Education for all 2000–2015: achievements and challenges', available from: https://reliefweb.int/report/world/education-all-global-monitoring-report-2015-education-all-2000-2015-achievements-and

Bennett, C. (2001) 'Genres of research in multicultural education', *Review of Educational Research*, 71(2): 171–217.

Bergamo, M. (2019) 'Quase 455 mil venezuelanos entraram no Brasil de 2017 a 2019, aponta governo. Folha de São Paulo, São Paulo, outubro de 2019', available from: www1.folha.uol.com.br/colunas/monicabergamo/2019/10/quase-455-mil-venezuelanos-entraram-no-brasil-de-2017-a-2019-aponta-governo.shtml

Bhabha, J. (2014) *Child Migration and Human Rights in a Global Age*, Princeton, NJ: Princeton University Press.

Candau, V. (2011) 'Diferenças culturais, cotidiano escolar e práticas pedagógicas', *Revista Currículo sem fronteiras*, 11(2): 332–344.

Freire, P. (1997) *Pedagogia da Autonomia: Saberes Necessários à Prática Educativa* (33rd edn), São Paulo: Paz e terra.

Instituto Unibanco (2018) 'O papel da gestão no acolhimento de alunos imigrantes', available from: www.institutounibanco.org.br/aprendizagem-em-foco/38/

Lucena, C. (2017) 'O espaço, a cultura e a integração ibero-americana: uma análise discursiva da construção de um espaço cultural compartilhado. Dissertação' (Mestrado em Letras), Recife: Centro de Artes e Comunicação, Universidade Federal de Pernambuco.

Medvedovski, N.S., Kerkhoff, H.V., DeMello Sopena, S., Santa Catharina, R.T., Santos Guimaraes, E. and Almeida, H. (2015) 'Diagnóstico rápido urbano participativo (DRUP): um relato sobre a ferramenta como instrumento para processos participativos em habitação de interesse social- uma ação extensionista', *Expressa Extensão*, 20(2): 99–116.

Novo, B. (2018) 'Direito dos refugiados e a nova lei de migração', Blog, Brasília-DF: *Conteúdo Jurídico*.

Oliveira, G. (2018) *Motherhood Across Borders: Immigrants and Their Children in Mexico and New York*, New York: New York University Press.

Revuz, C. (1998) 'A língua estrangeira entre o desejo de um outro lugar e o risco do exílio', in I. Signorini (ed) *Língua(gem) e Identidade: Elementos para uma Discussão No Campo Aplicado*, Campinas: Mercado de Letras, pp 213–230.

Rockwell, E. (2009) *La Experiencia Etnográfica: Historia y Cultura en los Procesos Educativos*, Buenos Aires: Paidós.

UNHCR (2018) 'Agências da ONU e exército Brasileiro recebem prêmio de direitos humanos por resposta humanitária à situação venezuelana', available from: www.acnur.org/portugues/2018/11/22/agencias-da-onu-e-exercito-brasileiro-recebem-premio-de-direitos-humanos-por-resposta-humanitaria-a-situacao-venezuelana/

UNHCR (2020) 'Venezuela', available from: www.acnur.org/portugues/venezuela/

5

The Inclusionary Potential and Spatial Boundaries of (Semi-)Public Space: Refugee Youth's Everyday Experiences in the Urban Fabric of Amsterdam

Ilse van Liempt and Mieke Kox

Introduction

Staring through the windows of a community centre in the east of Amsterdam, we see newcomers and their teachers leaving the different classrooms and heading to the central room. There, they meet other people, have a chat and intermingle while queuing for a warm, free lunch. Once they have received a plate, they try to find a seat to have their lunch on one of the six-person tables in the central room and continue their conversations or start a new one with other people. These newcomers with different nationalities, ethnicities, ages, gender and legal statuses (refugees and asylum seekers as well as unauthorised migrants), meet and interact with each other and with Dutch volunteers, neighbours and employees of the centre.[1]

Before the start of the COVID-19 pandemic, this scene could be observed in a community centre in the east of Amsterdam on a daily basis. It illustrates how newcomers are engaged in remaking everyday life in a new context after their migration. These processes are not only taking place in their own neighbourhoods, as sometimes is suggested in classical migration literature. They also take place in the dynamic space of the city, where there is a wide range of opportunities to make connections with others. As such (semi-)public spaces within cities offer great potential for the inclusion and participation of new groups (for example, Caglar and Glick Schiller, 2018; Darling and Bauder, 2019; Nettelbladt and Boano,

2019). However, participatory fieldwork among refugees in a community centre shows that it is not that straightforward for refugees to exploit the potential of public spaces in the city immediately after arrival.

Building new connections through (semi-)public space

Our conceptualisation of public space in this chapter refers to a variety of physical places (topographies) in the city, like streets, pavements, parks and squares, which are accessible to 'the public' (Carr et al, 1992). This accessibility is important and refers to the dimension of ownership that has traditionally been the distinguishing factor between the public and the private (Madanipour, 2003). This understanding suggests a somehow binary opposition between public and private space, whereas in practice the degree of 'publicness' of urban public spaces differs from place to place and from time to time, and is constantly shifting (Mitchell, 2003). There are, for instance, many semi-public spaces (Low and Smith, 2006) that are neither entirely public nor private. Examples include community centres or libraries with opening hours and of which you sometimes need to be a member to go in.

There is a large body of literature that acknowledges that public space can play an important role in the social life of cities (for example, Carr et al, 1992; Zukin, 1995; Lofland, 1998; Watson, 2006). Lofland (1998) describes public space as the site where one 'moves into a world of many unknown or only categorically known others (*biographical strangers*), many of whom may not share one's values, history, or perspective (*cultural strangers*)' (Lofland, 1998, p 9; original emphasis). In this literature, public space is conceptualised as inclusionary and accessible spaces where strangers can meet and people from different backgrounds can congregate, as a site of encounter, interaction and connection (Young, 1990; Lofland, 1998; Mitchell, 2003; Valentine, 2008; Wessendorf, 2013). In public space, one can thus be exposed to new people, information and cultural exchanges, with the potential for social contact across categorical differences that can reduce possible conflicts and tensions, as well as challenge discriminatory stereotypes (Valentine, 2008; Amin, 2012). Strangers are, however, also perceived as those posing a danger to society by their presence, which Ahmed (2000) calls 'stranger danger'. And these negative experiences and conflicts in public space, of course, ought not to be overlooked.

Research on encounters in public space also shows that the types of encounters vary in form. They can go from fluid, 'nodding relationships' (Kohlbacher et al, 2015) to more 'meaningful' encounters where we make new friends or build connections that can, for example, help to find a job or provide important knowledge. The simple fact of 'regular togetherness' (Wise, 2009) can thus facilitate fleeting relations and sometimes result in friendships across difference. Research on fluid encounters in public space shows that these encounters might seem random but may turn into public familiarity when they repeat themselves. For refugees, the recognition of language or visual appearance might create quick bonds in public space with people whom they assume share their cultural heritage. Stanley Milgram (1977, quoted in Lofland, 1998, p 60) calls such others '*familiar strangers*' (Lofland, 1998, p 60; original emphasis). In this chapter, we are not only interested to understand what type of social relations are built in (semi-)public spaces but also whether we can identify conviviality in these spaces and with people around them.

Conviviality speaks to an ability not only to invoke differences but also to stress similarities in urban exchanges. It refers to the ability to be at ease in the presence of diversity without restaging communitarian conceptions of the self-same ethnic and racial difference (Gillroy, 2004). The concept allows for exploring the inclusionary potential of public spaces for refugees. By focusing on these refugees' everyday use of, and experiences in, public space and the features that constitute conviviality when it is manifest, we hope to gain an inside perspective on how the dimensions of 'publicness' impact on their behaviour and experiences in public spaces in Amsterdam. This provides insight into how refugees make the city work for them and what they need for inclusionary and convivial public spaces.

Within the framework of conviviality, it is acknowledged that interactions performed are not always convivial. In public space, there is a lot of ignoring others, or what Lofland has called '*civil inattention*' (Lofland, 1998; original emphasis). Moreover, there is a growing concern that urban public spaces are becoming more *exclusionary* and hence less 'public' because of privatisation and surveillance practices that exclude citizens who 'do not conform to behavioural expectations in public space' (Squires, 2002; Kohn, 2004; Iveson, 2007, p 32). In public space, diversity and differences are thus 'celebrated' but also 'negotiated' (Watson, 2006; Valentine, 2008). Acknowledging the value of *all* encounters that make up the urban fabric of the city is necessary to explore both the potential for meaningful encounters and the dangers of subtle forms of exclusion and the resulting reinforcement of structural inequalities.

Methods

The second author conducted participatory research (for example, Cahill, 2010) in a community centre in the eastern part of Amsterdam to understand the 'cultures of communication' (Christensen and James, 2008) of the community being researched, with a particular focus on public space. From the beginning of 2020 up to April 2021 (with some disruptions due to the lockdowns during the COVID-19 pandemic), she spent 210 hours in total at this centre. The first month of the fieldwork, she participated in a wide range of activities that the centre offers, and she enjoyed lunch together with other participants. Later, she operated as a coach in the language cafes and held informal conversations with participants. Her background, as a white Dutch woman, fitted neatly with the dominant image of volunteers in the community centre. She was relatively young in comparison with other volunteers, which made it easy for refugees in the centre to level with her. Therefore, it was important to keep reminding participants of her role as a researcher alongside being a volunteer. Her approach resulted in contact with 77 refugees, asylum seekers and unauthorised migrants that varied from one single meeting in a language cafe to over 20 meetings and conversations with the same person. All observations and conversations are laid down in extensive fieldnotes.

The participatory fieldwork is supplemented with 18 interviews with young newcomers, who were all recruited in and through the community centre. The research involved 12 men and six women who varied in age from 19 to 37 years old. The respondents were refugees, asylum seekers and unauthorised migrants who left their home as they feared for their security and livelihoods. This includes asylum seekers with a so-called Dublin claim, that is, asylum seekers who are registered in another country in the Schengen area, after which the Dutch authorities have laid a claim on that country to accept the asylum seeker concerned. If that country does not respond within 18 months, the Dublin claim expires, meaning that an asylum seeker is eligible to claim asylum in the Netherlands after all. Some of the interviewees were waiting for their claim to expire in order to be able to claim asylum in the Netherlands. The respondents originate from countries such as Syria, Eritrea, Sudan and other countries that are known for their asylum migration. They had spent from between six months to over five years in the Netherlands. Some came – after their initial arrival in a reception centre – straight to Amsterdam, while others were housed in the city after their asylum procedure. Most interviews were held in a room in the community centre, but one interview was situated in the house of the respondent. The interviews lasted between 60 minutes and four hours, sometimes spread over two occasions. The interviews have been recorded and transcribed. Both the fieldwork notes and transcripts are analysed with Qualitative Data Analysis software (Atlast-Ti). A narrative analysis was applied, for which both the observational data and interview transcripts were used to construct and interpret the narrated experiences from a diverse group of people. For this contribution, we mainly focus on the role of public spaces in refugees' everyday lives.

Given the vulnerability of the research group, the study was submitted to and approved by the ethical committee of Utrecht University. Given the participatory approach and the confusion regarding the role of the researcher this may create, the researcher explained her role to the participants at the start of these activities to make sure that they understood that the information could – anonymously – be used for this study. Those newcomers who were approached for an interview all received an information sheet with some more information on the research and the voluntary character of their participation. They were reassured that participation was voluntary, to make sure that they did not feel obliged to participate, given their relationship with the interviewer. At the start of the interview they were also reassured that they could stop their participation in the study whenever they wanted to without any further explanation. Informed consent sheets were always signed before a formal interview took place. This resulted in very open interviews in a positive atmosphere. While respondents were sometimes a bit insecure due to their language proficiency, they were all sufficiently competent speaking in Dutch or English to be interviewed, and we made use of a translator app if a question was not entirely clear to the respondents. Sometimes, respondents became emotional while sharing their story. Then they were (repeatedly) reassured that it was up to them what information they wanted to share with the interviewer and that we could stop if they preferred. None of them wanted to stop, as sharing their story with someone who really listened to them was also often experienced as therapeutic. Research with vulnerable populations such as refugees holds many ethical challenges, and we were well aware of disparities of power. In this case, we tried to listen as much as possible and, where appropriate, we referred people to professional support organisations.

The study is situated in Amsterdam. This city had been selected as a site for fieldwork as it is historically known for being a liberal city with a long history of migration and tolerance towards different religions, lifestyles and mentalities, leading towards its current superdiversity (Uitermark, 2014). This city is often regarded as a sort of 'laboratory of diversity' (for example, Hannerz, 2000), and Amsterdam is generally proud to announce its tolerance towards 'strangers'. Its migration policies have long been an example of what was called 'a multicultural approach' (De Graauw and Vermeulen, 2016). However, like in many other European countries towards the end of the 1990s, the Netherlands started to adopt a 'failure of multiculturalism' discourse. Amsterdam, however, is still among the few Dutch cities where conservative and right-wing parties have not achieved major electoral victories, in contrast to some other cities in the Netherlands. Policymakers are also actively creating a counter-discourse in which migrants are not *a priori* seen as 'a problem'. Amsterdam's superdiversity and liberal culture is also reflected in its public spaces and might offer potential for the inclusion of newcomers in the city.

Refugee youth in public space: an insecure beginning

Our fieldwork in Amsterdam showed that young newcomers do not automatically exploit the potential of public spaces right from the start. Especially on arrival, young refugees and asylum seekers are rather reluctant to navigate public space. This is not the result of a lack of accessibility to or publicness of these places, as respondents do believe that they have the right to enter these spaces. This is directly related to uncertainty about their Dutch language skills and social norms. As Lofland (1998) argues, newcomers are confronted with both *biographical* and *cultural strangers* and might be insecure as to how to interact with these strangers. This becomes apparent straight after arrival when respondents had to use Google Translate for every single question, including asking someone in the street where they could find the police station or where they could claim asylum. We illustrate elsewhere how refugees deal with these insecurities and language barriers straight on arrival (Kox and van Liempt, 2022), but here we want to emphasise its impact on their use of public spaces in the Netherlands.

Lofland (1998) points at different elements that constitute 'strangers'. Our respondents' narratives add the importance of language to overcome barriers with strangers. A substantial number of our respondents were, for example, not sure (yet) whether they would understand a person they encountered language-wise and whether they would be able to make themselves clear, something that made them rather nervous and sometimes resulted in them not being able to talk at all. This situation made respondents insecure to encounter strangers in public spaces, even when their language proficiency improved and even if they believed that they had the right to access these spaces. Abrihet, an Eritrean youngster who had been in the Netherlands for a couple of years, explained, for instance, that he was still afraid to approach Dutch people:

> 'I've asked someone in the street for directions, but I got ignored even though I asked it politely. This makes me sad, and insecure whether I should speak Dutch in the streets. People don't understand me, and they didn't want to try to understand me. Here [at the community centre] people understand that my Dutch isn't that good yet and that I am still learning the language, but this is more complicated outside. People are there too occupied for me.' (Abrihet, informal conversation, 19 January 2020)

This experience made Abrihet – and some other respondents – rather reluctant to hang out in public spaces, while, at the same time, he was feeling lonely and longing for positive social encounters.

In line with this, some research participants talked about being insecure about social norms and doubted whether they should just greet someone or also talk to someone. Wise (2009) argues that regular togetherness may facilitate relations and sometimes friendships across difference, but this insecurity to hang out in public spaces makes it difficult to create such regular togetherness in the first year after arrival. Besides, some respondents expressed that their physical appearance made them afraid to go outdoors on arrival in the city, given possible confrontations with 'cultural strangers' (Lofland, 1998) and experiences of everyday racism. Amir, an Arabic-appearing man from the Middle East explained, for instance: "When I just arrived in the Netherlands, I was afraid to go outside. I had the idea that people were looking at me because of my Arabic looks and my beard. I thought that people might not trust Arabic people given everything that happened" (Amir, interview, 2 October 2020). Here, he is referring to several terrorist attacks that were committed by Muslims in western Europe in recent years that made him afraid that people would distrust Muslims. Amir's experience aligns with the findings of Ahmed (2000) around 'stranger danger' and, more specifically, Shaker Ardekani et al (2021, p 17), who discuss that Muslims in Amsterdam perceive 'frequent and long looks which resonate feelings such as being judged or unwelcomed'. Other respondents also emphasised that it was not only their own fear of going out and feeling (un)comfortable in public space but that they also sometimes experienced racism and discrimination, something that impacted their ideas on the accessibility of some public spaces. Saleh, a 30-year-old Arabic man, provided several examples of negative experiences, including his visit to a club where his access was rejected:

'Maybe in January or maybe in February, I don't know, I was going with two of my friends to a club. ... But when I go and stand in the line ... oh, we were not accepted. I ask, "Why?" No. I already knew his reasons, but he didn't want to say it. He wouldn't want to say it. I didn't ask to enter. They sent some police there, I asked them about the situation, and they said, "I can't do anything." ... I really don't want to feel the racists anymore. So, I'm afraid to go there. So I don't go there.' (Saleh, interview, 4 December 2020)

He believed that the reaction he got was directly related to his physical appearance as others believed him to be Moroccan. This made him – in his view – prone to discrimination given the negative image of this group in the Netherlands, which negatively impacts Moroccan youngsters as well (Bouabid, 2018). Saleh discussed these experiences in the context of racism, something that made him reluctant to visit clubs or similar places during his stay in the Netherlands and impacted his wider feelings about navigating public spaces. This example clearly shows the exclusionary character of public space, in this case caused by surveillance practices for specific persons who do not conform to behavioural expectations in public space (Squires, 2002; Kohn, 2004; Iveson, 2007, p 32).

Strategies to feel more comfortable to navigate public space

Research participants referred to an adjustment period that varied from a couple of weeks to several years. During this period, they used different strategies in order to become more comfortable to navigate public space. The most important strategy was to learn the language in order to feel more at ease with encountering others, but they also looked for information on Dutch habits and culture, tried to get to know (the street plan of) their neighbourhood/city and looked for social initiatives or institutions for newcomers. As such, they wanted to overcome the differences from the aforementioned strangers and adapt to the receiving society as this would – in their view – enable them to more easily participate in public life. Amira, a Syrian woman who feels very lonely given the lack of social contact – especially during the COVID-19 pandemic – explained that she was currently focusing on improving her language skills: "I am alone. I don't have contacts with other people because my Dutch language is complicated. ... So I have to learn the language. I have to start talking! After the pandemic, I have to go and talk to my neighbours, people at the sport school. I have to" (Amira, interview, 24 March 2021). Therefore, she has increased her efforts to learn the language. While all research participants are eager to learn the language, this was not a straightforward process. This was especially the case during the pandemic when language schools moved their classes online, community centres were closed and social contacts were discouraged. Berat, a highly educated man, had been in the Netherlands for about two years and was frustrated and disappointed in himself that it took him longer than expected to learn the language, especially as he believes that he needs the language to create friendships and become part of the city. Respondents do not only want to become more familiar with the language, but also with the social norms that they see in the Netherlands. During language cafes and informal conversations, we repeatedly received questions on the habits and customs of Dutch society. All these strategies are aimed at adjusting to these norms and make it easier to navigate public spaces or society as a whole.

Young refugees' use of public and semi-public spaces

Once research participants had improved their language proficiency and become more familiar with the city, they started to feel more secure in public spaces and especially in semi-public spaces. The fieldwork shows that semi-public spaces such as the community centre where we conducted our research have an important role in the process of adjusting to the city and increasingly using 'full' public spaces. Semi-public spaces have important educational functions as they help newcomers to improve their language skills, to discuss their opportunities to access the labour market and to meet other people. They also facilitate the regular togetherness that Wise (2009) discusses and contribute to building relationships, something that is more complicated in 'full' public spaces.

The semi-public space that we studied has an atmosphere that is similar to what Gillroy (2004) describes as being 'unremarkable' in relation to diversity. This means that respondents feel less afraid to talk Dutch in these spaces, less afraid to make mistakes, more at ease to express their concerns and needs, and to interact with others. For example, Sohail, an Afghan man, explained how he sees differences in conviviality during the language cafe in the community centre under study:

> 'I see other people talking to each other [in public space] and I would like that as well. I cannot do that though and I am looking for ways how to approach this. Here, I don't have this problem. Here, there are people who want to talk to you and who are here to help you with the language. Then, it is less problematic if you make a mistake. There are a lot of teachers here, but it is not like that in the streets. There I am afraid to make mistakes. Someone called me "Mr Perfectionistic" because I want to create perfect sentences, which complicates communication as well.' (Sohail, informal conversation, 15 March 2021)

The community centre under study is clearly organised around conviviality. It attracts people who are open to new contacts and who are less concerned with language barriers. The centre functions as a second home or – in the words of Amir – a "second family" to some respondents and stimulates their confidence. However, such spaces seem temporary to some extent; research participants use the space mainly in the first period after arrival when they are still in the arriving period, but do not seem to need these anymore once they are more settled in society. As they do not consider themselves a 'refugee' anymore, are occupied with working life or are fed up with being identified as a refugee only, they seem to move on. This might take several years, however, and people might – even after a period of more than a year – sometimes still come back if they are confronted with specific questions and do not know where else to go for advice and/or support. Semi-public spaces may be regarded as a stepping-stone to other public spaces. Respondents explained how going to the community centre helped with making use of a wider range of public spaces.

After their adjustment period, most refugees become more mobile and restrict themselves less to their own neighbourhoods, especially if they have a bike on which to move around the city. Research participants are particularly fond of the parks in Amsterdam. Depending on the neighbourhood where they or their friends are living, they choose a park to hang out together, play football, go running, observe other people, let their kids play or drink coffee or tea or read a book in the sunshine. Elra, a 26-year-old Eritrean woman, who lives together with her husband and two kids in Amsterdam, told us:

> 'I've been outside a lot during the lockdown. We went to a play garden in the neighbourhood, the small swimming pool in the Vondelpark. That is really nice, the kids love to go there. They like being outside. In Eritrea, we used to do that all the time, but here we don't have an outdoors place at our apartment.' (Elra, interview, 29 January 2020)

During the language cafes, we regularly discussed the activities that newcomers had been doing over the weekend. For some, this included visiting friends or family members in the Netherlands, but most often they reported doing homework for their language classes, cleaning their houses and visiting the park. In summertime, they also picnicked or barbequed there, although the latter has recently been prohibited in some parks due to COVID-19 restriction measures. While they do not explicitly argue that these activities in public spaces help them in identifying with the city, as Goffman (1959) argues, being in public spaces and participating in these spaces does offer some freedom and contributes to feelings of being part of the city.

Apart from socialising and recreational functions, public spaces are also used by newcomers to manage stress. Most respondents experience stress while they try to become part of, and participate in, the city and society. They are often struggling with the language and integration requirements, experiencing difficulties in accessing the labour market and feeling lonely, given the lack of a strong social network in the Netherlands. In addition, many had traumatic experiences in their home country or during the journey, something they still need to live with after arrival. Unauthorised migrants are also confronted with all kinds of deprivations due to the lack of a legal status and their efforts to obtain a residence permit (see Kox et al, 2020). Sports are a way to deal with this stress, as came to the fore during two informal conversations with Shir, a youngster without legal status in the Netherlands, who expressed some anger and frustration about the injustices he experienced:

> 'So much happened to me, there is so much going on in my head. That's why I go outside sometimes to run and scream it out. I don't care if people are looking at me, I just keep on running. It is a way to

get rid of the stress and empty my head. ... Sports is way better than a psychologist. They don't have the experience that I do have. This means that they cannot help me. A day in the gym is way better for me. The treadmill is my psychologist.' (Shir, informal conversation, 17 February 2020)

Sporting pursuits function as a coping mechanism in this case. Most research participants go running, walking or cycling, and some made use of gyms before these were closed during the COVID-19 pandemic. Some respondents also went to a bench at the Amstel River to calm down, as the running water helps them to relax and sometimes reminds them of home. In contrast, buzzy places like Dam Square can also be restorative when people feel and enjoy the buzz of the city and actively feel part of it (van Liempt and Staring, 2021).

Encounters in (semi-)public spaces

The previous section has shown that newcomers access different types of public spaces, which all have different meanings for them, varying from entertainment to coping, from personal development to social interaction, and from education to a second home. However, despite the research participants' frequent visits to these spaces and the social function of part of these spaces, a substantial number of research participants regret the lack of social encounters with 'local' people in these spaces. Most of them want to interact with 'Dutch' citizens, as this helps them to become part of the city and feel at home, but they argue that it is rather complicated to have such encounters in public spaces. Maryam, a Syrian woman who has been in the Netherlands for almost three years, explained:

'People are very friendly here. They say, "Hi". They don't do that in my country. We only say "Hi" to people we know, but not to people we don't know. People here, they do that. They are very nice. ... But ... an example. I live in Amsterdam East. I have neighbours from the Netherlands, Turkey, Syria and Italy. They live close together, but they do not talk to each other. In my country you say each morning "Hi, hi," and you have a coffee together, maybe in the door or in the street. That's good for the feeling of a human being. ... In my country, every day a friend will ask you how you are doing. Whether you have time for a coffee, to talk. That is good for the people's psychology. But here, people are only occupied with work.' (Maryam, interview, 25 March 2021)

This woman – like other respondents – misses the street culture that characterises her home country: neighbours meeting each other in the streets to have a talk and drink or eat something together at several moments during the day (see also van Liempt and Staring, 2021). They miss these types of interaction. Due to what Lofland (1998) calls 'civil inattention', research participants mainly hang out with people from their own ethnic backgrounds or other newcomers. As a consequence, their social interaction with 'Dutch' people remains limited to superficial small talk. While some participants do succeed in building more diverse relationships after their arrival or have become a member of mixed sports teams, several respondents argue that Dutch people are really nice and friendly, but difficult to interact with, at least at a more in-depth level. In their view, Dutch people always say 'Hi' and greet you when you pass them in the street, but it is difficult to actually engage at a deeper level with them. Ali, a Sudanese man who was frustrated by the lack of interaction he experienced and who was longing for some more friendships, explained:

> 'I have been living in the same neighbourhood for three years. Every day, I go to the same shop. Almost every day I see the same people, but they don't recognise me! When I was living in [a smaller city] for six months, I was going to one supermarket, the Aldi, every day. There, they knew me. If I came, they paid some attention to me. They greeted me and knew who I was. In Amsterdam, you can walk through the same streets every day, they just don't see you. ... If I have seen you once, twice or three times, then I know you. If I see you, I smile at you and ask you, "How are you doing? How was your day?" Have a little chit chat. But here, they don't do that! ... I have a neighbour with a dog, I have been talking once or twice with him. I say, "How are you doing? I live here as well, for almost one year." She said, "I've seen you," so I ask, "If you've seen me, why don't you say 'hello'?" She says: "I don't have time. I work." OK then.' (Ali, interview, 27 January 2021)

While it was difficult for him to concretely explain the lack of social interaction, he (along with other respondents) blamed this on the individualistic culture and the stress that people have due to their full agendas. In contrast with their home countries, they believe that it is not common here to build new ties in the street. This fits with the findings of Vermeulen (2021), who points at the closed culture that characterises the Netherlands, which may bring about doubts among refugees whether they will ever be fully accepted by Dutch society and able to establish close relationships.

The repeated questions on building relationships, creating ties and participating within Dutch society that we received during the language cafes show that contacts with the Dutch language and people are considered important by these newcomers and that they regret the lack of more convivial spaces. If they were allowed to change one thing in the city, some would create new public or semi-public spaces that would stimulate building new ties, such as a cafe for youngsters, where it would be common to go by yourself or introduce the street culture that they are used to in their home countries. Especially during the pandemic when sport clubs, gyms and cafes were closed, it was more complicated to establish such relationships. In semi-public spaces like the community centre where we conducted our research, it seems easier to build relationships, and the specific atmosphere where one feels safer and more comfortable to, for example, make mistakes helps. But even here it seemed difficult to transfer these contacts outside the semi-public space to other places and to integrate these in their everyday lives. They argue that Dutch people are too occupied, but also point at their own insecurity, given their newness in the Netherlands, their unfamiliarity with the Dutch culture and habits relating to how to establish new relationships. While some of the research participants did succeed, most are still struggling to become part of Dutch society.

Conclusion

Public spaces in theory offer lots of potential for building relationships with the city and with other people, but we have shown in this chapter that it is not self-evident for refugee youth who are new to the city to immediately exploit the potential of public space. Some research participants struggled to make meaningful encounters. Semi-public spaces such as the community centre where we conducted our research can fill an important role in providing a safe space where people feel less reluctant to encounter others and where interaction across difference is often commonplace (Wessendorf, 2013). Some of the insecurities that come with not speaking the language yet and/or not knowing the norms and rules of behaviour in public space can be crossed in these semi-public spaces. Such spaces – and the activities offered at these spaces – may influence the extent of interethnic contact and contribute to these newcomers' integration processes in society (see also Heringa et al, 2014). As such, these semi-public spaces have 'democratic possibilities' (Gillroy, 2004, p 140) where interaction from human being to human being takes place much more.

While semi-public spaces where encounters are more facilitated and organised can be helpful for newcomers in the city, this study, however, also shows that it continues to be difficult to transmit these relationships beyond the spaces where conviviality happened. This illustrates that conviviality is spatially bound to specific (semi-)public places, which comes at the expense of respondents' feelings of being part of the city and hampers their senses of belonging in Amsterdam. Conviviality is thus a useful and hopeful term, but persisting patterns of exclusion in the city should not be overlooked or ignored. Acknowledging the fact that community centres and/or places where language courses are offered can function as safe places from where bridging to urban public life can take place is important.

At the same time, the findings presented here concern research participants who were confident enough to visit the community centre that functioned as the starting point for this study. This raises important questions on how refugees, asylum seekers and unauthorised migrants who do not have the capability and/or courage to visit (semi-)public places like the community centre will navigate public spaces and encounter others. Including these accounts would give a more complete understanding of how public space is navigated and experienced and will most likely give more insights into various forms of exclusion in the city, especially as these refugees, asylum seekers and unauthorised migrants might experience more need for semi-public spaces in order to lower the threshold to – eventually – navigate public spaces in the city. This differentiation should be represented in further studies, as urban integration policies might – and need to – benefit from such understandings.

Note

[1] Asylum seekers are persons who left their countries in order to seek protection from persecution and serious human rights violations but who have not been recognised as refugees and granted protection (yet). Refugees left their countries for similar reasons but are already granted protection and recognised as refugees. Unauthorised migrants are persons without a valid authorisation to reside in a country's territory. This group consists of – among others – destitute asylum seekers, visa overstayers and labour migrants working in the informal economy.

References

Ahmed, S. (2000) *Strange Encounters: Embodied Others in Post-Coloniality*, London: Routledge.

Amin, A. (2012) *Land of Strangers*, Cambridge: Polity Press.

Bouabid, A. (2018) 'De Marokkanenpaniek; een geintegreerde morele paniekbenadering van het stigma "Marokkaan" in Nederlands', Dissertation, The Hague: Boom.

Caglar, A. and Glick Schiller, N. (2018) *Migrants and City-Making: Dispossession, Displacement and Urban Regeneration*, Durham, NC: Duke University Press.

Cahill, C. (2010) '"Why do they hate us?" Reframing immigration through participatory action research', *Area*, 42(2): 152–161.

Carr, S., Francis, M., Rivlin, L.G. and Stone, A.M. (1992) *Public Space*, Cambridge: Cambridge University Press.

Christensen, P. and James, A. (2008) 'Introduction: researching children and childhood: cultures of communication', in P. Christensen and A. James (eds) *Research with Children: Perspectives and Practices*, New York: Routledge, pp 1–9.

Darling, J. and Bauder, H. (2019) *Sanctuary Cities and Urban Struggles: Rescaling Migration, Citizenship, and Rights*, Manchester: Manchester University Press.

De Graauw, E. and Vermeulen, F. (2016) 'Cities and the politics of immigrant integration: a comparison of Berlin, Amsterdam, New York City, and San Francisco', *Journal of Ethnic and Migration Studies*, 42(6): 989–1012.

Gillroy, P. (2004) *After Empire: Melancholia or Convivial Culture?*, London: Routledge.

Goffman, E. (1959) *The Presentation of Self in Everyday Life*, New York: Doubleday.

Hannerz, U. (2000) 'Cities as windows on the world', in L. Deben, W. Heinemeijer and D. van der Vaart (eds) *Understanding Amsterdam: Essays on Economic Vitality, City Life and Urban Form*, Amsterdam: Het Spinhuis, pp 157–172.

Heringa, A., Bolt, G., Dijst, M. and van Kempen, R. (2014) 'Individual activity patterns and the meaning of residential environments for inter-ethnic contact', *Tijdschrift voor Economische en Sociale Geografie*, 105(1): 64–78.

Iveson, K. (2007) *Publics and the City*, Oxford: Blackwell.

Kohlbacher, J., Reeger, U. and Schnell, P. (2015) 'Place attachment and social ties: migrants and natives in three urban settings in Vienna', *Population, Space and Place*, 21(5): 446–462.

Kohn, M. (2004) *Brave New Neighborhoods: The Privatisation of Public Space*, London: Routledge.

Kox, M. and van Liempt, I. (2022) "I have to start all over again", The role of Institutional and Personal Arrival Infrastructures in Refugees' Homemaking Processes in Amsterdam, *Comparative Population Studies*, 47: 165–184.

Kox, M., Boone, M. and Staring, R. (2020) 'The pains of being unauthorized in the Netherlands', *Punishment & Society*, 22 (4): 534–552.

Lofland, L. (1998) *The Public Realm: Exploring the City's Quintessential Social Territory*, New York: Aldine de Gruyter.

Low, S. and Smith, N. (2006) *The Politics of Public Space*, London: Routledge.

Madanipour, A. (2003) *Public and Private Spaces of the City*, London: Routledge.

Mitchell, D. (2003) *The Right to the City: Social Justice and the Fight for Public Space*, New York: Guilford Press.

Nettelbladt, G. and Boano, C. (2019) 'Infrastructures of reception: the spatial politics of refuge in Mannheim, Germany', *Political Geography*, 71: 78–90.

Shaker Ardekani, R., van Lanen, S. and van Hoven, B. (2021) '"No one likes that judgmental look like you are a terrorist": sensorial encounters with the Muslim other in Amsterdam', *Geoforum*, 120: 14–21.

Squires, C. (2002) 'Rethinking the black public sphere: an alternative vocabulary for alternative public spheres', *Communication Theory*, 12(4): 446–468.

Uitermark, J. (2014) 'Integration and control: the governing of urban marginality in Western Europe', *International Journal of Urban and Regional Research*, 38(4): 1418–1436.

Valentine, G. (2008) 'Living with difference: reflections on geographies of encounter', *Progress in Human Geography*, 32(3): 323–337.

van Liempt, I. and Staring, R. (2021) 'Homemaking and places of restoration: belonging within and beyond places assigned to Syrian refugees in the Netherlands', *Geographical Review*, 111(2): 308–326.

Vermeulen, F. (2021) *Open armen en dichte deuren Percepties van Syrische en Eritrese statushouders over hun sociaal-culturele positie in Nederland*, The Hague: Sociaal Cultureel Planbureau.

Watson, S. (2006) *City Publics: The (Dis)enchantments of Urban Encounters*, London: Routledge.

Wessendorf, S. (2013) 'Commonplace diversity and the "ethos of mixing": perceptions of difference in a London neighborhood', *Identities. Global Studies in Culture and Power*, 20(4): 407–422.

Wise, A. (2009) 'Everyday multiculturalism: transversal crossings and working class cosmopolitans', in A. Wise and S. Velayutham (eds) *Everyday Multiculturalism*, Basingstoke: Palgrave Macmillan, pp 21–45.

Young, I.M. (1990) *Justice and the Politics of Difference*, Princeton, NJ: Princeton University Press.

Zukin, S. (1995) *The Culture of Cities*, Oxford: Blackwell.

6

Navigating 'Purdah' Culture in Urban Space: The Restricted Lives of Young Married Rohingya Refugees in Malaysia

Mohd Al Adib Samuri and Peter Hopkins

Introduction

Asylum seekers and refugees in Malaysia are usually urban residents, living in urban areas as opposed to designated refugee camps (Nungsari et al, 2020) as there is no such place provided by the government. Over the last three decades, many Rohingyan refugees have settled in the suburbs of Kuala Lumpur (Huennekes, 2018), particularly in shared low-cost flats and affordable houses, becoming a close-knit community. Urban areas were chosen as a place of residence due to the availability of work, particularly in the informal economy sector; this also enabled the mobility of refugees, accessibility to community-based activities, and proximity to international agencies and local non-governmental organisation (NGO) offices. However, the purdah culture, a social norm adhered to strongly by many Rohingya, has impacted their lived experience in urban settings, particularly among vulnerable young refugees. Many aspects of Rohingya refugees' lives are restricted, including schooling, employment and access to medical services as they adhere to their culture uncompromisingly.

Previous research on Rohingya refugees living in long-term or short-term settlements focused heavily on legal rights, personal challenges and struggles faced in their host countries. While several studies also discussed purdah culture as a barrier to refugees' access to healthcare (Ripoll, 2018; Parmar et al, 2019; Guglielmi et al, 2021), gaps remain in relation to how young married refugees survive in urban areas and obtain work, education and healthcare in a new host country. As Rohingya refugees tend to adhere to purdah culture, especially newly arrived refugees, it is important to understand how this practice impacts their lives.

In this chapter, we explore how young married Rohingya refugees navigate the purdah culture in urban Malaysia. The lives of migrants are in limbo, including in Malaysia, due to the slow progress of judicial hearings or state bureaucratic processes regarding their legal status and resettlement (Mountz et al, 2002). As Griffiths (2014) notes, asylum seekers wait for long periods for a decision, and many live in constant fear of sudden changes and are uncertain of when they will hear the outcome of their application for refugee status. In this period of 'waiting', some Muslim refugees seek to marry a person who shares their language and culture, or reunification with family, which challenges their integration into the host country (Brunner et al, 2014). These studies provide insight into why refugees such as the Rohingya refugees in this study prefer to marry among themselves, even though they are struggling to survive during this period of waiting.

In this chapter, we discuss our study as well as the literature review on Malaysian refugee policy and the Rohingya's purdah culture. We then explore the findings of the research, which examines marriage as a way for young Rohingya refugees to relocate to Malaysia. We also provide insights on young Rohingyas' restrictive experiences with space, for instance, their shared homes, schools and healthcare services.

The study

The findings we discuss here emerged from a larger study on child marriage in Malaysia, which explored the narratives of 120 young people who were married while underage, from various communities such as the Malay, Indian, Chinese, Indigenous people (Orang Asli in Peninsular and Bumiputera in East Malaysia), and Rohingya refugees. Through a study funded by the United Nations Children's Fund (UNICEF) Malaysia, we examined the driving factors behind child marriages in Malaysia and their effects on vulnerable groups. This study contributed important data and insights to UNICEF's advocacy activities to stop child marriage in Malaysia. We explore the lived experiences of one particular group – 20 young married Rohingya refugees – the majority of whom were marginalised and discriminated against because of their status as refugees.

The young refugees were selected by three female gatekeepers in the Rohingya community after being informed of the inclusive criteria for the study, in several cities, such as the Klang Valley, Kuantan and Penang. All participants in the study provided written consent, and we obtained the husbands' approval for the interviews with young Rohingya women. The interviews were conducted in English and Bahasa according to the gatekeepers' preferred languages, while the questions and answers were mediated and translated by them. Interviews were conducted by the female field researchers since the young female Rohingya preferred to speak with a person of the same gender. Most of the interviews were conducted in a closed room, where the male principal investigator and first author of this chapter remained outside. Although the rest of the participants were married to husbands with a wide age gap between them, the principal investigator was able to interview three young Rohingyan husbands about their perspectives on marriage. Each interview lasted no longer than 90 minutes. The transcriptions, codes and categorisations, using NVivo, were used to identify themes emerging from these interviews. To protect the privacy and confidentiality of our study participants, we used pseudonyms in this writing.

A brief analysis of the Malaysian legal context sheds light on this issue since the research participants were young married refugees living in Malaysia. The Islamic law in Malaysia, which also applies to Muslim residents and refugees, stipulates that the marriageable age for men and women is 18 and 16 respectively, and anyone under those ages seeking to marry must get permission from the Sharia court. After the legal reform in 2019, the Sharia court established a clear procedure for processing such applications for underage marriages. These include providing supporting documents, including a medical report, social welfare report and police report. Rohingya people often marry without obtaining the permission of the Sharia court and fail to register their marriage with the local Islamic authorities. They set up their own Islamic organisations in competition with each other to manage their religious affairs, which include solemnising a marriage, issuing marriage certificates and facilitating divorces (Kassim, 2015; Mamat and Razali, 2020). This complicates government efforts to reduce child marriage in marginalised groups such as the Rohingya.

Refugees in Malaysia: a background

In Malaysia, roughly 179,510 refugees and asylum seekers were registered with the United Nations High Commissioner for Refugees (UNHCR) as of the end September 2021. Some 154,880 refugees come from Myanmar, including some 103,030 Rohingyas, 22,470 Chins and 29,370 others fleeing persecution in Myanmar or who are from conflict-affected areas (UNHCR Malaysia, 2021a). The Rohingya fled Myanmar to escape oppression, violence, torture, unjust prosecution, murder and extreme poverty. Malaysia is an attractive transit country for Rohingya refugees, which is the largest refugee group, before they are resettled in another country. The easy access to Malaysia through its borders is a contributing factor to them being smuggled into the country. This involves dishonest or bribed officers of the Malaysian authorities, who allow migrants to be smuggled across the Malaysia–Thailand border (Nordin et al, 2020).

However, even though Malaysia has a large number of refugees, it is not obligated to come up with policies for refugees since it has not signed the 1951 Refugee Convention and its 1967 Protocol. As a result, Malaysian law has not adopted international law's definition nor recognises the rights of refugees. At the moment, there are no laws in the country that define refugees or recognise their rights, and the government does not appear to want to include this vulnerable group in any laws or grant them citizenship or permanent residency. It is the responsibility of international agencies such as UNHCR to grant refugee status, register them, process the application for resettlement and ensure the rights of refugees in Malaysian territories. As far as the Rohingya are concerned, they are all classified as refugees by UNHCR because of the decades-long conflict in Myanmar, regardless of how they reached Malaysian territory, including through people smuggling or marriage syndicates as in this study. As a result of the absence of a formal legal framework in Malaysia, refugees are not legally recognised, thus limiting their opportunities to participate in formal employment, economic activities, public schools and health services (Nungsari et al, 2020).

Malaysia's government initially adopted a liberal policy towards Rohingya refugees in the 1970s–1990s, when it hosted refugees from Indonesia, Bosnia, Cambodia and Myanmar. During that time, the Malaysian government issued several temporary documents to Rohingya refugees who had arrived in Malaysia before 1992. Nevertheless, the policy changed through legal reform when the country faced security and socioeconomic challenges, exacerbated by undocumented and irregular migrants, particularly between 2002 and 2005, which enabled authorities to impose harsh penalties, amnesty exercises, border rules and deportations (Kassim and Zin, 2011; Yesmin, 2016). After the eruption of conflict in Myanmar in 2012, Malaysia changed its refugee policy from liberal humanitarian to realist (Yesmin, 2016). The Malaysian authorities detained some Rohingya and provided minimal humanitarian assistance to those who had been recognised by the UNHCR. Malaysia's immigration authorities regularly checked Rohingyas' documents and detained some of them. The Malaysian government has pressed developed third countries to assist in addressing the Rohingya refugee issue, especially in expediting the resettlement process. Meanwhile, the Malaysian government is motivated to maintain a grey zone around Rohingya since they are part of the informal labour force, which plays an important role in Malaysia's economy (Hoffstaedter and Perrodin, 2019).

The Malaysian government also has limited engagement in refugee issues and has left the responsibility to the already overburdened UNHCR office (Hoffstaedter, 2017). Refugees in Malaysia, particularly the Rohingya, desperately seek UNHCR cards to prevent arrest and deportation to their country of origin, where their freedom and lives could be at risk. According to the Malaysian Home Office Minister, there are 179,383 UNHCR card holders in Malaysia, mostly refugees from Myanmar (*The Star*, 2021). The UNHCR card merely serves as identification of the holder, but it is not regarded as a driving licence, legal document, travel document or resident permit. The card does not grant immunity from the law (UNHCR Malaysia, 2021b). However, contrary to popular belief among refugees, the card does not confer a formal right to work in Malaysia because Malaysian laws do not recognise refugees, which forces most of them to work in the informal sector (UNHCR Malaysia, 2021c). With the UNHCR card, refugees in Malaysia can access medical care with half the cost subsidised by the government, as well as other essential support services provided by UNHCR and its partners. Due to the alleged widespread circulation of falsified UNHCR cards, the international agency developed a system called the UNHCR Card Verification Service, which allows Malaysian law enforcement to validate documents issued by UNHCR to refugees and asylum seekers in Malaysia.

Refugees' everyday lived experiences have been severely impacted by the authorities' policy towards them and the way that they are treated, even if they hold a UNHCR card. Despite these challenges, the Rohingya have managed to survive in Malaysian urban settings, where they stay in cheap apartments and quarters around major cities. The Rohingya and refugees from other countries have received limited assistance from international agencies, NGOs and the public. Purdah culture has a serious and concerning impact on the lived experience of Rohingya women and young people, including their relationship to public space.

The purdah culture

In some Muslim societies, gender segregation in public and private spaces is strictly practised by traditionalist and conservative groups. Based on the Islamic law concept of *mahram* (related individuals) and *non-mahram* (unrelated individuals), this gendered practice regulates and mediates the appearance, relationship and mobility of men and women in private and public spaces throughout their lives (Mazumdar and Mazumdar, 2001; De Backer, 2020; Nawratek and Mehan, 2020). Muslim women and girls' dignity and honour are seen to be protected and preserved through this restrictive practice. Muslim societies may use different words and notions that refer to the restriction of women who have similar ideas, but the degree of adherence to these practices may differ from one context to another because of differences in religious interpretation and practicality.

In the Rohingya context, the word 'purdah' literally means 'curtain'. Rohingya tradition practises strict gender segregation and restricts girls' mobility (Zaman et al, 2020), which means women are expected to stay at home and not interact with men outside their families. In addition, women and girls must wear a face veil and cover their body parts properly. A woman's exposure to a man unrelated to her or her appearance in public is considered undignified (Yonally et al, 2021). Purdah is often associated with religious values (Mim, 2020), which prohibit Muslim women from being seen by non-related persons. Accordingly, purdah is a source of pride, in that staying at home protects girls' honour and secures their marriage prospects (Guglielmi et al, 2021). Rohingya women and girls are only permitted to leave the house when accompanied by a male relative or spouse. As such, these girls are placed in a position where marriage presents an opportunity to leave their homes with their husbands. As a matter of fact, what the Rohingya have been practising has also been observed by some segments of Muslim communities in South Asia. This practice can also be found in several other displaced groups such as among Syrian refugees. Syrian society has an idea known as *sutra*, which literally means 'curtain' in Arabic, and can be interpreted as the social protection and preservation of girls' honour to prevent them from having a premarital sexual relationship. This idea also contributes to the incidence of child marriage in those vulnerable displaced groups, along with other identified driving factors (DeJong et al, 2017; Mourtada et al, 2017).

Purdah may be seen in varying degrees of observance, from casual to strong, by some Muslim women. In the past, literature has explored how socioeconomic factors may contribute to how people observe purdah differently. The richest families can afford to keep their women at home, while the poorest must send their women to work (Parmar et al, 2019). Purdah has restricted the poor family's ability to earn a decent income, even in the informal sector, making life in patriarchal society more difficult (Lata et al, 2021). On the other hand, in another study by Asadullah and Wahhaj (2017), women who are from lower-income households, less educated and illiterate disregard the purdah as poverty and see it as a push factor to find and participate in paid work. Desperate to earn a living, some poor Muslim women have broken the purdah norm and joined the labour market despite family opposition (Amin, 1997). Muslim women working as migrant workers in countries where purdah is not enforced have allegedly challenged this norm (Thambiah et al, 2016).

Purdah is not something that is adhered to equally by all Muslim communities in Asia. Comparatively, Muslim women in Malaysia and Indonesia have different views on the cultural norm of women's visibility in public spaces. Purdah, as practised by Rohingyas and other South Asian communities, is not observed by local Muslim women in the Southeast Asian region (Thambiah et al, 2016) as it is not a concept rooted in their culture, and there is no equivalent term in their language. Muslim women in Malaysia have no mobility restrictions in contemporary times and can actively engage in public spaces and activities, work and study outside the home. Having a contrast of religious practices in a host country like Malaysia makes the Rohingya adherence to purdah culture more challenging since they are at odds with local Muslims.

While many Malay Muslim women do not practise the purdah norm, they generally wear hijab in a variety of styles. Arguably, hijab is an expression of one's faith and fashion in Malaysia, and hijab facilitates women's mobility in public spaces such as the workplace, schools and mosques. Generally, Malay Muslim women of all ages, hijab-wearing or not, can enjoy the outdoors alone without male companions. Based on our observations in the Rohingya refugee community, it is interesting to note that some Rohingya women have adapted their style to the Malaysian hijab and traditional Malay clothing instead of their traditional style, which is a sign of assimilation into local society. Additionally, we found that Rohingya women who adhere to the Hanafi school of law that restricts women from attending mosques do not attend any nearby local mosques for daily prayers or Eid celebrations, compared to local Malay Muslim women, who regularly attend mosques for daily prayers and communal activities. There is a possibility that Rohingya women may interact with local Muslim women in their neighbourhood, provided they know the local language. Oftentimes, both men and women Rohingya refugees participate actively in religious and social activities organised by Rohingya community-based organisations near their houses without any participation from local Malay Muslims. The situation serves to strengthen the culture and values of the Rohingya people.

Fleeing into marriage

The increasing population of refugees in Bangladesh means that it is no longer considered as the best place for them to seek sanctuary, making Malaysia a possible alternative. Notably, previous research argued that Bangladesh has been affected by the Rohingya refugee crisis in many different ways, including by economic, political and environmental factors (Alam, 2018). People smugglers see opportunities in the conflict in Myanmar and offer desperate Rohingya people, both in Myanmar and Bangladesh, trips to Malaysia along with various schemes and promises with huge costs. Young girls are easy targets for these schemes. The first group comprises girls who have been arranged and mediated by family in Myanmar for marriage to Rohingya men waiting in Malaysia. The family may receive an amount of money from the prospective husband as payment for the travel. The second group comprises girls who will be sold to Rohingya men who are interested in marrying them without prior arrangement. The people smugglers will be contacted, and the potential husband will be negotiated with regarding the offer and price. Wahab (2018) argues that use of deception, human smuggling and forced marriages are the three worst forms of exploitation of Rohingyas in Malaysia. The girls in this study were anxious, overwhelmed and frightened on their journey to Malaysia, and they were fearful of their fate over the water and through the rainforest. Due to the constant patrolling of Malaysian and Thai maritime authorities on their borders, not all Rohingya manage to cross the border, but many manage to cross through what participants in the study described as 'rat holes'.

Those who managed to be smuggled into Malaysia described terrifying experiences during their journey. Nur, a 17-year old, described her traumatic memory of travelling to Malaysia. The girl spent a month in the rainforest of Thailand, waiting for a man willing to pay the costs of people smugglers. Nur said that she did not eat enough and developed skin diseases such as boils. She was sold by people smugglers to Rohingya men in Malaysia, who were not working at the time. The following day, her future husband took her to a shared house in Kuala Lumpur and married her the next day with the dowry still owing. Aminah, who was aged 16, the oldest of seven sisters, entered Malaysia via people smugglers with 12 other girls to be married there. Aminah found the journey to Malaysia to be very challenging:

'I was afraid to come to Malaysia since I heard there were so many deaths on the ships. Some ships sank at sea. In the days before I left Myanmar for here, I had three sets of clothes with me, some food and ten water bottles with me, all provided by one of the NGOs, SCF. During my time aboard the boat, I ate that food but did not get anything else for three days. Any time I ate food in Thailand, I got diarrhoea.' (Aminah, interview, 16 April 2017)

It appears that migration enabled parents or marriage brokers to set up an arranged marriage on behalf of Rohingya men already in Malaysia. According to Arafah, aged 22, she was forced to marry at 16 after her future husband paid her father MYR5,000 to smuggle her into Malaysia by boat. Although the first payment had been made and the bride had agreed to marry, the agent requested an additional MYR5,000 to facilitate their entry into Malaysia illegally. She explained that they would have to return the money to her future husband should their marriage contract be cancelled. Arafah was worried about marrying in Malaysia because she was not sure whether her husband would be able to look after her if he did not speak Malay. She was taken away from the agent by her future husband after the boat docked.

Girls were offered for marriage through the Malaysian-based Rohingya social network. Unmarried men are approached by people smugglers to get married to unaccompanied girls. In other words, the men are required to pay for the girls' travel expenses, which is often considered as the *mahr* (dowry) for the girls. Aiman, aged 18, a young Rohingya man, shared his experience of 'buying' a wife from people smugglers. Aiman said, "I got a call from people smugglers asking if I was interested in getting married or not. There was a girl coming unaccompanied. They texted me, 'No one wants her.' Then, I said, 'I'll take her'." This illustrates how people smugglers use marriage to facilitate migration, particularly of Rohingya girls and young women to Malaysia.

Confinement after marriage

Some Rohingya brides in Malaysia, particularly those who participated in this study, are restricted to their rooms and do not have access to public areas except when accompanied by their husbands. Rohingya refugees often share a house due to the high cost of living in urban areas of Malaysia, where the monthly rent exceeds their unstable income. Moving accommodation is often done to find cheaper rent and to be close to the husband's job. We observed that a 900 square foot flat was shared among 4–5 families where they shared toilets and a kitchen. The territory of shared homes was divided according to the agreed area within the house based on the contribution to the monthly rent. A larger contribution translates to a larger room. Curtains demarcate some areas in the rented houses we saw, showing their designated spaces. The interior of the houses was minimalist and bare, except for a comforter and pillow. In general, most of their houses are clean and tidy, even though the house is considered dilapidated. For many of them, privacy is a luxury they cannot afford, and housing issues become a stressor that endangers their wellbeing (Shaw et al, 2019).

Following the marriage ceremony, the child bride enters the rented room with her husband. These children were confined to the marital house where they were unable to do anything productive other than cooking and cleaning. The majority of young refugees we interviewed reported that their doors were locked from the outside when their husbands left for work. On entering their rooms, we found only one window connecting them with the outside world. They do not own or have access to a telephone and, if they do, they do not have the credit to make a phone call. Internet access that would enable them to communicate with others is out of their reach.

The husband is dominant in the Rohingya's patriarchal culture and controls his wife's life, both inside and outside the home. Wives are not permitted to leave the house to work (Kaveri, 2017), purchase groceries and other necessities. Sumirah, aged 17, who has been married for one year, says she wants to leave the house. She said, "I never went out, my husband never took me out, and I never came out because he never let me." In another interview, Umairah, aged 17, told us that only her husband can go to the store and buy groceries. For Rohingya women, jobs are not only a way of easing their husbands' burden, they are also a way of getting out of the house and into public spaces. Guglielmi et al (2021) found that Rohingya displacement may lead to shifts in norms for married girls. More active participation of married girls in skill-building and income-generating activities could instigate these changes. For example, Umairah, who wanted to become a seamstress so that she could earn an income, had never asked her husband for approval to work.

There are some Rohingya girls who are frustrated that their marriage is not going to provide them with a better future. Their ideal marriage is shattered by the hard and confined life in urban Malaysia. For instance, 15-year-old Halima was furious about having little option other than to marry after her father stopped supporting her as she was growing up. She recounted that her husband had been "as abusive ... as possible." For example, he beat her "when his guests said my food was bad." Since she had no family in Malaysia, she had nowhere to turn to for support. She was confined to her home, unable to work, as she was waiting for her husband to return home to prepare dinner for him. Her rental house was occupied by three families, with each family occupying its own space.

The presence of children in marriage was also seen as a contributing factor to the confined lives of Rohingya refugees since women in the Rohingya culture are expected to raise their children. Jamilah, who is aged 23 and married at the age of 16, said that "because there was no choice" to survive, she was locked up in her home with two children aged three and 12 months. "I wish to work in order to provide a better life for my two children," Jamilah said. She was just distressed by the fact that she needs to buy formula milk powder and cereal, which doctors recommended, while her husband could not afford this. In addition, her husband did not permit her to work outside the home since she needed to care for her two children, and they argued frequently about money. For Jamilah, whose husband works in the informal construction sector, earning MYR50 a day is not enough to live in a big city like Kuala Lumpur.

Research findings revealed that male Rohingya refugees are also anxious when they leave their houses. The presence of Rohingya refugees in public spaces makes them vulnerable to harassment and discrimination by authorities and members of the local community. Many Rohingya refugees are challenged by policemen, to whom refugees pay bribes to avoid jail (Nungsari et al, 2020). Fearing police encounters, Aiman often avoided going outside to work. The uncertainty has also prevented Rohingya refugees from travelling outside their homes. He said: "If the police arrest me, and I go to jail, who is protecting my wife? The police once extorted, saying, 'Give us money. I will take the money. If you don't give money, you have to go to jail'."

In addition to the confined and stressful living situation, some husbands are concerned by the uncertainty of their futures. In the early third trimester of her first pregnancy, Aminah, aged 16, recalled being beaten by her husband after just four months of marriage. Having lived in a shared home, her husband would lock the door of her room and beat, kick, slap and punch her, pull her hair, and sexually abuse her. Aminah had nowhere to complain and did not disclose the matter to other Rohingya women in her home. As for Aminah's marriage, she said, "I feel regret because I have no one to share my problems with." Aminah wanted to go beyond the house to shop for groceries and work outside the house. Nevertheless, she knew she would need her husband's permission to go out, saying, "It's up to my husband. If he permits me, I will go out."

Additionally, some Rohingya women in this study reported that they are forbidden from communicating with their neighbours, who are locals and members of their community, without the permission of their husbands. Their social circles are limited due to their limited ability to speak the local language. The women have not mingled with any local Malay Muslim women in their neighbourhood, let alone attended any local mosques for daily prayers or Eid celebrations. During the interview, Nur, 17, described her husband as having trust issues and said that she could not leave the house. Furthermore, her husband would stipulate what clothes she could wear when going out with him, and she could not meet anyone in her neighbourhood. Nur was warned that she would be beaten by her husband if he discovered that she had met someone. Nur only knew one of her local neighbours, but she did not know Malay, so they couldn't communicate.

Restricted from school

Rohingya children in Malaysia are unable to access formal education in Malaysia due to government laws and policies that do not recognise refugee rights. Children living as refugees are affected by this legal discrimination, especially their right to education, which will later limit their opportunities. This has led to international agencies and NGOs in Malaysia establishing various types of community schools close to the Rohingya communities (Letchamanan, 2013). Education is essential for refugee children in temporary settlements, particularly in conflict and post-conflict situations. In such situations, education is seen as a humanitarian response to protect children's wellbeing, enhance their learning opportunities and foster their overall development (Shohel, 2022).

Community-based schools, however, do not offer the same facilities and quality of education as government schools in Malaysia. Community-based schools lack the resources and basic teaching facilities necessary to teach refugee children. They also lack funding, transportation, meals, paperwork and teaching equipment (Nordin et al, 2020). The curriculum of these established schools differs from Malaysia's national curriculum standard. In most schools, the focus was only on Islamic education and the recitation of the Quran. Additionally, its facilities are basic, and its management largely relies on financial assistance from international agencies, NGOs and the public. Although the schools provide free education to their students, several Rohingya parents find it difficult to send their children to school due to incidental costs such as transportation, books, food and stationery. It is difficult to attract children to the school, as refugee parents and youth prioritise work over education (Farzana et al, 2020). Rohingya children can learn, play, interact and build their identity as Rohingya Muslims at this learning centre since there are no local children or other refugees present.

Rohingya girls usually attend school only until they reach puberty following the purdah culture (Bakali and Wasty, 2020). Their families typically stop allowing them to attend school when they are close to menstruating and make them stay at home. Girls can no longer play or go to public places such as shops, playgrounds or school. Rohingya girls are, therefore, restricted from acquiring knowledge, including Quran recitation and Islamic studies, compared to their male peers. Only those with knowledgeable family members can continue to study at home. Sumirah, aged 17, reported that she wasn't allowed to return to school after puberty at 11 and was only able to study at home with her uncle, who was a religious teacher. She and her siblings were forbidden to leave their house by their parents. Sumirah said, "If you grow up, it's about menstruation, so at school people will ridicule you." Although she enjoyed attending school, she realised that women who have reached puberty need to be prepared for marriage and motherhood.

In this study, most participants remembered learning experiences at a madrasa school in Myanmar, before conflict forced them to flee persecution. Umairah, aged 17, said she went to a Quran school in Myanmar for two years until she was eight years old. Even though her family was unable to send her to school, she remembered how fun it was to play with friends there. In Malaysia, she attended an UN-sponsored community school for two years, but she stopped learning when the school closed. Umairah's desire to learn was still there after marriage, but her ability to do so was hindered by the presence of a restrictive patriarchal culture.

When Rohingya girls get married, they lose their opportunities to gain education since they are forced to take care of their families and raise their children. For instance, Kavira, aged 17, whose father died when she was a young girl, had to emigrate to Malaysia when she was 15 in order to marry. She did not receive a *mahr* (dowry), but the cost of her debts coming to Malaysia was borne by her husband in lieu of the dowry. She went to school in Myanmar, but quit because she could not afford it, since her family's sustenance depended heavily on her elder brother's earnings. When asked whether she was interested in going back to school in Malaysia, she replied,

"How do you learn if you have children?" Her one-and-a-half-year-old son has prevented her from going to school or leaving the house.

In addition to religious studies at a madrasa, they do not have access to academic and secular learning that might stimulate their interest in the wider world and equip them with knowledge and skills needed in life. Fifteen-year-old Halima recalled her five years of schooling in a town near her village in Myanmar. Her father sent her to school every day since there were no schools in her village. In addition to security concerns following the conflict, none of the girls in her village attended school, so she was forced to drop out. Halima and her husband were smuggled into Malaysia because they did not have permission to marry in Myanmar at the age of 14. Halima expressed her desire to study in Malaysia instead of marrying if given the chance. Halima remembers herself as a smart kid at school, "because I was often number one in class." Although she is still childless, she does not plan to continue studying even though she is aware of her natural intellectual ability.

All young Rohingya refugees hope that their children will be able to go to school in Malaysia. As discussed by Arshad and Islam (2018), refugees are concerned about the consequences of limited education, and want to ensure that their children receive an education. Ruqayyah, aged 18, who no longer attends school in Malaysia, prays that her child can study in Malaysia. Ruqayyah explained, "If they don't have an education, they can't write. We don't have enough education, so if we have kids we want them to have it." Having fled to Malaysia with the help of people smugglers, Ruqayyah was forced to stop studying in a madrasa in Myanmar at the age of 12. Ruqayyah said that she learned to recite the Quran at the madrasa, but did not learn to read or write, even though her father was a religious teacher. Rohingya children realise that the religious instructions they received do not prepare them well for their lives. Access to education – including its spaces and amenities – is very limited, and they hope that this will one day be possible for their children.

Access to public health facilities

In accordance with the purdah culture, Rohingya women rely heavily on their husbands for health-related decisions, including choosing healthcare facilities and family planning (Ripoll, 2018; Parmar et al, 2019). Even though Malaysia has excellent medical facilities, patriarchal values dictate access to healthcare for Rohingya women in urban areas. The husband is the only person permitted to make decisions on the type, location and cost of the treatment. A husband can also take his wife to treatment facilities, such as hospitals or clinics, but it is forbidden for women to leave their homes for treatment without permission and accompaniment. Some study participants who did not have UNHCR cards preferred private health facilities over government hospitals since they were cheaper. Since husbands oversee finances, men hold the power to decide whether to seek healthcare or not; the number of children and the use of contraceptives are affected by the husband's employment status as well as his financial status.

Wives are restricted from making their own reproductive health decisions or from negotiating with their partners about issues such as the number of children, the use of contraceptives, the frequency of sexual relations and the time gap between pregnancies. Many refugees are also unaware of the types of contraception that are offered and subsidised by government health facilities. Considering that only men are allowed to go out, the choice of contraceptive pills is easier for families since they can be purchased over the counter at the pharmacy, and wives don't have to travel to a health facility for another type of contraception. For example, Kavira, aged 17, told us that only her husband would go to the pharmacy to buy contraceptives. Her sister-in-law told her about contraception after she had given birth to her first child, and she had no idea about it before or during the beginning of their marriage. In fact, Kavira did not discuss where she would give birth with her husband when she was about to give birth. Since she does not hold a UNHCR card, her husband decided to go to a private hospital nearby, which was much cheaper than government hospitals, which do not subsidise non-citizens. "The child has already pooped in the womb," doctors told Kavira, and she was handed over to her husband for a decision regarding a caesarean. Kavira underwent surgery to give birth to the child according to her husband's decision, and she was hospitalised for three days.

It is significant that Rohingya refugees are so committed to family planning due to their low economic standing. Their traditional view about a large number of children as endorsed by religion is challenged when they realise that the cost of raising a child is so high in the urban areas of Malaysia. Jamilah, 23, who already has two children, said that she is serious about taking contraceptive pills with the approval of her husband. Jamilah said, "I need to save money before I can have a child." Halima, aged 15, also explained why she took contraceptive pills in the first year of her marriage, saying that she and her husband did not know Malay well enough to obtain health services in Malaysia. As soon as her husband had "little savings", she stopped taking contraceptives and was ready to start a family. The young mother knew she was at risk due to her age, but she "still wish[es] to have children because I was confined at home". Halima and her husband went to a private clinic to find out about their chances of becoming pregnant after being advised by someone in the community. It is evident from these two stories that saving and wise money usage are crucial aspects of having children because the Rohingya community puts a lot of pressure on newlyweds to prove their fertility.

The participants, being young and vulnerable refugees, were not ready to become pregnant physically, psychologically or financially. They were surprised to encounter so many difficulties during pregnancy and worried that they would not be able to secure money for the delivery. Seventeen-year-old Sumirah said she was terrified to learn that she was pregnant because she did not have enough money to give birth. "If I wanted to go, he would ask for ten to 12 grand, so I don't have any money," she said. Her abusive husband works as a fuel pump attendant at a petrol station and earns only MYR1,000–1,200 a month. "Whenever I see my husband, I am sad. Whenever there is not enough money, I am sad too." Sumirah, who is three months pregnant, says she has no one in Malaysia that she can talk to about pregnancy concerns. Having lost contact with her mother in Myanmar, she cannot ask her questions about women's issues. Yasmeen, aged 16, was nervous about having a baby due to the financial problems her family was facing. "I will face more difficulties if I have a baby," she said. She determined that, if she had a daughter, she would not want her to be married during her childhood. Yasmeen regrets getting married at the age of 15, she said, "because I was too young; to marry under the age of 18 is not a good idea".

In addition to buying contraceptive pills for their wives, men also get contraceptives such as condoms to prevent their wives from getting pregnant. Ahmad, who is 19 years of age and married at 16, says he initially did not know anything about family planning because no one had told him since he was living alone in Malaysia. Ahmad said, "After having a child, you know how to be a father. My brother-in-law has advised me to be a good father. You have to take good care of your children." Ahmad admits to regularly wearing condoms to prevent his wife from getting pregnant. As a husband, he refused to let his wife work because she had a child to take care of. He said, "Babysitting is better than a working wife." Nevertheless, Ahmad admitted that if they have to, he will let his wife work as long as someone can take care of their child. Ahmad also mentioned the cost of healthcare in Malaysia, which is so expensive because he and his wife do not have a UNHCR card. Visits to a clinic will cost him an average of MYR100 each time, which is equal to two days' wages.

Conclusion

We have examined gendered and sexist patriarchal cultural norms that restrict the participation of women in certain spaces. Some Rohingya refugees live in very distressing conditions in urban Malaysia, where they are denied many basic rights, such as access to formal employment, public education and healthcare. The experiences of some of the Rohingya refugees in urban Malaysia demonstrate that their shared religious identity does not qualify them for citizenship and equal treatment or rights, and, therefore, they are confined to marginal spaces. Their vulnerability is exacerbated as a result of adhering to the restrictive purdah culture, a social norm that restricts women's everyday experience and shapes their relation to the public and private sphere. In this study, we found that some young female married Rohingya refugees are pushed to the fringes of society, with no freedom of movement or access to any spaces outside their rented rooms. Some young newly migrated Rohingya seem to hold strongly to their cultural norms derived from traditional gender roles.

The findings of our study should not be viewed as a homogeneous representation of the Rohingya refugees' experiences in Malaysia or elsewhere, as many individuals may have received support or been subject to different conditions. The adherence to cultural norms and values varies on an individual basis, especially when survival is at stake. Based on the interviews presented in this chapter, some of these women did not mind breaking the purdah norm by helping to earn a living outside the home or by attending school. In their interviews, they indicated that they were willing to negotiate between their cultural norms and a decent standard of living, since their rights are not legally recognised in the host country. In this context, international agencies and civil society organisations should engage women and their spouses with regard to their economic potential to be able to access the job market and education. Local Malay Muslim women who actively participate in the job market and public sphere could serve as role models to these women refugees so they would understand that their faith and culture should not be a hindrance to having a better life.

To improve the lives of young married Rohingya refugees, more culturally sensitive policies and programmes – that promote equality between men and women – are needed to help them, particularly to empower vulnerable girls who are currently confined to the private sphere. For instance, these women may require subsidies for childcare, public transportation and children's food in order to learn new skills, complete an academic study or join the informal job market. Men who allow their wives to learn and work outside the home should also receive some form of incentive, such as acceleration of the resettlement process or a financial grant or microcredit to start a small business. To eliminate the gender discrimination experienced by Rohingya women, the sexism and patriarchy supported by purdah culture needs to be overturned through community engagement and education. Moreover, it is necessary to engage with Rohingya community leaders regarding the urgent need for societal change that will promote gender equality, including with regard to accessing public spaces. Stakeholders should start by helping to develop a community-based campaign under the leadership of their religious leaders, illustrating how purdah is a cultural construct that can be modified, and by supporting women working and learning outside the home.

Acknowledgements
This research was funded by Universiti Kebangsaan Malaysia (GUP-2019-068) and UNICEF Malaysia (PP-2016-002).

References
Alam, M. (2018) 'Enduring entanglement: the multi-sectoral impact of the Rohingya crisis on neighboring Bangladesh', *Georgetown Journal of International Affairs*, 19: 20–26.

Amin, S. (1997) 'The poverty-purdah trap in rural Bangladesh: implications for women's roles in the family', *Development and Change*, 28(2): 213–233.

Arshad, M. and Islam, A. (2018) 'A scattered life: the lived experiences of Rohingya refugee mothers in Malaysia', *Al-Shajarah: Journal of the International Institute of Islamic Thought and Civilization* (ISTAC): 107–122.

Asadullah, M.N. and Wahhaj, Z. (2017) 'Missing from the market: purdah norm and women's paid work participation in Bangladesh', IZA Discussion Paper No. 10463. https://doi.org/10.2139/ssrn.2895311

Bakali, N. and Wasty, S. (2020) 'Identity, social mobility, and trauma: post-conflict educational realities for survivors of the Rohingya genocide', *Religions*, 11(5): 241–255.

Brunner, L.R., Hyndman, J. and Mountz, A. (2014) '"Waiting for a wife": transnational marriages and the social dimensions of refugee integration'. *Refuge: Canada's Journal on Refugees*, 30(1): 81–92.

De Backer, M. (2020) 'Street harassment and social control of young Muslim women in Brussels: destabilising the public/private binary', *Journal of Gender-Based Violence*, 4(3): 343–358.

DeJong, J., Sbeity, F., Schlecht, J., Harfouche, M., Yamout, R., Fouad, F.M., et al (2017) 'Young lives disrupted: gender and well-being among adolescent Syrian refugees in Lebanon', *Conflict and Health*, 11(1): 25–34.

Farzana, K.F., Pero, S.D.M. and Othman, M.F. (2020) 'The dream's door: educational marginalization of Rohingya children in Malaysia', *South Asian Journal of Business and Management Cases*, 9(2): 237–246.

Griffiths, M.B.E. (2014) 'Out of time: the temporal uncertainties of refused asylum seekers and immigration detainees', *Journal of Ethnic and Migration Studies*, 40(12): 1991–2009.

Guglielmi, S., Mitu, K. and Seager, J. (2021) '"I just keep quiet": addressing the challenges of married Rohingya girls and creating opportunities for change', *The European Journal of Development Research*, 33(5): 1232–1251.

Hoffstaedter, G. (2017) 'Refugees, Islam, and the state: the role of religion in providing sanctuary in Malaysia', *Journal of Immigrant & Refugee Studies*, 15(3): 287–304.

Hoffstaedter, G. and Perrodin, L. (2019) 'Life in limbo: refugees in Malaysia', in S. Lemière (ed) *Illusions of Democracy: Malaysian Politics and People*, Amsterdam: Amsterdam University Press, pp 183–200.

Huennekes, J. (2018) 'Emotional remittances in the transnational lives of Rohingya families living in Malaysia', *Journal of Refugee Studies*, 31(3): 353–370.

Kassim, A. (2015) 'Transnational marriages among Muslim refugees and their implications on their status and identity: the case of the Rohingyas in Malaysia', *Islam and Cultural Diversity in Southeast Asia*, 175–202, available from: http://repository.tufs.ac.jp/bitstream/10108/93077/1/B182-09.pdf

Kassim, A. and Zin, R.H.M. (2011) *Policy on Irregular Migrants in Malaysia: An Analysis of its Implementation and Effectiveness*, PIDS Discussion Paper Series, available from: www.econstor.eu/handle/10419/126870

Kaveri (2017) Being stateless and the plight of Rohingyas. *Peace Review*, 29(1), 31–39.

Lata, L.N., Walters, P. and Roitman, S. (2021) 'The politics of gendered space: social norms and purdah affecting female informal work in Dhaka, Bangladesh', *Gender, Work, and Organization*, 28(1): 318–336.

Letchamanan, H. (2013) 'Myanmar's Rohingya refugees in Malaysia: education and the way forward', *Journal of International and Comparative Education*, 2(2): 86–97.

Mamat, Z. and Razali, R.M. (2020) 'Pengurusan perkahwinan masyarakat Rohingya di Malaysia menurut perspektif undang-undang dan Syariah', *Kanun: Jurnal Undang-Undang Malaysia*, 32(2): 243–274.

Mazumdar, S. and Mazumdar, S. (2001) 'Rethinking public and private space: religion and women in Muslim society', *Journal of Architectural and Planning Research*, 18(4): 302–324.

Mim, N.J. (2020) 'Religion at the margins: Resistance to secular humanitarianism at the Rohingya refugee camps in Bangladesh', *Religions*, 11(8), 423–440.

Mountz, A., Wright, R., Miyares, I. and Bailey, A.J. (2002) 'Lives in limbo: temporary protected status and immigrant identities', *Global Networks – A Journal of Transnational Affairs*, 2(4): 335–356.

Mourtada, R., Schlecht, J. and DeJong, J. (2017) 'A qualitative study exploring child marriage practices among Syrian conflict-affected populations in Lebanon', *Conflict and Health*, 11(1): 53–65.

Nawratek, K. and Mehan, A. (2020) 'De-colonizing public spaces in Malaysia: dating in Kuala Lumpur', *Cultural Geographies*, 27(4): 615–629.

Nordin, R., Sahak, S. and Ishak, M.K. (2020) 'The plight of refugees in Malaysia: Malaysia as a transit country in protecting refugees' rights', *Journal of Nusantara Studies*, 5(1): 378–394.

Nungsari, M., Flanders, S. and Chuah, H.Y. (2020) 'Poverty and precarious employment: the case of Rohingya refugee construction workers in Peninsular Malaysia', *Humanities and Social Sciences Communications*, 7(1): 1–11.

Parmar, P.K., Jin, R.O., Walsh, M. and Scott, J. (2019) 'Mortality in Rohingya refugee camps in Bangladesh: historical, social, and political context', *Sexual and Reproductive Health Matters*, 27(2): 1610275.

Ripoll, S. (2018) 'Social and cultural factors shaping health and nutrition, wellbeing and protection of the Rohingya within a humanitarian context', Institute of Development Studies/UNICEF, available from: https://opendocs.ids.ac.uk/opendocs/handle/20.500.12413/13328

Shaw, S.A., Karim, H., Bellows, N. and Pillai, V. (2019) 'Emotional distress among Rohingya refugees in Malaysia', *Intervention*, 17(2): 174.

Shohel, M.M.C. (2022) 'Education in emergencies: challenges of providing education for Rohingya children living in refugee camps in Bangladesh', *Education Inquiry*, 13(1), 104–112.

Thambiah, S., Chakraborty, K. and Sarker, R. (2016) 'Negotiating male gatekeeper violence in team-based research on Bangladeshi migrant women in Malaysia', *Gender, Place and Culture: A Journal of Feminist Geography*, 23(8): 1150–1163.

The Star (2021) 'Home Minister: 179,383 UNHCR card holders in Malaysia according to government figures', available from: www.thestar.com.my/news/nation/2021/06/10/home-minister-179-383-unhcr-card-holders-in-malaysia-according-to-gov039t-figures

UNHCR Malaysia (2021a) 'Figures at a glance in Malaysia', available from: www.unhcr.org/en-my/figures-at-a-glance-in-malaysia.html

UNHCR Malaysia (2021b) 'Know the myths from the facts: nine things about the refugee issue in Malaysia', available from: www.unhcr.org/en-my/news/latest/2021/4/606563ac4/know-the-myths-from-the-facts-nine-things-about-the-refugee-issue-in-malaysia.html

UNHCR Malaysia (2021c) 'Contact UNHCR in Malaysia: queries on employment of refugees', available from: www.unhcr.org/en-my/contact-unhcr-in-malaysia.html

Wahab, A.A. (2018) 'The colours of exploitation: smuggling of Rohingyas from Myanmar to Malaysia', *Akademika*, 88(1), available from: http://ejournal.ukm.my/akademika/article/view/15433

Yesmin, S. (2016) 'Policy towards Rohingya refugees: a comparative analysis of Bangladesh, Malaysia and Thailand', *Journal of the Asiatic Society of Bangladesh*, 61(1): 71–100.

Yonally, E., Butler, N., Ripoll, S. and Tulloch, O. (2021) *Review of the Evidence Landscape on the Risk Communication and Community Engagement Interventions among the Rohingya Refugees to Enhance Healthcare Seeking Behaviours in Cox's Bazar*, Brighton: Social Science in Humanitarian Action Platform.

Zaman, S., Sammonds, P., Ahmed, B. and Rahman, T. (2020) 'Disaster risk reduction in conflict contexts: lessons learned from the lived experiences of Rohingya refugees in Cox's Bazar, Bangladesh', *International Journal of Disaster Risk Reduction*, 50: 101694.

7

Inclusive Urban Planning and Public Space for Refugee Youth in Pursuit of a Just City in Amman, Jordan

Rana Aytug

Introduction

Cities emerge from, are shaped by and develop as a result of migratory movements and increasing urban diversity. Among this growing migrant population, the arrival of young refugees in urban settings with important differences such as class, race, language, trauma, education and family backgrounds (Marshall et al, 2016, p 3) has a transformative effect on the demographic, cultural, political and economic characteristics of cities. Incoming migration brings to cities a surplus of benefits such as needed skills, cultural diversity and entrepreneurship, which can boost creativity, innovation and economic growth (Price and Chacko, 2012, p 13). Simultaneously, many young refugees face difficult challenges in becoming active participants in the economic, cultural, social and political lives of their communities; these challenges can include lack of residency rights, lack of political representation, inadequate housing, restrictions to work or low-paid, insecure or hazardous work, limited access to state-provided services such as health or education, religious intolerance, discrimination based on race or gender, and social exclusion (Price and Chacko, 2012, p 34). Furthermore, ongoing anti-immigrant attitudes and contested relationship dynamics between newcomers and receiving communities can be perceived as 'dangerous mobilisers in a context where the centre no longer holds' (Sassen, 2013, p 3).

The prevalence of injustice in cities demands a persistent and revitalised pursuit for innovative ideas and solutions that can contribute to creating an inclusive city for all city inhabitants, including young refugees. An inclusive city is one that listens, values and places the challenges, needs and aspirations of its people at the centre of policy and design. An inclusive city provides multiple channels and platforms that enable city inhabitants to participate in shaping the spatial and material character of the cities they inhabit. Most importantly, an inclusive city encourages ongoing and constructive conversations between local planning authorities and the communities they serve around what constitutes a just and inclusive city. Ultimately, an inclusive city is one that values local communities as partners in shaping and managing the city. While this vision of an inclusive and just city can seem detached from the reality of how cities generally function and perform, cities devoid of inclusive urban policies and practices will continue to fuel injustices and lead to further segregation. In the pursuit to confront and manage such challenges, among a range of fundamental questions, cities will need to ask: how can the city engage refugee youth, who are often marginalised and excluded from urban planning processes?

To advocate for inclusion in urban planning processes, planning authorities will need to develop and test guidelines and instruments for engaging all city inhabitants in decision-making processes. In line with this, they will need to develop mechanisms to manage, enforce, implement and monitor these processes, while raising awareness of the potential benefits of building inclusive and just cities. In practice, this means that planning authorities will need to commit to embedding the value of inclusion at all stages of the planning process through their plans and actions. Inclusive planning as a tool for building just and inclusive cities must be driven by the requirement and acceptance of a diversity of voices. In other words, to encourage inclusion and belonging in urban public space, local planning authorities will need to explore inclusionary planning processes that enable city inhabitants to participate meaningfully as partners in the decision-making process and have a say in how public urban spaces are created and managed. Inclusionary planning at its best captures diverse challenges, needs and aspirations that can contribute to the creation of inclusive urban public spaces that serve to promote and strengthen a sense of belonging. Faced with this opportunity, cities will need to invest resources and pave channels for collaboration that engage the skills, talents and experiences of diverse individuals and groups, particularly young refugees, in ways that enable them to exercise their agency as partners in creating an inclusive and just city.

In this chapter, I discuss the capacity of inclusive urban planning to build inclusive and just cities for refugee youth. Inclusive planning is a political process that can and should enable the conditions for all city inhabitants, including refugee youth, to shape the spatial and material character of the cities they live in. Building on the key ideas presented thus far, I will discuss the theoretical dimensions of the inclusive city, urban planning and the urban public space through the lens of inclusion. The significance of this theoretical knowledge for building inclusive cities in this chapter resonates with the insight I have gained from interviews conducted with young refugees in the city of Amman. These findings capture a glimpse into the everyday experiences of refugee youth in the city in an effort to shed light on the transformative potential of inclusive planning as a tool for nurturing inclusion and belonging in urban public space. The surrounding discussions highlight the dominant norms and practices driving traditional urban governance and opportunities for facilitating refugee youth experiences of socio-spatial inclusion. They highlight the interdependent relationship between the inclusion of minority and marginalised communities in urban planning, through approaches such as intercultural place-making, and the creation of inclusive public spaces that strive to challenge prevailing socio-spatial injustices, inequalities and forms of exclusion. Building on these discussions, I address the criticality and necessity for inclusive urban planning as a call for action – to encourage alternative and innovative ways to rethink urban politics, engage the urban political will of refugee youth and re-envision public space for a more socially just city.

The intercultural, inclusive and just city – more than 'just' public space

The new urban condition and shortcomings in urban planning models over the last decades call for 'culturally sensitive urban development models' (UNESCO, 2015, p 4). These models are expected to 'rehumanise' urban environments through adopting approaches that serve to increase social cohesion, and counter social and spatial segregation and the uneven distribution of wealth, while aiming for equitable distribution and access to urban resources and more integration and connection among residents (Duxbury et al, 2016, p 6). It would be unrealistic to assume that any one urban development model on its own is capable of tackling all urban inequalities and injustices. However, approaches such as intercultural place-making and discussions surrounding the intercultural city can offer practical insights that can shed light on how a culturally sensitive urban development model would ideally function and perform.

The intercultural city stems from the notion that each individual has something to contribute to shaping, making and co-creating the city and its urban public spaces (Wood, 2012, p 7). It acknowledges that communities thrive through contact and interaction, not in isolation, and that all cultures attain the right to survive, flourish and contribute to the diverse landscape of the society in which they are present (Bathily, 2019, p 10). This calls for the recognition of and engagement with all forms of difference in the city and preparedness on the part of all who design, build, manage and use urban spaces (Bathily, 2019, p 42). Intercultural place-making is perceived as a collaborative act between citizens and local planning authorities that holds the capacity to facilitate dialogue, exchange and reciprocal understanding between people of different backgrounds (Wood et al, 2006, p 9). As such, the intercultural city, which is akin to the inclusive city, recognises intercultural place-making as a core value for building social inclusion and as a right to the city.

The contested relationship between city inhabitants and urban authorities runs through the history of urban planning across a diverse range of geographical contexts (Sandercock, 2000; Low and Iveson, 2016, p 11). This contested relationship has contributed to the exclusion of certain citizens and to depriving them of their rights to the city. In this light, Lefebvre's conceptualisation of the right to the city (1996) is far more than an individual right to the resources that the city embodies – it is the exercise of a collective power over the processes of urbanisation (Harvey, 2003, p 1). The right to the city signifies the right for all city inhabitants 'to appear on all the networks and circuits of communication, information and exchange' (Lefebvre, 1996, pp 194–195). Thus, the focus of intercultural place-making on diversity and participation serves to provide opportunities to exercise the right to the city. Cities lacking opportunities to exercise the right to the city contribute further to fuelling urban alienation: urban alienation through which segregation (by class, neighbourhood, profession, age, ethnicity or gender) becomes commonplace, and public space extremely rare and inaccessible, can make the city 'unliveable' (Lefebvre, 1970, p 92).

While public space can be defined in different ways – in principle and not necessarily in practice – most commonly public space includes areas that are accessible to all members of the public in a given society (Orum and Neal, 2010, p 1). Outdoor areas such as parks, streets and sidewalks as well as public buildings like schools and libraries are often included in definitions of public space. Public space can be recognised as any physical (or virtual) area where individuals and groups can interact with one another in a shared space. However, 'being in public' does not necessarily equate to interaction or to 'being public' (Iveson, 2007). Spaces commonly referred to as public space are intimately intertwined with 'power and meaning and symbolism' and therefore people experience and interpret the public space differently depending on their position within society (Massey, 1994, p 3). For example, newcomers to a city can embody the exteriority of the urban system since the 'rules' of participation and engagement are commonly defined by the 'host' (Arciniegas, 2016, p 13).

The urban public space has been described as a site of heterogeneity and encounter (Darling and Wilson, 2016, p 12). Young refugees are prone to experiencing discrimination and exclusion in urban public spaces, which can be traced back to a number of intersecting and overlapping diversity factors such as race, ethnicity, dress, religion, language, gender or skill level (Price and Chacko, 2012, p 13). While scholars have pointed out that alienation and exclusion are typical traits of urban life (Lefebvre, 1970; Meer and Modood, 2012), the urban environment is a fertile ground for emerging forms of civic engagement in response to challenges like an imbalance of power among urban stakeholders (Domaradzka, 2018, p 609).

Efforts to confront processes of discrimination, segregation and exclusion and to pave channels for participation in the social, cultural, economic and political life of the city (Low and Iveson, 2016, p 14) are at the core of building inclusive and just cities. Through a critical engagement with such processes of inquiry, multiple inequalities, prejudices and injustices can emerge, which can shed light on how 'discriminatory practices operate in and across scales, places, and temporalities' (Hopkins, 2014, p 1575). Hence, examining justice in the city through the lens of inclusive planning has the potential to 'wrest from space new possibilities' (Sandercock, 2000, p 219), while raising a greater sense of 'political consciousness' that can contribute to increased levels of acceptance for others and greater equality (Fainstein, 2005, pp 15–16).

Methodology

In this chapter, I draw from semi-structured and walking interviews that were conducted in 2019 during a period of fieldwork in Amman for my PhD research. My research examined the relationship between mobilising youth in urban politics and sustaining peace in the diverse city. The city of Amman was chosen as a case study considering its prominent position as a diverse city with a significantly youthful population. Close to 70 per cent of Jordan's population are youth below the age of 30 (OECD, 2018a, p 1).

Jordan's diverse demographic and development over the course of its history is largely attributed to its geopolitical significance and regional migratory movements. Jordan remains the second largest refugee host per capita worldwide (89 refugees per 1,000 inhabitants) with 751,275 refugees documented from 57 different nationalities, of whom 82 per cent are living in urban areas (UNHCR, 2018, p 1). These characteristics positioned the city of Amman as an informative case study through which transferable insights into the core themes of my research were gained.

Youth is a relational concept encompassing a fluid and transitional phase in life, and therefore it is not possible to define youth based on chronological age; however, for the purpose of this research it was necessary to identify an age group. The age group 18–35 was identified in consideration of the Jordanian context of the case study, where the age of 18 offers a basic threshold that entitles youth to a set of civic and political rights, as they become eligible for voting in elections and forming associations, non-governmental organisations and political parties (OECD, 2018b, p 25). While the Jordanian National Youth Strategy encompasses youth up to the age of 30, during fieldwork it became apparent that the research would benefit from expanding the age group, and thereby the diversity of views, to encompass the age bracket provided by the League of Arab States, which goes up to the age of 35 (OECD, 2018b, p 27).

During fieldwork, I interviewed 31 young people (aged 18–35) from across the host and migrant youth community and 16 local planning officials over the course of two visits, spanning from mid-January 2019 to the end of February 2019 and during October 2019. In this chapter, I draw from eight semi-structured interviews conducted with a selection of refugee youth living in Amman governorate (outside of refugee camps), namely from Palestine, Syria and Sudan. These particular interviews have been chosen for the purpose of this chapter as, through the lived experiences of young refugees living in Amman, they demonstrate the role and value of inclusive urban planning and the transformative potential of urban public space.

Interviewees were contacted in advance via email or phone to request their participation primarily through gatekeepers in civil society organisations. Considering that I would be asking youth to share their perceptions surrounding urban diversity and their role in urban politics amidst a politically and spatially contested environment, the referral of participants through a trusted contact significantly contributed to building a foundation of trust from the onset. Out of the eight semi-structured interviews referenced in this chapter, the four walking interviews I have drawn from serve to prompt discussions that explore the connections between self and place. The locations in which walking interviews were conducted (Hashemite Plaza in East Amman and Abdali Boulevard in West Amman) were identified following their frequent mention by research participants during semi-structured interviews. Hashemite Plaza is located in the downtown area of Amman, and research participants characterised the space as being frequently visited by low-to-middle-income social groups. On the other hand, according to participants, Abdali Boulevard represents a contemporary and modern side to the city of Amman and is characterised as a space frequently visited by middle-to-high-income social groups. The socioeconomic attributes specific to each location prompted enriching discussions to unfold naturally, elicited by the surrounding environment.

On returning from fieldwork and beginning the transcription process, I embarked on the process of thematic analysis and fine-tuned the list of emerging themes and subthemes emerging from my data. The findings of this research were entirely dependent on being granted access into the lived experiences of research participants through the stories, perspectives and insights they shared with me. The process of building and maintaining trust made this exchange possible. Ethical considerations were fundamental to the research process. I needed to be sensitive to the possible ways in which participation in the research might impact participants (Somekh et al, 2011, p 4). I also needed to carefully consider relations of power, control, inclusion and exclusion and the ways in which these concepts speak to identities in different ways and to different people in different contexts (2010 p 59). For example, when identifying interview locations, it was essential that youth participants proposed the public locations where we would meet and the day and time most suitable for them. Another ethical concern coupled with walking interviews was that confidentiality cannot be assured if the walking interview is in a public place, as the researcher would be seen alongside the interviewee and others in the public space may overhear certain parts of the conversation (Kinney, 2017, p 2). During the walking interviews, I was mindful of avoiding attention from others in the public space who may overhear particularly sensitive parts of the conversations. To address this, I remained aware of our surroundings and would direct our walk towards a quieter and less occupied zone when needed. Despite such considerations, which I have attempted to mitigate, walking interviews alongside semi-structured interviews served as a highly productive way of accessing a local community's connections to their surrounding environment (Evans and Jones, 2011, p 857). Furthermore, as an Arabic speaker, I was able to conduct my interviews in both English and Arabic, and sometimes in Arabic only. This flexibility in language enabled the participants to freely express their views without linguistic barriers.

In pursuit of an inclusive city

This section serves to connect the theoretical knowledge presented thus far in this chapter with the insight I have gained from interviews conducted with young refugees in the city of Amman. This insight highlights the dominant norms and practices driving traditional urban governance and presents opportunities that inclusive planning can deliver for facilitating refugee youth experiences of socio-spatial inclusion. The excerpts I have chosen to highlight in this section provide a glimpse into the everyday lived experiences of refugee youth in the city of Amman and speak to the challenges and potentials of inclusive planning in pursuit of a just and inclusive city.

Following a prolonged civil war and outbreaks of violent conflict in his home country, Sudan, a young man aged 25, whom I will call Ali, fled to Amman, Jordan with, as he poignantly profoundly described it, "nothing, but maybe some hope". Ali left his home, family, friends and education behind. The threat to his life overshadowed the risk and uncertainty coupling his escape. Ali said that he did not have any expectations for the life that awaited him in Amman. As he put it, "We [other Sudanese refugees] just wanted to escape the terrible circumstances there. It was a matter of life and death ... so we accepted whatever was offered to us." Ali shared that, in the time leading to his escape, his mother passed away and, as the eldest among his siblings, it fell on his shoulders to look after and support his younger brothers. He shared with me that since his arrival in Amman he has had to work illegally, as the financial support he receives monthly from the United Nations High Commissioner for Refugees (UNHCR) is not enough to cover his basic needs, let alone to help him support his family. He also shared with me that as a consequence of being caught by authorities illegally working he has been jailed on four occasions.

> 'In Sudan, I had never seen a jail or even visited one. You need to eat and drink, and when you don't have enough for that, what else are you supposed to do and from where do you get money? You have to look for a job. You are a refugee; you do not have an opportunity. In jails you hear terrible things, they tell you that you are worthless. ... I still have dreams. God willing, I can carry on my education and live like everyone else is.' (Interview, October 2019, Sudanese man, aged 25–29)

Since Jordan is not a signatory of the 1951 refugee convention, refugees are limited from fully integrating in their local communities with equal rights. However, based on a memorandum of understanding with the UNHCR, basic rights such as education and healthcare are secured on registration of migrants with the Ministry of Interior and entities responsible for overseeing the reason for being in Amman (El-Abed, 2017, p 3). However, the restrictions surrounding the right to employment severely limits refugees from economically integrating in their local communities and securing an income for a sustainable livelihood (El-Abed, 2017, p 24). This excerpt highlights that, in the absence of critical integrating factors such as the right to employment and economic activity, young refugees are further marginalised and excluded from being active members of the local community. As one young woman shared:

> 'Unfortunately, in our part of the world, living in dignity has become a dream. We can't be productive without feeling that we are living dignified lives. All youth want is to live in dignity, to work, to be productive, to be able to pay their bills ... and the reality is that most of our youth are struggling. They can't find jobs.' (Walking interview, October 2019, Syrian woman, aged 25–29)

As both participants suggested, when the 'basic needs' provided are insufficient and fall short of securing the bare minimum required to lead an independent and dignified life, often many young refugees are forced to seek work illegally. This represents a vicious cycle, and leads to feelings of entrapment, which are also reflected in statements that young refugees made, such as "Everything is a problem. Paying for healthcare, paying for bills, for transportation. ... Even though I am not in jail, I feel like I am trapped" (interview, October 2019, Sudanese man, aged 25–29). The restrictions that prevent young refugees living in Amman from working and therefore integrating into the local community has a ripple effect and negatively influences notions of belonging and inclusion at the urban scale. In this light, one young man shared the following:

> 'If I was allowed to work, I would feel that I am a part of the community. I would meet people and maybe go out. I would know the city better. But I don't have money. If I want to go to Dead Sea or any historical place, I don't even have the transportation costs. One day, if I leave Jordan and I am asked if I ever visited the Dead Sea, they won't believe I haven't. I don't even have enough for my rent so how can I go out to places? That's why refugees are not part of the community.' (Interview, October 2019, Sudanese man, aged 25–29)

The sense of exclusion coupled with the injustices refugee youth experience exemplify why migrant inclusion is a significant, polarising and highly politicised issue. The exclusion of youth from attaining fully fledged rights raises a multiplicity of questions surrounding not only the scale at which migrant policies ought to be formulated and implemented but also the ways in which migrant inclusion can be measured, managed and encouraged (Price and Chacko, 2012, p 13). As the participant quoted inferred, the ideal of an inclusive city is intertwined with notions of inclusion in urban public space, and, as a consequence of poor socioeconomic conditions, young refugees are often marginalised from accessing the urban public space. This observation speaks to Massey's argument that people experience and interpret spatial social relations differently as a result of their position within society (1994, p 3). Acknowledging that refugee youth (who make up a diverse social group) do not share a uniform experience of the city has implications for how difference in the city is perceived and can be managed. As the participants indicated, there is a limit to the use of public space for building inclusion, considering that even in the most carefully designed public spaces, the marginalised and those who are prejudiced against them remain distant (Amin, 2002, p 968).

In this light, refugee youth made statements such as: "The country [Jordan] can't offer us anything because you are already a burden on them. ... It has to look after its own people" (interview, October 2019, Sudanese man, aged 25–29); and "We can never be treated as ordinary residents. We have accepted our status as refugees because we need to be protected and so you will always be a refugee" (interview, October 2019, Sudanese man, aged

25–29). From such statements, it can be inferred that by severing channels of dialogue and collaboration refugee youth are further marginalised, and local planning authorities miss the opportunity to engage refugee youth as equally valuable members of the community, who embody diverse skills, talents and experiences that are vital for building an inclusive and just city.

At the core of building a shared commitment to a political community is the criticality of understanding how young people, particularly newcomers, identify and develop a sense of belonging to the city. As Hopkins has suggested, a sense of identity and community for many young people 'is shaped by where they live, the territorial affiliations they hold and the tensions that exist between them and groups of young people from neighbouring communities' (2010, p 119). In this light, one participant shared: "This government doesn't count me as a citizen. However I feel that I belong here [Amman]. My childhood, my school, my university, my friends ... all this is a part of my life in Amman, so I feel that makes it more home [than Syria]" (walking interview, February 2019, Syrian woman, aged 30–35). This quote captures the contested nature of identity and belonging for many refugee youth. The participant acknowledged the absence of her citizenship rights as a Syrian national living in Jordan, which conflicts with her sense of belonging in Amman, which is attributed to relevant markers such as childhood memories, her school, university and friendships. As such, it is critical to investigate what 'citizenship beyond the state' (Gordon and Stack, 2010, p 130) can offer for refugee youth. In the absence of state citizenship, and thereby the denial of equal rights, intercultural place-making in the inclusive city serves as an opportunity to investigate how active citizenship at the urban scale can be nurtured. Discussions on the right to the city offer solid ground for such an investigation, considering that the right to the city is an exercise of collective power over processes of urbanisation (Harvey, 2003, p 1) and exercising agency in the matters affecting the lives of all who inhabit the city. Thereby, intercultural place-making, which is akin to exercising the right to the city, can contribute to forming a political community. Another participant speaks to this opportunity:

> 'If the government created public events or programmes for us [refugees] to take part in and if we felt that we were treated equally to other residents, and they made us feel at home, we could feel that we are part of the community. But we do not feel this way now.' (Interview, October 2019, Sudanese man, aged 25–29)

In light of this view, local planning authorities in Amman would benefit from developing sustainable guidelines and instruments for engaging refugee youth at all stages of the planning process, including planning, execution and monitoring, while raising awareness among all city inhabitants of the potential benefits of building inclusive and just cities. While the transformative potential of inclusive planning for refugee youth is clear, the widespread shortfalls in realising democratic participation cannot be ignored. In practice, inclusive planning can be seen as an uphill battle. Often, urban governance is typically organised around hierarchical bureaucratic agencies, guided by strict mandates and limited knowledge of the real issues facing city inhabitants (Innes and Booher, 2000, p 18). As the following participant observed: "The first mistake was not including youth in planning, and the second mistake was not including them in implementing plans. They do not listen to our voices" (walking interview, October 2019, Syrian man, aged 25–29).

Research participants generally acknowledged that participation in urban planning in Amman is predominantly top-down and that efforts to engage youth were largely inconsistent and tokenistic. Moreover, they suggested that efforts to date lack sustainability and have little to no influence on building social inclusion. The current *Amman 2025* master plan was developed between 2006 and 2008, with the aim of being an evolving document that would do more than just guide the physical development of the city. Inspired by international best practice, *Amman 2025* set out to deliver metropolitan, urban and community planning. Using participatory approaches and in contrast to previous plans, it solicited key institutional issues such as civic engagement and the building of Greater Amman Municipality (GAM)'s institutional capacity (Zeadat, 2018, p 173). However, considering the implications of Amman's growing and shifting population in the time since, the city requires an updated strategy that responds to its population growth (Zeadat, 2018, p 152). An updated strategy ought to prioritise and respond to building social cohesion and inclusion across the migrant and host community and to focus on actively engaging its youthful population. Theoretical advances surrounding inclusionary planning suggest that the way in which local communities engage in the planning process can have a profound impact on notions of inclusion and belonging. In this light, one participant shared:

> 'If you want to do anything for youth, you need to get them involved. Whenever they see that the city is working with them, you raise their sense of awareness and interest and they will take care of it, whether it is a programme or a project. Anyone who is engaged in the preparation phase of a project, programme or a plan will be more loyal to the execution and sustainability of the project. Youth are really committed. If you work with them, you gain their loyalty and you ensure that their energy runs the project.' (Walking interview, October 2019, Syrian man, aged 30–35)

As this participant infers, local planning authorities can play a key role in promoting civic engagement, social inclusion, participation and representation (Price and Chacko, 2012, p 34) among refugee youth by prioritising and endorsing inclusive planning approaches. However, as Arnstein argues, there is a critical difference between 'going through the empty ritual of participation' and having the real power to influence and shape outcomes (1969, p 216), which implies that planning authorities need to persistently and consistently engage refugee youth at all stages of the planning process. While research participants commonly acknowledged the significance of connecting in public spaces and in participating in municipality-level projects, they also addressed that their exclusion was coupled by an absence of trust in local planning authorities and an absence of transparency and accountability in the plans that are delivered.

> 'Greater Amman Municipality is killing any space that has the potential to be a public space because we are a community living in fear as opposed to opportunity. They think that if they create spaces where people can get together. ... I don't know, they just start naming the problems instead of the opportunities. They [GAM] worry about the public space becoming a gathering spot for people that might ruin it or use it for protests. ... You see they always imagine the dark scenarios and that is how they function.' (Walking interview, February 2019, Palestinian woman, aged 25–29)

The participant critically argued that GAM has contributed to making the city 'unliveable' (Lefebvre, 1970, p 92) through limiting and tightly controlling access to urban public spaces, which severs the potential for interaction. Many young people interviewed suggested that limited and tightly controlled public spaces reflected the government's efforts to prevent individuals and groups from congregating, out of fear that this would enable protests to become commonplace. Others suggested that young people were viewed as a threat to social order by public authorities and provided examples of how public spaces were heavily secured, which limited their accessibility to those spaces. In this vein, Wood and Landry suggest that some environments are more conducive to interaction than others, and that strategic interventions can capitalise on the transformative potential of urban public space to transform avoidance and indifference into engagement and cooperation (2008, p 320). However, this issue cannot be simply resolved by providing space that is accessible for all. For example, the research highlighted that refugee youth tend to avoid visiting urban public spaces that attract diverse members of the local community and instead prefer to visit spaces (whether public or private) that enable them to interact with other refugees. In this light, one participant shared:

'We have friends from Somalia, Yemen and some Syrians. Most of us meet at the UN Refugee Agency support centre or other centres that have activities going on for refugees. It is not really possible to meet others in other places, because you can't tell if they are a refugee. However, if you meet at the UN Refugee Agency support centre then you know that they are a refugee as well. It becomes easier to start a conversation because you know that they have drank [sic] from the same cup you have and so it is easier to become friends.' (Interview, October 2019, Sudanese man, aged 30–35)

While purposefully set up spaces such as the UN agency support centre are necessary and vital for enabling refugees to build a sense of community with others who can relate to a shared experience, initiatives that complement such services through providing opportunities for refugee youth to interact with the wider community are equally important. One way for new forms of interaction to occur is to create the conditions that facilitate them through inclusive planning. Inclusive planning approaches such as intercultural place-making advocate for collaboration between local planning officials and city inhabitants, whose needs, challenges and aspirations as well as skills, talents and lived experiences are valued as a fundamental attribute of the diverse city. Inclusive planning can help deliver planning outcomes that promote social justice through creating social and cultural spaces that are accessible and that enable increased interaction between diverse individuals and groups based on an understanding of diverse community needs and aspirations. By acknowledging diversity as a source of innovation, creativity and economic vitality, local planning authorities can help foster and promote cultural practices in urban public space through deliberated policies and programmes that support cultural practices of migrant communities and enable cultural expression (Price and Chacko, 2012, p 57). In this way, inclusive planning can offer a channel for young refugees to contribute to shaping the future of the cities they inhabit, which in turn provides an opportunity for diverse cities to thrive.

Conclusion

This chapter has underlined the necessity and criticality of inclusive planning in contributing to creating an urban future that is just and inclusive. While there is no single solution that will guarantee an inclusive city, without a critical understanding of the complex and contested nature of diversity in the city, which young refugees contribute to shaping, and in the absence of inclusive planning approaches such as intercultural place-making, opportunities for building inclusion in the city can be lost. In this light, I am reminded of Maalouf's observation that there is no miracle cure to address complex challenges, for '[t]he world is a complex machine that can't be dismantled with a screwdriver. But that shouldn't prevent us from observing, from trying to understand, from discussing, and sometimes suggesting a subject for reflection' (2000, p 29).

Maalouf's observation speaks to Jacob's description of the city as a metaphor for 'an immense laboratory of trial and error, failure and success, in city building and city design' (Jacobs, 1961, p 6). In this sense, cities and their public spaces can serve as sites on which 'solutions' can be tested. As Healey observes, knowledge is created anew when we exchange perceptions, understandings and experiences (1992, p 241). Therefore, it is not possible to predefine a set of tasks that planning must address, 'since these must be specifically discovered, learned about, and understood through intercommunicative processes' (Healey, 1992, p 241). Rather, the process of learning how to plan inclusively is made possible through the act of collaboration between planning authorities and city inhabitants. For refugee youth, who are commonly marginalised and excluded from actively participating in urban planning processes, inclusive planning offers an opportunity to constructively contribute to shaping the spatial and material character of the city, and for planning authorities it simultaneously provides an opportunity to understand and respond to the needs, challenges and aspirations of the diverse communities they serve. This act of collaboration supports cities to create governance structures and mechanisms that aim to enhance the integration of migrants and minorities and facilitate their contribution to the development of the city (Bathily, 2019, pp 5–6).

While the voices shared in this chapter emerge from the city of Amman, the discussions they have stirred shed light on the criticality and necessity of inclusive planning as a core value of urban policy and design across all cities. By capturing glimpses into the lived experiences, challenges, needs and aspirations of young refugees, each voice in this chapter echoes the urgency for cities to continuously ask: how can we engage refugee youth, who are often marginalised and excluded from urban planning processes? In this vein, cities will also need to ask: how can the design of urban public spaces encourage diverse individuals and groups to interact in ways that contribute to building inclusion in the city? Considering that the quality of interaction in urban public space is a reflection of the status of social inclusion in any given society, it is therefore imperative for urban public spaces to shape and be shaped by inclusive planning practices such as intercultural place-making.

The pursuit for an inclusive city calls for genuine, consistent and sustained participatory and collaborative processes and practices in urban governance that involve the concerted efforts of all city inhabitants (Price and Chacko, 2012, p 13). In this sense, planning authorities must look at how participation varies for diverse individuals and groups and across different geographical contexts. They will also need to acknowledge how urban policies and design impact the lives of all city inhabitants, including refugee youth. Planning authorities need to look past conventional planning approaches and be willing to challenge the status quo of top-down planning. Urban policies need to step outside their hierarchical and bureaucratic shells, and, instead, policymaking needs to emerge through and represent the dynamic diversity of lived experiences, aspirations, skills and talents that make up the social fabric of cities, and the design of urban public spaces needs to be driven and shaped by this dynamic diversity that all cities embody.

Ensuring the full inclusion of all city inhabitants is bound to be an ongoing challenge for all cities. However local planning authorities have a responsibility to enable open channels for communication and participation that reach far and wide into the diverse communities they serve. Planning authorities need to experiment and identify creative and innovative means to collaborate with all sectors of society and merge informal and formal processes of co-creating space. They need to be open to critique and accountability in order to build foundations of trust as well as to cultivate opportunities for sharing, learning and exchange. Without open channels for participation in city life, opportunities for communication, dialogue and exchange with city inhabitants cease. In this way, the sustained prevalence and effectiveness of open channels of participation in city life will significantly influence the social and spatial connections refugee youth experience, which is fundamental to the pursuit of a just and inclusive city.

References

Amin, A. (2002) 'Ethnicity and the multicultural city: living with diversity', *Environment and Planning A*, 34(6): 959–980.

Arciniegas, C.O. (2016) 'Paradoxical integration: the in-between space of [non] belonging', in G. Astolfo and K. Pallaris (eds) *Seeing the City Anew: Designing for Refugee Integration Volume*, 8: 13–31.

Arnstein, S.R. (1969) 'A ladder of citizen participation', *Journal of the American Planning Association*, 35(4): 216–224.

Bathily, A. (2019) *The Intercultural City Step by Step: A Practical Guide for Applying the Urban Model of Intercultural Inclusion*, Strasbourg: Council of Europe.

Darling, J. and Wilson, H.F. (eds) (2016) *Encountering the City: Urban Encounters from Accra to New York*, London: Routledge.

Domaradzka, A. (2018) 'Urban social movements and the right to the city: an introduction to the special Issue on urban mobilization', 29(4): 607–620.

Duxbury, N., Hosagrahar, J. and Pascual, J. (2016) *Agenda 21 for Culture: Why Must Culture Be at the Heart of Sustainable Urban Development?*, Barcelona: United Cities and Local Authorities.

El-Abed, O. (2017) *City Migration Profile: Greater Amman Municipality*, vol. Mediterran, available from: www.uclg.org/sites/default/files/amman_city_migration_profile_executive_summary_en.pdf

Evans, J. and Jones, P. (2011) 'The walking Interview: methodology, mobility and place', *Applied Geography*, 31(2): 849–858.

Fainstein, S.S. (2005) 'Cities and diversity: should we want it? Can we plan for it?', *Urban Affairs Review*, 41(1): 3–19.

Gordon, A. and Stack, T. (2010) 'Citizenship beyond the state: thinking with early modern citizenship in the contemporary world', *Citizenship Studies*, 11(2), available from: www.informaworld.com/smpp/title~content=t713411985

Harvey, D. (2003) 'The right to the city', *International Journal of Urban and Regional Research*, 27(4): 939–941.

Healey, P. (1992) 'Planning through debate: the communicative turn in planning theory', *Town Planning Review*, 63(2): 233–249.

Hopkins, P.E. (2010) *Young People, Place and Identity*, London: Taylor & Francis.

Hopkins, P.E. (2014) 'Managing strangerhood: young Sikh men's strategies', *Environment and Planning A*, 46(7): 1572–1585.

Innes, J.E. and Booher, D.E. (2000) *Collaborative Dialogue as a Policy Making Strategy*, UC Berkeley IURD Working Paper Series, available from: https://escholarship.org/uc/item/8523r5zt

Iveson, K. (2007) *Publics and the City*, Oxford: Blackwell.

Jacobs, J. (1961) *The Death and Life of Great American Cities*, New York: Random House.

Kinney, P. (2017) 'Walking interviews', *Social Research Update*, 67(1–4), available from: http://sru.soc.surrey.ac.uk/

Lefebvre, H. (1970) *The Urban Revolution*, translated by Robert Bononno, Minneapolis, MI: University of Minnesota Press.

Lefebvre, H. (1996) *Writings on Cities*, edited by E. Kofman and E. Lebas, Oxford: Blackwell.

Low, S. and Iveson, K. (2016) 'Propositions for more just urban public spaces', *City*, 20(1): 10–31.

Maalouf, A. (2000) *In the Name of Identity*, New York: Penguin Group

Marshall, E.A., Roche, T., Comeau, E., Taknint, J., Butler, K., Pringle, E., Cumming, J., Hagestedt, E., Deringer, L. and Skrzypczynski, V. (2016) *Refugee Youth: Good Practices in Urban Resettlement Contexts*, Victoria: University of Victoria.

Massey, D. (1994) *Space, Place, and Gender*, Bristol: Polity Press

Meer, N. and Modood, T. (2012) 'How does interculturalism contrast with multiculturalism?', *Journal of Intercultural Studies*, 33(2): 175–196.

OECD (2018a) *OECD Youth Well-Being Policy Review of Jordan Presentation of the Report of the Youth Inclusion Project*, Paris: EU-OECD Youth Inclusion Project.

OECD (2018b) *Youth Well-Being Policy Review of Jordan (EU-OECD Youth Inclusion Project)*, available from: www.oecd.org/dev

Orum, A.M. and Neal, Z.P. (2010) *Common Ground? Readings and Reflections on Public Space*, New York: Routledge.

Price, M. and Chacko, E. (2012) *Migrants Inclusion in Cities: Innovative Urban Policies and Practices*, Barcelona: UN-Habitat.

Sandercock, L. (2000) 'When strangers become neighbours: managing cities of difference', *Planning Theory & Practice*, 1(1): 13–30.

Sassen, S. (2013) 'When the center no longer holds: cities as frontier zones', *Cities*, 34(1–4): 67–70.

Somekh, B., Burman, E., Delamont, S., Meyer, J., Payne, M. and Thorpe, R. (2011) 'Research in the social sciences', in B. Somekh and C. Lewin (eds) *Theory and Methods in Social Research* (2nd edn), London: SAGE, pp 2–13.

UNESCO (2015) *Habitat III Issue Papers: 4 – Urban Culture and Heritage*, New York: UNESCO.

UNHCR (2018) *Fact Sheet: Jordan*, available from: www.unhcr.org

Wood, P. (2012) *Intercultural Place-Making*, Venice: Symposium at Università Iuav di Venezia, 21–22 June.

Wood, P. and Landry, C. (2008) *The Intercultual City: Planning for Diversity Advantage*, New York: Routledge.

Wood, P., Landry, C. and Bloomfield, J. (2006) *Cultural Diversity in Britain: A Toolkit for Cross-Cultural Co-Operation*, York: Joseph Rowntree Foundation.

Zeadat, Z.F. (2018) *A Critical Institutionalist Analysis of Youth Participation in Jordan's Spatial Planning: The Case of Amman 2025*, Edinburgh: Heriot-Watt University.

8

Sense of Belonging among Tibetan Refugees in India: A Case Study of the Bylakuppe Settlement in Karnataka, India

Anne Bramwell-Grent and Ajay Bailey

Introduction

The Tibetan refugee diaspora has faced protracted displacement since 1959. After the Chinese People's Liberation Army crushed a Tibetan uprising – a result of a decade of coercive Chinese communist state policy and constant human right violations in the Tibet region (Anand, 2003) – an estimated 80,000 Tibetans followed their spiritual leader, the 14th Dalai Lama Tenzin Gyatso, in his flight into India (Dolma, 2019). Consequently, Tibetan refugees were accommodated in refugee settlements all over India and largely still reside there (Smith, 1996; Ahmad, 2012). Both the Tibetan government in exile and the Indian government agreed to keep the Tibetan refugees in settlements isolated from Indian society. The main objective for this was the preservation of the Tibetan culture and to avoid admixture with the local population (Bentz, 2012). Meanwhile, Tibetans largely remain officially stateless, as they are not recognised by the People's Republic of China – currently governing the Tibet region as a part of China – nor have documents of any other country. Tibetans rarely claim Indian citizenship, arguably because of the social pressure from fellow Tibetan refugees and discouragement from the Central Tibetan Administration (CTA). This liminal stage of statelessness has led to lack of career opportunities and ability to integrate and travel abroad (Falcone and Wangchuk, 2008).

In the past five decades, an increasing number of Tibetans have been born in exile. For this generation of Tibetan refugees, the homeland is imagined through oral histories, religion and everyday cultural practices (Falcone and Wangchuk, 2008; Prakash, 2011; Dolma, 2019). The older generation of refugees have continued many of the everyday religious practices of Tibet, such as spinning prayer wheels and hanging prayer flags, during the past decades, whereas most of the youth increasingly characterise themselves as a mix between Tibetan, Indian and Western cultures. Younger Tibetans in exile engage with Indian popular culture such as Bollywood films, which present them with social tensions between old and new ways of viewing certain aspects, such as romance and marriage (Lau, 2010; Swank, 2011). Tibetan youth in many of the settlements are caught between visible and invisible boundaries that exist between Tibetan and anti-Tibetan views (Piltz, 2006). This inherent ambivalence towards a return to Tibet, in addition to constant 'othering' by the people outside the settlement, and aspirations to move to Western countries, shapes the often ambiguous, multiple and contested nature of attachment and sense of belonging.

Overall, this chapter aims to gain an understanding of the feelings of belonging that Tibetan youth in India experience towards different localities – including India, Tibet and Western countries. There will be a focus on socio-spatial inclusion and exclusion, in particular urban spaces and ways in which this differs between generations.

Tibetan migration towards India

While some of the Tibetan refugees who followed the Dalai Lama in his flight eventually sought refuge in Nepal and Bhutan, for most of them India was the destination in the long arduous journey. In the years since, a steady flow of Tibetans is migrating to India. It is estimated that around 130,000 Tibetans live outside of Tibet, and India hosts about 95,000 of them (CTA, 2010). Geographic proximity, the willingness of the Indian government to host the refugees and diasporic networks have led to many waves of migration from Tibet to India. Many Tibetans also believe that the proximity of the Dalai Lama is the only thing that can bring happiness when in exile; the settlement of this spiritual and political leader in India is an important pull factor for Tibetans to reside in this country. Equally important is that the headquarters of the Tibetan government in exile was established in Dharamshala, making India the locus of Tibetan political life in exile. Lastly, the refugee settlements that were established in India enabled Tibetan refugees to live among themselves to ensure that the Tibetan identity is not lost (Bentz, 2012).

Tibetan migration first began to take shape in 1949, when communist China's invasion of Tibet was followed by ongoing human rights violations. Fundamentally, three migration phases can be traced in the history of Tibetan displacement (Ahmad, 2012).

The first phase began in 1959, when the Chinese People's Liberation Army crushed the Tibetan uprising against the Chinese communist authorities (Federal Office for Migration Switzerland, 2013). Communist China annexed Tibet, which resulted in the previously mentioned escape of the 14th Dalai Lama, followed by an exodus of 80,000 Tibetans through the Himalayas into India (Ahmad, 2012). The second phase of Tibetan displacement began in the early 1980s, caused by three major events. Firstly, the Bhutanese government forced the exiled Tibetans living there to owe allegiance to the country by accepting its citizenship and adopting Bhutanese culture. After India's approval, approximately 3,100 Tibetans migrated from Bhutan to India. Secondly, after Tibet was opened to trade and tourism between 1986 and 1996, another estimated 25,000 Tibetans arrived in India (Ahmad, 2012). Thirdly, in 1988, when martial law was proclaimed in Tibet, many were forced to leave the country (Federal Office for Migration Switzerland, 2013). The third phase of Tibetan displacement can be said to have started in 1996 and continues until the present date and comprises today's Tibetan new arrivals. However, this phase is not as distinct and can be seen as an extension of the second phase (Federal Office for Migration Switzerland, 2013). Prakash (2011) states that roughly 3,000 refugees per year make the rather dangerous crossing over the Himalayas into India. Many of the refugees are young children sent away by their parents to find a better life in India.

In this chapter, we explore the multiple senses of belonging that Tibetan youth experience while living in a refuge settlement in Karnataka, India. Our key research question is: 'How do Tibetan refugees perceive and reflect their sense of belonging towards the Indian society?' Although this study did not have an intended focus on youth, the findings indicate that younger Tibetan refugees – approximately until the age of 30 – generally differ from older refugees in their sense of belonging towards Indian society. The empirical sections present the experiences, attachments and senses of belonging that are ambiguous, multiple and contested.

Conceptualisation of belonging

A sense of belonging can be defined as a 'personal, intimate, feeling of being "at home" in a place' (Antonsich, 2010). Essential aspects of this concept are cognitive stories – narratives that people tell themselves and others about their identity – as well as desire for attachments – a longing for becoming-other (Yuval-Davis, 2006; Antonsich, 2010). This emotional and social notion of belonging, however, is inevitably conditioned by the politics of belonging. Antonsich (2010), drawing on Fenster (2005) and Yuval-Davis (2006), explains: 'Belonging should be analysed both as a personal, intimate, feeling of being 'at home' in a place (place belongingness) and as a discursive resource which constructs, claims, justifies, or resists forms of socio-spatial inclusion/exclusion (politics of belonging)' (Antonsich, 2010, p 1). By merely focusing on the sense of belonging, one risks treating belonging as an individualistic matter, disregarding the social and political context within which it is immersed. Antonsich (2010) elaborates:

> To be able to feel at home in a place is not just a personal matter, but also a social one. In fact, if one feels rejected or not welcomed by the people who live in that place, her/his sense of belonging would inevitably be spoiled. This means that one's personal, intimate feeling of belonging to a place should always come to terms with discourses and practices of socio-spatial inclusion/exclusion at play in that very place and which inexorably conditions one's sense of place-belongingness. (p 12)

While analysing the sense and politics of belonging, the importance of locations, geographically and socially, have to be taken into account. In the geographical sense, belonging is always related to a place and is therefore always located. These locations are always multiple, fluid and (re-)created with experiences of the people who inhabit these spaces. This entails that people are inclined to have different belongings globally that can change over time (Anthias, 2013). The notion of social locations – the combination of factors such as gender, race and age – is also crucial to the concept of belonging. Each person belongs to multiple social locations, which co-constitute each other. These social locations are linked to multiple axes of differences, which equally change and are contested over time and, as well, they differ between spaces (Yuval-Davis, 2006).

Hou et al (2018) identify four aspects that impact belonging: social capital, economic integration, the receiving society's receptivity and exposure to the host society. Each of these aspects contains several indicators that influence the notion of belonging. These indicators are not conceptualised to be fixed, normative or unproblematic. They provide a frame by which we can observe and understand the different senses of belonging.

Firstly, social capital refers to immigrants' social ties. Commonly used indicators are bonding and bridging social networks. Hou et al (2018) state that bonding social networks – 'ties with other members of the same immigrant or ethnic group' (p 7) – might strengthen immigrants' identification with the source country, while bridging social networks – 'relationships beyond a tight-knit community' (p 7) – tend to enhance the development of sense of belonging towards the receiving society. However, the way in which both bonding and bridging social relations shape feelings of belonging very much depends on the nature of these social ties. Emotionally dense ties with friends and family, which are stable, significant and take place through frequent interactions, tend to generate a sense of belonging. Conversely, weak ties, for example occasional everyday encounters in public spaces, are not sufficient to enhance a sense of connectedness to others on which belonging relies (Amin, 2002; Antonsich, 2010).

Secondly, Hou et al (2018) contend that economic integration offers a reflection for immigrants' participation in the receiving society. Along these lines, Antonsich (2010) argues that being fully and successfully integrated into the economy of the host country is an essential factor in generating feelings of attachment, from a material perspective as well as in relation to making a person feel that she has a stake in the future of the place where she lives. Therefore, the socioeconomic position of immigrants in the host country is more likely to play a role in developing their sense of belonging.

Along these lines, it is important to state that legal factors, such as citizenship and resident permits, are an essential dimension of belonging, as these factors produce security. If one is entitled with rights to work, to stay, one can participate in and actively shape one's environment (Antonsich, 2010).

Thirdly, the aspect of receiving society's receptivity indicates how the host country welcomes and treats immigrants (Hou et al, 2018). Commonly used indicators for this are perceptions of the social climate towards immigrants in the host country and discrimination. The development of a sense of belonging is hampered by discrimination and a negative social climate towards immigrants (Antonsich, 2010; Hou et al, 2018). These indicators also relate to the politics of belonging, as they are based on narratives of inclusion and exclusion.

Lastly, exposure to the host society emphasises the contacts that immigrants have with the majority group of the receiving country. Important indicators for this are proficiency in the host country's language, age at immigration, length of residence and commitment to remain in the host country (Antonsich, 2010; Amit and Bar-Lev, 2015; Hou et al, 2018; Raijman and Geffen, 2017). Language proficiency is not only a symbol of national identity and cultural solidarity, but also relates to particular ways of understanding and defining situations and meanings – thus evoking a sense of community. However, language can also be activated in the politics of belonging, by increasing the gap between 'us' and 'them'. The indicators such as age at immigration and length of residence revolve around the importance of autobiographical factors, such as memories and personal experiences, which attach a person to a place. Particularly, childhood memories play a crucial role, as the place where a person grew up often continues to be a central part of that individual's life (Antonsich, 2010; Raijman and Geffen, 2017). Furthermore, a lengthier tenure in the country is (normatively) expected to weaken immigrants' sense of belonging to other places and enhance feelings of attachment towards the host society (Amit and Bar-Lev, 2015).

Scholars have thus far predominantly focused on Tibetan social and cultural practices. Chen (2012) states that it is important to highlight exiles' feelings for local places in India itself, instead of merely focusing on the sentiment towards their homeland. This study offers such a new perspective by focusing on the relations between Tibetans in exile and their Indian social environment, which is often neglected by scholars (Lau, 2010). More specifically, this study focused on acquiring an in-depth understanding of the varied and contested senses of belonging of Tibetan refugees towards the Indian society.

Data for this study were collected in the Bylakuppe settlement in Karnataka State, located in the south of India, as it is the first and one of the biggest settlements in the country (Prakash, 2011). The methods used were participant observation, in-depth interviews and photography. In total, within this study, we conducted 39 interviews with male and female Tibetan refugees and a wide variation of ages.

Study site: the Bylakuppe settlement

The government of Karnataka allocated 3,000 acres of land to the 3,000 Tibetans of the initial population of Bylakuppe (Bentz, 2012). These distributed lands were largely uninhabited and consisted of dense forests with wild animals. The Indian government employed and paid the Tibetans to clear these forests (Kantharaj, 2006). In addition to Bylakuppe, there are three more Tibetan settlements in Karnataka, which are located in Hunsur, Kollegal and Mundgod.

Today, Bylakuppe officially consists of two separate settlements, often referred to as the old and new camp. The old camp is called the Lungsung Samdupling settlement and has around 15,600 residents. Established in 1960, it is the oldest settlement in India. The new camp, Dickyi Larsoe, was set up in 1969 and has a smaller population of approximately 4,700 people (Kantharaj, 2006; Tsekyi and Thimmaiah, 2014). The settlement is divided into 23 villages, of which 16 villages belong to the old camp and seven to the new camp (CTA, 2018). These villages are located about two to three kilometres apart from each other in the old camp and four to six kilometres in the new camp (Prakash, 2011). The villages are numbered in sequence according to the order in which they were initially formed, and each has its own Tibetan name as well. Each village consists of approximately 30 families, ranging from four to 14 family members (Prakash, 2011; CTA, 2018).

Bylakuppe is also home to some of the largest monasteries of Tibet, such as Sera, Namdroling and Tashi Lhunpo. These monasteries play an important role in both the preservation of Buddhism and community development. The Sera monastery is the biggest among them, with an occupation of almost 3,000 monks (CTA, 2018). This monastery is the re-establishment

Figure 8.1: Tashi Lhunpo monastery

Source: Anne Grent (2018)

of one of the most important monasteries existing in Tibet (Arpi, 2011). Tashi Lhunpo (Figure 8.1), inaugurated by the Dalai Lama in December 2015, is the newest monastery in Bylakuppe (CTA, 2018).

Furthermore, many Tibetan schools can be found within the settlement, such as the S.O.S. Tibetan Children Village. This school serves simultaneously as a boarding house and an education facility. These schools appear to be well organised and full of supplies (Prakash, 2011).

Participant recruitment

The strategies for this research included the use of gatekeepers and snowball recruitment. The use of gatekeepers – people with a prominent and recognised role in the local community (Hennink et al, 2011) – was a central form of participant recruitment in this study. One of the gatekeepers was a prominent monk from the Sera monastery, who introduced us to his fellow monks and to families that he was acquainted with. The second gatekeeper was the headmaster of a monastic secondary school, who introduced us to the teachers at the school and some of his friends. By selecting multiple gatekeepers and using snowball recruitment as an additional recruitment strategy, this study was attentive to any potential problems in the gatekeepers' selection of participants, as gatekeepers might purposely select participants whom they would like the researcher to include in the research (Hennink et al, 2011).

In total, 39 participants were recruited. These participants broadly varied in age, as 15 of them were between 15 and 31 years old, and 24 participants ranged from 32 to 87. Unfortunately, women were underrepresented in this study, as merely four participants were female. It was challenging to include more women in the study. This can largely be explained by the fact that both the researchers and the gatekeepers were situated in the camp where the Sera monastery is located. Mainly male Tibetan monks live here, which made it more difficult to build rapport with women before asking them to participate. Although the underrepresentation of women in this study is unfortunate and arguably jeopardises the validity to a certain extent, the interviews themselves revealed no explicit differences between the perceptions of women and men. Nonetheless, in order to more clearly include the lived experiences of women, future research should be especially aware about gender dynamics when designing a data collection strategy.

Additionally, the data regarding economic integration is biased, as Tibetans who work in Indian society are likely to be excluded from the study, as most of them do not live in Bylakuppe due to a lengthy daily commute to Indian cities. Within the settlement, however, efforts were made to include participants from a wide range of educational levels and professions, for example monks, electricians, postmen, accountants, students and teachers, in an attempt to reflect the socioeconomic diversity within Bylakuppe.

Observation and interviews

In order to gain an understanding of the context being studied, participant observation was applied throughout the fieldwork period. Schensul et al (1999) define this method as 'the process of learning through exposure to or involvement in the day-to-day or routine activities of participants in the research setting' (p 91). A field diary was maintained in which both elements of the physical environment – involving the surroundings of the setting and providing a written description of the context – as well as a description of the participants and recorded activities and interactions that occur in the setting were included. Short summaries of informal conversations and observations were added to the fieldnotes as well. This concerns the informal conversations during social gatherings that were considered relevant for this study.

Furthermore, in-depth interviews were conducted with Tibetans who live within the Bylakuppe settlements. According to Hennink et al (2011), in-depth interviews allow researchers to identify individual perceptions, beliefs, feelings and experiences. With this reasoning, this method is suitable to investigate the perceptions of Tibetans about their sense of belonging.

Participants in the study continuously reflected on their temporary state of living in the settlement, some wishing to go to a third country and some with a long-term wish to return to Tibet. The subject of the questions in the interview included daily life at the settlements, perceptions of both Tibet and India, the social and economic interaction with people outside the settlements and future migration plans.

The interviews were of varying lengths and depths of information, although some participants were more able than others to answer the rather broad and often challenging questions about, for instance, their perceptions of Indian society. Important to note is that some participants were significantly more fluent in English than others, which generally enabled them to give more extensive and nuanced answers and to express their thoughts and feelings better. In some cases, interviews were conducted with the help of a translator. Overall, depending on the aforementioned circumstances, some interviews took about half an hour, whereas others lasted for more than one hour.

Data analysis

The data of this study was analysed through thematic analysis as developed by Braun and Clarke (2006). This analytic approach was selected as it enables researchers to identify patterns within the data, which is useful given the explorative nature of this study. The thematic analysis by Braun and Clarke (2006) includes six phases: familiarisation with data; generating initial codes; searching for themes among codes; reviewing themes; defining and naming themes; and producing the final report. The main categories include: elements of Indian culture in daily life; elements of Tibetan culture in daily life; commitment to remain in India; languages; opinion on Indian citizenship; non-Bylakuppe residents' perception of Tibetans; Bylakuppe residents' perception of Tibetans; and contacts with Indians. These categories were grouped together into themes that are present in the results section in this chapter.

Senses of belonging of Tibetan youth

While analysing the findings of this study, it became evident that a distinction between Bylakuppe and non-Bylakuppe residents was required. Bylakuppe residents are Indian people who are native to the Bylakuppe area and live near the Tibetan settlement. This group is generally more accommodating of the Tibetans and knows the history of the settlement. Non-Bylakuppe residents, on the other hand, are generally not familiar with the history of Tibetan refugees, as they usually do not get in touch with Tibetans on a regular basis.

Social capital

Social capital relates to the social ties of Tibetans, which are likely to shape and encourage feelings of attachment towards the Indian society (Hou et al, 2018). Both bridging social networks (ties with Indian people) and bonding social networks (relationships with fellow Tibetans) are considered relevant for an assessment of social capital. As bonding social networks are evident, given the fact that all participants live among fellow Tibetans, this paragraph will elaborate on their bridging social networks. Furthermore, there will be a focus on the nature of these ties, as mainly emotionally dense ties tend to influence feelings of attachment (Amin, 2002; Antonsich, 2010).

Younger participants indicated frequent engagement in encounters with non-Bylakuppe residents. Most of these participants were born in India and, after being educated in Tibetan schools until 12th grade, pursued their studies in Indian cities such as Mysore or Bangalore. Metok (teacher, 27 years) explained: "When I was in college, I was the only Tibetan in my class. All the other 60 students were Indians. I made so many Indian friends there." Tsering (teacher, 28 years) said that he even has more Indian than Tibetan friends: "In college, all my friends were Indians. I had the best moments of my life at college. I explored so many things. I have even fallen in love with an Indian lady."

These ties are generally emotionally dense, as they are often taking place through frequent interactions during their studies. Furthermore, the younger refugees who have learned the local language establish more ties with local youth groups.

While non-Bylakuppe residents were predominantly regarded as friends, participants generally thought of their ties with Bylakuppe residents as mainly procedural, reciprocal and task oriented. Lobsang (monk, 39 years) stated: "I just talk and drink tea with Indian people, but we are not friends." Sonam (postman, 41 years) said: "I would consider the relationship with local Indians more as a business deal. We need them, we pay them. It is of a business deal from two sides."

In Bylakuppe, one can clearly notice the economic functions that Bylakuppe residents occupy in the settlement. Many participants said that the *autos* (auto rickshaws) in Bylakuppe are always driven by Bylakuppe residents (Figure 8.2). Consequently, participants often get in touch with them when they use the *autos* to travel in the settlement and to the nearby town of Kushalnagar. Kushalnagar is the largest urban area and commercial centre for the district of Kodagu. Additionally, shops and hotels within the settlement reportedly and visibly often employ Bylakuppe residents. This increases their interaction and reciprocity between the refugees and the local residents. Moreover, these ties can largely be characterised as weak ties, as

Figure 8.2: Indian autos in Bylakuppe

Source: Anne Grent (2018)

they are generally based on everyday encounters in public spaces, and thus are arguably not sufficient to enhance a sense of connectedness to others on which belonging relies. In this public place, belongingness is procedural and bereft of strong bonds that makes the coexistence of these groups viable, as there a sense of reciprocity.

Economic integration

Investigating economic integration of participants enables us to reflect on the participation of Tibetan refugees in Indian society (Hou et al, 2018). We identified a difference between educational integration and occupational integration. While most young refugees migrated to Indian cities for higher education, many participants reported that they faced difficulties in finding a job in these cities. They faced certain obstacles in their job search, given their official statelessness. Due to a lack of job opportunities within Indian society, participants often return to the Tibetan settlements for work, even though they often would prefer otherwise. Tsering (teacher, 28 years) explained: "The problem for us is that our official status is still that of refugees. I thought maybe I should go and enter the Indian market, but that is difficult with a refugee status."

In addition, Tashi illustrated the way belonging-related politics – through practices of socio-spatial exclusion – negatively impact the occupational integration of Tibetan refugees:

> 'Being separated from India, not being an Indian citizen, there are certain things you can't do and certain jobs you can't get. Like for example government jobs, or in the military, in the navy, armed forces, whatever. As a Tibetan, you can't get a job there, because we are not Indians. Our young people, they have to go in private companies for jobs. Privately, they employ us. All the government things are blocked for us. Starting a business is easier when you are a citizen; it is more difficult if you are not a citizen.' (Retired, 64 years)

Under certain circumstances, it is possible for Tibetan refugees to apply for an Indian passport. This would enable them to expand their employment opportunities. Some participants emphasised the communal disadvantage of applying for an Indian passport. Phuntsok explained: "Once we have an Indian passport, then the whole purpose of being in India in exile is lost. The reason why we have a separate school system, separate parliament, separate Tibetan administration is to preserve our Tibetan identity" (teacher, 51 years). Mainly younger participants, however, do not always agree with the notion that documents are central to one's identity. Yangkey said:

> 'In order to keep our identity, it is not necessary to keep Tibetan documents specifically. It is the 21st century; we have to move on. Even though it is so important to keep our Tibetan culture and Tibetan rituals going, it is not necessary to keep the Tibetan documents to prove that you are from the Tibetan community. You are not Tibetan because you got a green book. It is not necessary to show them. ... There are some people who really need to apply for Indian citizenship in order to ease their personal issues. Not because they don't like the Tibetan identity, it is not because they hate Tibetans. They did that because they need to do that.' (Teacher, 30 years)

Tsering highlighted the differing opinions between his generation and the generation of his parents by saying:

> 'Since my childhood days, my parents have been telling me the same thing: there is a reason why you are still a refugee, there is a cause you have to fight for. One aspect is that I want to do great business, and then one is my family's wish to serve the country, to fight for our own country. So, I am still in the middle. I am still not able to decide.' (Teacher, 28 years)

This statement shows that multiple social locations – son, young man – can arguably result in ambiguous and ambivalent feelings of attachments towards Tibet.

Receiving society's receptivity

The receiving society's receptivity relates to the ways in which a host country welcomes and treats immigrants. Discrimination and a negative social climate towards immigrants discourage the development of a sense of belonging (Antonsich, 2010; Hou et al, 2018). Both younger and older participants said that they have experienced discrimination in Indian society to a certain degree. However, it is important to point out that participants solely noted instances of discrimination on an individual level. They reported no problems that have occurred on a community level.

Participants sometimes experience discrimination by non-Bylakuppe residents in the form of name-calling. Young Tibetans arguably must deal with this more often, as they usually live in Indian cities during their studies. Gyemtsen (school prefect, 19 years) explained: "I met lots of Indian people who thought of our Tibetan face as a yellow type, so they call us 'chinkies'. They treat us differently this way." Participants explained that '*chinkie*' means something along the lines of 'Chinese person' or 'flat eye'.

Besides name-calling, participants occasionally feel like they are being stared at in an inappropriate manner. Dorje (administrator, 38 years) said that it makes him feel uncomfortable whenever this happens. "In the settlement, we don't feel like outsiders. But when you move out of the settlement into the city, at that time I sometimes feel like an outsider."

Moreover, one could argue that young refugees can be expected to develop ambivalent feelings of attachment towards Indian society during their studies. While they acknowledge making close Indian friends during this period of their life, they are simultaneously more exposed to discrimination.

Other than the discrimination by non-Bylakuppe citizens, discrimination by Indian government officials is also an issue that participants often mentioned. It was stated multiple times in both interviews and informal conversations that Tibetans experience difficulties with processing paperwork, as they feel like they are regarded as foreigners. For example, it frequently takes more time for them than for Indian citizens to acquire necessary signatures. In addition, they are often expected to pay more money, as Tsundue commented:

> 'They [government officials] always try to extract more from us than from the locals. Whenever you have to do some work, they come up with high prices. If the official amount is 50 rupees, and everybody has to pay 50 rupees, they will ask more from us. Because we look

different, and then they think we are better off than people from their own society, they consider us as outsiders.' (Teacher, 26 years)

Multiple participants implied that discrimination by non-Bylakuppe residents and Indian government officials are fuelled by a lack of awareness of the Tibetan identity and heritage. Participants mentioned that, whereas Indian people around Bylakuppe are familiar with Tibetans, in bigger cities – such as Bangalore and Mysore – Tibetans form a minority group. Pema explained: "Some people know about Tibetans. For them it is not that much of a problem. Some don't know about us. They think of us as outsiders or foreigners" (teacher, 26 years). These narratives of exclusion by Indian government officials are likely to reduce feelings of attachment towards Indian society.

Exposure to host society

Exposure to the host society includes the contacts that immigrants have with the majority group (Hou et al, 2018). Language proficiency and commitment to remain in India are two relevant topics to consider when assessing the exposure of Tibetan refugees to Indian society.

When considering language proficiency, a distinction has to be made between the local language, Kannada, and the national language, Hindi. Participants who did not grow up in Bylakuppe generally have little knowledge of the Kannada language. This makes it very difficult for them to connect with Bylakuppe residents, which is identified as one of the reasons why these ties are often regarded as merely business relationships. Kelsang (10th grade student, 18 years), said: "I don't even know how to say, 'What is your name?' in Kannada. I just know how to count to three. But I forgot about it now." Dolma (shop owner, 43 years) explained: "Mostly in Bylakuppe itself, Tibetans speak Kannada very fluently. People do get better relations with the local people by learning the Kannada language."

Younger participants who have attended school in India tend to be more proficient in the national language, Hindi, than in the local language, Kannada, although they often do not speak Hindi fluently. Yama (12th grade student, 19 years) explained: "We learn Hindi in class 6, 7 and 8. Only three years. We learn the alphabet and some words." Some participants said that they learned Hindi from Bollywood movies, which the majority of the participants like to watch. Tsetan (teacher, 33 years) said: "When I was in school, I used to love movies. Most of the movies are Hindi. I learned Hindi by seeing movies."

Consequently, those who understand Hindi are able to maintain friendships with non-Bylakuppe residents and can arguably gain more insights into the Indian culture that is distributed through movies. Those who do not, however, are likely to experience an invisible political boundary that separates a perceived 'us' from 'them' and constructs Tibetans as clearly demarcated from Indians.

In terms of their commitment to remain in India, many participants stated that they view India as their second homeland. Tsetan (teacher, 33 years) said: "I must say that India has become my country, my second homeland." This feeling of India as a second homeland may be enhanced by the fact that a large share of the participants was born in India or arrived as children or young adolescents. This results in their socialisation taking place in India and a lengthier tenure in the host country. The place where a person grew up often continues to be a central part of that individual's life (Antonsich, 2010; Raijman and Geffen, 2017). Tashi (retired, 64 years) explained: "My entire life, as a child, education and working, everything was in India. So, I am a Tibetan, but in my heart, I am an Indian in that sense."

Despite the efforts of both the Indian government and the Tibetans to preserve the Tibetan culture within the refugee settlements, Indian cultural influences can be witnessed in Bylakuppe. One can, for instance, see advertisement posters for Bollywood movies, and it is very common for restaurants to serve both Indian and Tibetan food. Participants consume Indian foods such as *puri*, *parotta* and *dosa*, as well as Tibetan foods such as *tsampa*, *momos* and *thukpa*. Some participants even prefer Indian food to Tibetan food. When Pema was asked what kind of food he prefers, he answered:

> 'Definitely Indian. I was born and raised in India. I always had the Indian diet, which is rice and all these things. I didn't have our own diet much. In the sense of food, I am more towards Indian food. They have multiple cuisines, whereas in Tibetan society there are hardly eight to ten cuisines. That's it. So, there is more choice in Indian food. And we are used to Indian food. When we were in school, there was Indian food, rice and dahl. Dahl is not grown in Tibet at all, but now we are used to it.' (Teacher, 26 years)

Although India is often regarded as a second homeland, many first-generation refugees – those who were born and have lived in Tibet – often reported a strong wish to return. They wish to see their families again. Second-generation refugees, however, have never been to Tibet themselves and expressed different opinions about their homeland. Rigzin, a second-generation refugee, explained that he merely has ideas about Tibet from the stories of others and pictures:

> 'I was born in India. People say that we are Tibetans. The first thing that came to mind was "Where is Tibet?" I wonder what our capital

Lhasa looks like, the Potala and everything. It is just the pictures I can see, not the reality. We don't have freedom yet.' (Accountant, 28 years)

Moreover, some young refugees explicitly stated that they do not feel the need to return to Tibet. They perceive the current Tibet region as backward with a lack of healthcare, employment and education facilities. Consequently, returning to Tibet would mean that they would have to lower their living standards. Moreover, many observe that the Chinese have influenced Tibet too much. As years go by, a free Tibet increasingly feels like a distant dream to them. Sonam elaborated on this:

'It is not Tibet anymore. The Chinese completely changed it. It is not like you can see lots of yaks and sheep, see these rivers and forests. It is not anymore. The Chinese have polluted it. It is not like the old Tibet; it has been changed so much. They just literally destroyed everything. From the monasteries, to the daily lives of people, to the landscape, or even the rivers and forests. There is nothing to see in Tibet now. It is just the name Tibet, but it does not feel like my land anymore.' (Postman, 41 years)

Furthermore, many young Tibetan refugees expressed a desire to move to Western countries such as in Europe, the United States and Australia. They largely believe that there are more opportunities for them in those countries. Lhundup (teacher, 23 years) said: "I am planning to join one of the universities in Australia. I am still working on this. I don't give up. I was a big dreamer when I was in school, and I will remain a big dreamer." Tashi explained this phenomenon:

'Now, slowly what is happening is that going back to Tibet as a free people is becoming more and more difficult. Young people don't see that happening now. So many young Tibetans are looking towards the West to settle. Not so much India. If they get a visa today, they will go. They see the West to be wonderful, the land of milk and honey, money to be picked from the trees. Everything is shiny, wonderful, clean, spotless, you know. They see that. They want to go there. So that is what they do. There is a huge effort to try to go anywhere. Holland, Germany, French [sic], Denmark, Sweden or whatever; it does not matter. Not towards Tibet; nobody goes to Tibet.' (Retired, 64 years)

However, once Tibetans go to the West, they usually continue to support the Tibetan community in India. Nyima (employee of the Tibetan Agricultural Co-operative Society, 38 years) said: "Tibetan people use to go abroad and work. They send money to their parents over there. They sometimes build a house for their parents." Dawa (college student, 21 years) added that he would like to study abroad, but afterwards return to India to serve the Tibetan community: "If I get the opportunity to study abroad, I go there and then return to the Tibetan community to serve here."

Along these lines, influences of the Western culture are apparent in Bylakuppe – especially when it comes to music. When sitting in *coffee cafés* (coffee shops) or while walking through the streets, one can hear Justin Bieber blaring from the speakers. Ngawang (employee, animal care non-governmental organisation, 41 years) said: "I love Western music. To be honest, nowadays, the younger generation of Tibetans is more attracted to the Western culture." With regard to this, Rinchen (provider of internet services, 28 years) reasoned: "It is not like because I am Tibetan I only should like Tibetan songs. That is not necessary." Belonging here involves a conflict between what is expected and what is practised by the young people. The ways in which young Tibetans weave together different cultures, norms and practices shows their ability to switch between cultures. A deeper reading of these practices highlighted the freedom that they have to express themselves, which they may not have had if they had been in Tibet.

Participants generally expressed appreciation for Tibetan, Bollywood and English music equally – reflecting the mix of Indian, Western and Tibetan influences in their daily life. Dolma (shop owner, 43 years) said: "I listen to Hindi, Tibetan and English music, all mixed up. I don't have a preference." At musical concerts, Tibetan, Bollywood and Western dances are performed, as shown on an advertisement poster for a musical concert.

This range of cultural influences that can be witnessed in Bylakuppe indicates that Tibetans are in the process of developing feelings of attachment towards multiple locations: Tibet, India and, increasingly, Western countries.

Conclusion

Tibetan refugee settlements in India were initially designed to be temporary, but after all these decades the dream of a free Tibet remains distant (Palakshappa, 1978; Ahmad, 2012). Whereas older Tibetans often still feel a strong attachment towards their homeland, a different perspective is noticeable among the youth. For many of them, Tibet is an imagined homeland, as they have never been to Tibet themselves and have only got to know it through stories of others. Some of them regard contemporary Tibet as a backwards region with too many Chinese influences. However, although the nature of their sense of belonging towards Tibet might be changing, Tibetan youth still sustain feelings of attachment towards their (imagined) motherland. For younger Tibetans born in the settlements, this sense of attachment is imagined and reiterated through everyday practices of culture, oral histories and political activism. Although many of them were born and raised in India, they identify themselves as refugees. Hereby, it is important to note that refugeeism is a continually political phenomenon, which is consistent with the reality of Tibetans in India. They largely refuse to apply for Indian citizenship, which indicates that their paper identity as Tibetan refugee is an important symbol of loyalty to their motherland (Voe, 1981). A broader reading shows that the liminal state of being could end with the application of Indian citizenship. For younger people, the chance of resettlement in a third country is further reduced when they change nationalities.

Tibetan youth are also developing a sense of belonging towards the Indian society that surrounds the settlement. Many young Tibetan refugees were born and socialised in India: they study in Indian cities, befriend non-Bylakuppe residents and are fond of Indian music, movies and food. However, they simultaneously face difficulties with connecting to Bylakuppe residents, are generally not fluent in Hindi and even less so in Kannada, occasionally experience discrimination and have rather limited employment opportunities in Indian society. These obstacles hinder developing an attachment to the local groups and generate ambivalence in terms of their position, location and identity in relation to Bylakuppe and non-Bylakuppe residents. This is reflected in their reluctance to apply for Indian citizenship. Practices of socio-spatial inclusion and exclusion shape personal development and add to the liminal existence of Tibetans in India.

The results also indicate that multiple social locations and positions – for example, son, young man, Indian educated, liberal views, aspirations to live in a Western country – result in ambiguous and ambivalent feelings of attachment towards Tibet. While the older refugees encourage the youth to keep their refugee status to fight for a free Tibet, the youth are eager to expand their opportunities in Indian society. If they, for instance, wish to start a business in India, it would be necessary for them to apply for an Indian passport.

Additionally, young Tibetan refugees in India are increasingly dreaming of pursuing their ambitions in Western countries, such as in Europe, the United States and Australia. They believe they will be granted more opportunities there than they currently have in India or would have in Tibet. They are also being encouraged by Tibetan refugees who reside in the West already. Furthermore, by earning money in the West, they believe that they will be able to support the Tibetan community in India and their struggle to return to Tibet.

To better understand the ways in which participants develop a sense of belonging towards Indian society, it is helpful to reflect on the multiple routes and pathways to forming identity/identities. Young Tibetan refugees in India seem to occupy a 'third space' between Tibetan, Indian and Western. This notion of a third space is derived from the 'third space theory' of Homi

Bhabha. In such a space, people are constantly (re-)constructing their own identity through interactions with others, without becoming either this or that (Bhabha, 1990; English, 2002).

Additionally, Edward Soja (1996), building on Henri Lefebvre, defines the third space as 'a purposively tentative and flexible term that attempts to capture what is a constantly shifting milieu of ideas, events, appearances and meanings' (p 2). This encompasses perceived space – in Lefebvre's terms 'spatial practice', influenced by experiences and conceived space or 'representations of space', the existing properties of a location. Within these spaces is a lived space – 'representational space', changed and appropriated by the imagination. In Soja's (1996) words: 'Thirding produces what might best be called a cumulative trialectics that is radically open to additional otherness, to a continuing expansion of spatial knowledge' (p 61).

Essentially, the voices of the third space view culture as unfixed, while remaining cautious of the politics of history and location (Lavie and Swedenburg, 1996). Western societies used identity politics to unify themselves and frame colonialised populations as the Other. The opposing postmodernist celebration of fragmentation, however, has failed to acknowledge the power relations between the centre and margins that still remained.

As for young Tibetans in India, power relations still constrain them to stay in the settlements and fight for the Tibetan cause, while their motherland remains inaccessible to them. In the meantime, the perceived opportunities they will have in the West are tempting. Whereas Tibetans generally do not appear to spatialise their belonging in Indian neighbourhoods, the third space they seem to inhabit can be observed in their daily lives within the settlements. In the Tibetan restaurants and coffee shops, for instance, Tibetan, Indian and Western music is played alternately, while the youth often sing along to all the songs. At home, most of them watch Tibetan, Bollywood and Hollywood movies and enjoy them equally. This entails that they are likely developing a sense of belonging towards Tibet, India and the West simultaneously, as one identity does not exclude the other, but they are being constantly renegotiated. Hereby, the importance of analysing diasporas as a process whereby refugees can shape their identities is stressed (Patterson and Kelley, 2000).

Ultimately, this research contributes to a more comprehensive understanding of belonging by applying the concepts of sense of belonging and politics of belonging to the context of the Tibetan refugee diaspora in Bylakuppe. Whereas belonging has been seen as an important aspect in academic literature since at least the 1950s, scholars have only recently started to critically unpack the multiple senses of belonging (Hou et al, 2018). Raijman and Geffen (2017) argue that further examination of a sense of belonging would complement our understanding of diasporas. As the struggle for a free Tibet continues, so does the struggle for seeking a sense of belonging for the Tibetans in India and abroad. As the 14th Dalai Lama advocates, "Give the ones you love wings to fly, roots to come back, and reasons to stay." Similarly, our understanding of belonging needs to be more comprehensive and open to multiple interpretations and freedoms to reach a common goal of wellbeing.

References

Ahmad, J. (2012) 'Tibetan diaspora in India: longing and belonging', *The Tibet Journal*, 37(4): 35–45.

Amin, A. (2002) 'Ethnicity and the multicultural city: living with diversity', *Environment and Planning*, 34(1): 959–980.

Amit, K. and Bar-Lev, S. (2015) 'Immigrants' sense of belonging to the host country: the role of life satisfaction, language proficiency, and religious motives', *Social Indicators Research*, 124(3): 947–961.

Anand, D. (2003) 'A contemporary story of "diaspora": the Tibetan version', *Diaspora: A Journal of Transnational Studies*, 12(2): 211–229.

Anthias, F. (2013) 'Identity and belonging: conceptualisations and political framings'. *KLA Working Paper Series*, 8(1): 1–22.

Antonsich, M. (2010) 'Searching for belonging: an analytical framework', *Geography Compass*, 4(6): 644–659.

Arpi, C. (2011) 'Tibet studies', *Asian Ethnicity*, 12(3): 235–248.

Bentz, A. (2012) 'Being a Tibetan refugee in India', *Refugee Survey Quarterly*, 31(1): 80–107.

Bhabha, H. (1990) 'The third space: interview with Homi Bhabha', in J. Rutherford (ed) *Identity, Community, Culture, Difference*, London: Lawrence & Wishart, pp 207–221.

Braun, V. and Clarke, V. (2006) 'Using thematic analysis in psychology', *Qualitative Research in Psychology*, 3(2): 77–101.

Chen, S.T. (2012) 'When "exile" becomes sedentary: on the quotidian experiences of "India-born" Tibetans in Dharamsala, North India', *Asian Ethnicity*, 13(3): 263–286.

CTA (Central Tibetan Administration) (2010) *Demographic Survey of the Tibetans in Exile*, Dharamsala: Planning Commission.

CTA (Central Tibetan Administration) (2018) *Department of Home*, available from: http://centraltibetanreliefcommittee.org

Dolma, T. (2019) 'Why are Tibetans migrating out of India?', *The Tibet Journal*, 44(1): 27–52.

English, L. (2002) 'Third space: contested space, identity, and international adult education', *Adult Education and the Contested Terrain of Public Policy*, 2(1): 117–122.

Falcone, J. and Wangchuk, T. (2008) '"We're not home": Tibetan refugees in India in the twenty-first century', *India Review*, 7(3): 164–199.

Federal Office for Migration Switzerland (2013) *Focus India: The Tibetan Community in India*, available from: www.sem.admin.ch/dam/data/sem/internationales/herkunftslaender/asien-nahost/ind/IND-ber-tibetan-community-e.pdf

Fenster, T. (2005) *Gender and the City: The Different Formations of Belonging*, Hoboken, NJ: Blackwell.

Hennink, M., Hutter, I. and Bailey, A. (2011) *Qualitative Research Methods*, London: SAGE.

Hou, F., Schellenberg, G. and Berry, J (2018) 'Patterns and determinants of immigrants' sense of belonging to Canada and their source country', *Ethnic and Racial Studies*, 41(9): 1612–1631.

Kantharaj, C. (2006) *A Sociological Study of Tibetan Women Entrepreneurs in Karnataka with Special Reference to Bylakuppe Settlement*, available from: http://shodhganga.inflibnet.ac.in/handle/10603/86271

Lau, T. (2010) 'The Hindi film's romance and Tibetan notions of harmony: emotional attachments and personal identity in the Tibetan diaspora in India', *Journal of Ethnic and Migration Studies*, 36(6): 967–987.

Lavie, S. and Swedenburg, T. (1996) 'Between and among the boundaries of culture: bridging text and lived experience in the third timespace', *Cultural Studies*, 10(1): 154–179.

Palakshappa, T.C. (1978) *Tibetans in India: A Case Study of Mundgod Tibetans*, New Delhi: Sterling Publishers.

Patterson, T.R. and Kelley, R.D. (2000) 'Unfinished migrations: reflections on the African diaspora and the making of the modern world', *African Studies Review*, 43(1): 11–45.

Piltz, A. (2006) *Internet and Public Identity among Tibetan Youth*, available from: www.anpere.net/2006/8.pdf

Prakash, L.O. (2011) 'Tibetan refugees in India: the case of Bylakuppe in Karnataka', *The Indian Journal of Social Development*, 11(2): 503–515.

Raijman, R. and Geffen, R. (2017) 'Sense of belonging and life satisfaction among post-1990 immigrants in Israel', *International Migration*, 4(2): 1–21.

Schensul, S.L., Schensul, J.J. and LeCompte, M.D. (1999) *Essential Ethnographic Methods: Observations, Interviews, and Questionnaires*, Lanham, MD: Altamira Press.

Smith, W. (1996) *Tibetan Nation: A History of Tibetan Nationalism and Sino-Tibetan Relations*, Boulder, CO: Westview Press.

Soja, E. (1996) *Thirdspace: Journeys to Los Angeles and other Real-and-Imagined Places*, Oxford: Blackwell.

Swank, H. (2011) 'A wanderer in a distant place: Tibetan exile youth, literacy, and emotion', *International Migration*, 49(6): 50–73.

Tsekyi, T. and Thimmaiah, N. (2014) 'Demographic status of Tibetan settlements in Karnataka', *International Journal of Advanced Research in Management and Social Sciences*, 3(10): 21–30.

Voe, D.M. (1981) 'The refugee problem and Tibetan refugees', *The Tibet Journal*, 6(3): 22–42.

Yuval-Davis, N. (2006) 'Belonging and the politics of belonging', *Patterns of Prejudice*, 40(3): 197–214.

9

Negotiating Identity in Urban Space: Everyday Geographies of Syrian Students in Istanbul

Seyma Karamese

Introduction

More than three million Syrian migrants are now living in Turkey, escaping from the harsh conditions of war in their country (Erdoğan, 2018). Many of the migrants are young people, and spatial experiences of young migrants are often different from adult experiences (Evans, 2008, p 1659). A particularly important youth group are Syrian students, who are the subject focus in this chapter. Syrian students have a visible presence in the social life of Istanbul and negotiate various forms of exclusion/inclusion in everyday geographies of the city. Therefore, in this chapter, I focus on the everyday spaces of Syrian students and examine the encounters and identity negotiations that occur in those spaces. My principal question is, 'How do Syrian students construct and negotiate identities in their everyday geographies, and how does this impact on their sense of place in Istanbul?'

In this research, the urban spatial experiences of young refugees have a central position. And urban space is conceptualised as a 'negotiated reality' (Anderson, 1991, p 28). Since places are the essential creator of difference, people experience othering and difference in shared places of cities. Elias and Scotson (1994) in their study use the concepts of 'established' and 'newcomers' to articulate the logic behind the power relations constructed between residents (insiders) and newcomers (outsiders/migrants). Through stigmatising the zones of newcomers and attributing bad behaviours to them, native people exclude them from society. However, migrants also negotiate space. As a result, encountering is not fixed but open to surprise (Ahmed, 2009) and unpredictable. And it can have transformative capacity (Wilson, 2017).

I use 'encounter' here to mean a meeting between those with different identities (ethnicity, nationality, gender, for example) and suggest that encounters can transform the meaning and making of urban space (Wilson, 2017). Among the various populations negotiating their identities through encounters, youth identities are especially dynamic, as they are often highly adaptable to changes in the urban environment (Dwyer, 1998). I use 'space' and 'place' interchangeably as the combination of material, metaphorical, real and imagined spaces controlled, perceived, practised and created by young Syrians. Considering the dynamic and social construction of space, Massey focuses on encounters in terms of experiences, memories and associations within space. In this regard, 'space does not exist prior to identities/entities and their relations ... identities/entities, the relations "between" them, and the spatiality that is part of them, are all constitutive' (Massey, 2005, p 10). In other words, the city is not the given place where encounters live, but rather consists of encounters (Amin, 2006). Besides, the encountering and feeling of exclusion or inclusion cannot be understood without power relations between the majority and minority. Spatiality is thus a vital dimension of the organisation of social power (Cresswell, 1996).

Symbolic interactionism focuses on how individuals' behaviours are contextual, thus directing scholars' attention to the socio-spatial interactions of members within groups. The identity of human beings is always in a state of becoming and it is expressed and performed within a space, so it is argued that place-based social relations are vital for the continuity of self and the development of groups. Habitus is critical during this interaction as well because 'the habitus is not only a structuring structure, which organises practices and the perception of practices, but also a structured structure: the principle of division into logical classes which organises the perception of the social world' (Bourdieu, 1984, p 170). As habitus is generally developed from an early age and is shaped by the place where one lives, moving to a new place requires the development of new habitus, and this helps one to deal with new environments and situations (Easthope, 2009, p 74). In addition to new habitus, possibilities for the production of social and cultural capitals are also important (Bourdieu, 1984). As a result, with the interactions, negotiations or encounters of different groups, the possibility of producing new habitus and capitals by labelling a group or space, there is always a possibility of inclusion or exclusion into the spaces of the host country.

Socioeconomic backgrounds of Syrian students

Research into the profile of Syrian students in Turkey in 2018 showed that Syrian students had been in Turkey for an average of 5.5 years (Erdoğan, 2018). Different routes and means to enter Turkey were used, including arrival by plane from another country, arrival in Mersin province by ship from

Lebanon, entering at a formal checkpoint, entering illegally without passing through a checkpoint at the border, and coming to the border in a car with relatives. The students were under the status of temporary protection, and, due to this protection regime, their rights and overall status were not clear.

However, some had succeeded in obtaining Turkish citizenship or a residence permit and they benefited in terms of legally being able to find work and having citizenship rights (Hamsici, 2019). Participants had varied levels of education and different schooling experiences. The students who were between 18 and 20 years old completed their high school education in Turkey, so they often had the advantage of speaking Turkish to a higher standard than the older students. This younger group's motivation to migrate was generally to help the social and economic standings of their families, and it included both men and women. However, those aged between 22 and 26 years old were often men and had come to Turkey to avoid military service or because of threats to their human rights. Generally, after learning Turkish, they looked for employment, and then they looked for education opportunities in Turkey. Some participants were able to evidence the education level they had achieved in Syria and were able to continue their education in Turkey. However, most had to start university courses at the first stage, as they did not have official papers to prove their Syrian qualifications. All the participants either spoke English or Turkish fluently in daily life.

The socioeconomic level of participants and their families is currently lower than their level in Syria (Erdoğan, 2018). In the Turkish context, the socioeconomic background of Syrian migrants is not high. However, most of the participants saw education as the first step to improving their socioeconomic standing.

The universities at which the participants study include private and state institutions. To be admitted to study at a Turkish university, one must pass the YOS exam (foreign student exam). Generally, foreign students attend private courses to pass this exam, and most need financial support for their education (Harunoğulları et al, 2019, p 832). The majority of participants were accepted at private universities through scholarships, and they have tried to cover any other costs by working part time, generally in low-paid jobs.

Methodological approach

My methodology involved a qualitative approach. I utilised in-depth interviews and participant observation, which allowed me to engage in the complex social world of my target group. My personal experiences in the field showed how interviewing and observing go together and cannot be easily separated. Observations helped me to begin to understand the everyday social worlds of the students, and in-depth interviews allowed me to fill the gaps and gather personal narratives about the meaning of urban spaces.

For instance, during participant observations, I did not initially understand why female students preferred to meet in Turkish cafes rather than Syrian ones. However, through conducting interviews, I learned that the female students feel more comfortable answering questions in Turkish cafes. In this regard, using an in-depth interview is an efficient method of gathering more detailed information about experiences and practices of people (O'Reilly, 2012). I conducted in-depth interviews with 30 Syrian students, all over the age of 18, 13 of whom were men and 17 women. To access students, I used a snowballing sampling method and to protect confidentiality I have used pseudonyms. Participant observation in the field lasted eight months and primarily involved note-taking.

The positionality of the researcher is another important dimension of qualitative research. In particular, positionality is related to the insider/outsider status of the researcher (Ergun and Erdemir, 2010, p 34). For this research, my identity produced both insider and outsider positions. For instance, being a migrant, a student in another country and a Muslim produced an insider position, while being Turkish and speaking another language produced an outsider position. However, since identities of researchers are negotiated and fluid, my student and migrant identity sometimes became more dominant, while, on other occasions, being Turkish became more important.

During the research, I activated my personal experiences of being a young Turkish immigrant. Since the UK was not my first experience in terms of living abroad – I had lived in Germany for two years without speaking the German language – my experiences as a young migrant helped me more than I expected. Moreover, common experiences, my gender and emotions helped to build close relations. Being a woman made it easy to talk to the female respondents. My female participants told me that they found the interview to be therapeutic, and it made them think about things in their daily lives they had not thought about before.

Negotiating identities in various spaces in Istanbul

The research reveals that Syrian students have a variety of spatial experiences and strategies of place-making. To reflect this diversity, I examine various types of spaces, which I call 'segregated space', 'judicial space', 'private space', 'comfort zones', 'open spaces' and 'cooperational space'. These categories of spaces were drawn from the data collected and the themes that emerged from the data analysis and coding.

Segregated spaces

From the past to the present, the Fatih district has been recognised as a religious neighbourhood. It has a structure in which different religious communities and religious non-governmental organisations (NGOs) are located. In addition to these religious identities, it is also surrounded by mosques and religious historical buildings in which religious people come together.

However, with the arrival of many Syrian migrants, the religious identity of this district is shifting. The perceptions of the neighbourhood, especially for Turkish people, has changed in recent years. When I talked with Turks and Syrians during fieldwork, they generally considered Fatih to be associated with Syrian migrants. This has resulted in the neighbourhood having a negative reputation to some extent, and it being a space of segregation between Turks and Syrians. Norbert Elias and John L. Scotson (1994), in their study, use the concepts of 'established' and 'newcomers' to articulate the logic behind the power relations constructed between residents (insiders) and newcomers (outsiders/migrants). Through stigmatising the zones of newcomers and attributing bad behaviour to them, residents exclude them from society.

In this regard, despite the common assumption, Fatih is thus not always a space of belonging and comfort for Syrian youth. As the area is associated with migration and social problems, many Syrian students are reluctant to be identified as a migrant from Fatih. Many of the students now only make brief visits to Fatih, mainly for shopping in Syrian markets or eating in Syrian restaurants. "When I first came, I was only familiar with Fatih. I could not get out of there because I don't speak Turkish. But now I've learned the language, I've learned everywhere. Now I'm uncomfortable when I am staying in Fatih because you're only dealing with Syrians there" (Abdullah, man, 22, graduate student).

Hasan, an undergraduate student, explained the importance of the Fatih district when he first arrived in Turkey. It was an area where he had religious and family connections, so it helped him settle in the city. However, he added that Fatih was not the Istanbul he saw in TV series, and that disappointed him. He explained that, only speaking Arabic and only having Syrian friends, and not being able to see Maiden's Tower and the seaside – one of the main tourist attractions of Istanbul – made him uncomfortable. When he decided to leave Fatih and its isolation, his life started to change. It helped him to learn Turkish more quickly and enabled him to interact with more Turks. Thus, these segregated spaces often push students to another space in the city, which I have labelled 'comfort zones'.

Comfort zones

Contrary to how one may imagine it, Syrian students in the research did not like to spend a lot of time within segregated spaces. They see these spaces as temporary and prefer to escape to what I have called their 'comfort zones'.

This not a form of spatial displacement, but rather an active strategy of the students to escape forms of labelling and exclusion.

Halit clarified the difference between segregated places and comfort zones:

> 'As you know, everyone is Arab in the Fatih district. Even if they are not Syrians, they are seen as Syrian because of their language. When you get there, you only see immigrants. Am I not an immigrant? I'm also, but I want to see everybody, I want to forget I'm an immigrant. In Taksim or Besiktas, I'm getting into the crowd. I see people from different cultures. I'm like anyone else. No one says that he is Syrian, our country returned to Syria.' (Halit, man, 23, graduate student)

In these 'comfort zones', they feel less labelled, and they have encounters with many different groups of people, and, as such, they feel more integrated into society and have more of a sense of belonging to Istanbul. As in the findings of Phillips' research into British Muslims (2006), the students generally prefer to be in places that are mixed and diverse, rather than in places that are labelled as Syrian. As Phillips shows in her research, British Muslims generally preferer to live in mixed neighbourhoods, rather than self-segregating. Diversity is coined as comfortable here.

Hasan, in the following statement, explained the meaning of comfort zone when referring to the district of Üsküdar:

> 'I was sitting there in a cafe when I discovered Üsküdar. There were people from different groups. There were people from each group. Conservatives, Islamists, Kemalists, Nationalists were all together. It was beautiful. I improved my Turkish there. Even I used to smoke [with] my friends in cafes when we were chatting. Üsküdar has peace of mind. This peace is not anywhere else. When I get out of the subway and breathe the Üsküdar, I take a deep breath ... and I feel like I'm back home. I feel I am in my country.' (Hasan, man, 21, undergraduate student)

This quotation illustrates how the students often feel comfort and greater anonymity in spaces of difference. Amin (2006, p 1012) discusses the meaning of 'small achievements in the good city' by paying attention to civil exchanges and the importance of creating spaces of interdependence to improve intercultural relations. Amin's thinking around 'micro-publics of everyday social contact and encounter' (2002, p 959) has a crucial role in the everyday geographies of Syrian students. Nigel Thrift (2005, p 147) sees encounters in everyday life as 'reservoirs of hope', which make it possible for strangers to connect and to make connections with Turkish people. The students give importance to these micro-level encounters in mixed neighbourhoods by producing social relations.

Judicial spaces

Everyday interactions between people are imbued with uneven power relations. Thus, interaction between various groups or individuals in the city cannot always count as a meaningful encounter (Valentine, 2008, p 333). Instead of convivial coexistence, power imbalances can prevent successful social encounters and even lead to practices of self-segregation within certain places (Phillips et al, 2014, as cited in Huizinga and van Hoven, 2018, p 311).

Hana (18) was one of the students in whom I first observed this practice of self-segregation within public transportation. I met with her on a bus when I was travelling to the airport. As I got on the bus, I went towards the back in order not to disturb anyone. In the back seats, I sat next to a Syrian woman, whom I had difficulty even seeing in the corner. I understood that she was Syrian because of her headscarf style. When I greeted her and started chatting, I realised how timid she was at the beginning of our conversation. We chatted in English during our long journey, and she explained that she was a foreign student preparing for university exams. She was talking very quietly, as if she didn't want to be heard. When I asked why she was sitting in the back and speaking like that, the answer I got was very revealing. She said that it was "in order not to be noticed, or rather not to be disturbed". I have chosen the word 'judicial' to describe the power relationship between the majority (native Turks) and minority (Syrians), which makes meaningful encounters difficult. I call these 'judicial spaces', where close physical contact is possible, and there are symbolic 'courts' in these places, which are created by the discomfort of physical contact and closeness between different people. Public transportation, cafes and restaurants are some examples of such places. These places are symbolic courts in that people are being judged and tried. The judges – Turkish people – base their judgement, on 'evidence', such as speaking Arabic and dressing like Syrians. When they see such pieces of evidence, they often start to judge and discriminate. What the accused can do, however, is to remove the evidence.

Meryem shared an experience of being 'judged' while waiting in the queue to pick up a delivery with her friend:

> 'We were speaking Arabic while waiting in [a] queue to receive cargo. When the women just in the back realised that we were Syrians, they immediately started to discuss [how] cargo could be delivered to us even though there is a war in Syria. Again, judgements had begun about us in terms of our economic support, how we are primitive people and [there is] "unnecessary" social support from [the] Turkish government to Syrians. On the other hand, we had to speak Turkish among ourselves and talked about the fact that our university books had arrived and how we were educated migrants. How easy it is to

judge without knowing anything about people? We all have to prove ourselves.' (Meryem, woman, 18, YOS student)

Rama explained the judgement she faced in public transport while doing her own ironic social experiment:

'We did a social experiment with my friend. One day we spoke Arabic in the subway, people looked at us critically and started to say "These Syrians are everywhere. They occupied our country." The following day, we spoke English very fluently and one of the Turkish women said "Wow. Look at these girls, how they are educated." I am the same, but attitudes are totally different. It is really ridiculous.' (Rama, woman, 20, undergraduate student)

Goffman (1959) argues that the self cannot be explained by inner experiences alone because it is socially constructed, and it depends on the context. He introduces the concepts of the theatre (backstage/front stage) and the game. If actors draw positive attention to these roles, they maintain them to affect others. In other words, in everyday life, humans behave like actors, choosing to develop roles as part of a strategic game. While people engage in 'front stage' behaviour, they are aware that others are watching; 'backstage behaviour' refers to what we do when no one is looking (Cole, 2019). In this analysis, the backstage of the students' everyday life is where they can express themselves and their identities openly. Homes as private spaces are good examples of the backstage, which I will discuss in the following section. However, I consider judicial space as a 'front stage', in which different groups or individuals interact, and people behave like performance actors to maintain or conceal certain identities.

Private spaces

Homes are a backstage, where Syrian students act free of the expectations and norms dictated by front stage behaviour, where they are often judged. According to Valentine (2008, p 329), public spaces are regulated by 'political correctness', and migrants may feel anxious to express their own values. However, in 'privatised' spaces such as houses, it can be easier to express one's own values and cultural identity. In this study, I found that Syrian students can express themselves more freely at home. In this way, home spaces turn into a place of otherness because they do not have any connections with native Turks. Turkish people generally do not visit their homes. Moreover, they have little or no relations with their neighbours and generally complain about the discrimination experienced within apartment blocks.

When I was a guest in the homes of Syrian students, I noticed how they express themselves more comfortably than in the streets. During participant observations, I saw that one group of students, who were afraid to show that they were Syrians outside, did not hesitate to display their Syrian culture at home. Speaking Arabic, drinking Arabic coffee, wearing local Syrian clothes were indispensable components of their houses. However, the houses can also be seen as an isolation area, where there is no interaction with the Turkish population.

Bilal, whom I met in an NGO where he was working as a volunteer for children, was a very social person in his daily life, and he expressed spatial-based differences between Turkey and Syria in discussing the meaning of home:

> 'Here is different from Syria. In Syria, we have neighbours, we have big gardens and we have neighbourhoods. Everyone was familiar with each other. We were sitting, chatting and eating together. But now no one knocks on our doors even if at religious festivals. I do not know my neighbours. When we first have come to this house, we distributed dessert to introduce ourselves. But then nobody visited us.' (Bilal, man, 26, graduate student)

Amr, who lives with other Syrian students from the university, added that even if there is an interaction with Turkish people in daily life, homes are not the places where that happens. Instead of private spaces, public ones are the places of meeting and encounter: "I have Turkish friends, but we meet outside. Neither they nor we visited each other. I do not know why it is like that. Only Arab friends come to our house to [play on the] PlayStation, eat and [have] free time but no Turks" (Amr, man, 22, graduate student). Therefore, it could be argued that there is a clear border between outside (public space) and inside (home). The home is where they try to produce continuity of cultural values, and it could be considered that they have turned their house into a place where they maintain their Syrian identities freely.

Cooperational space

By moving to a new place, migrants enter a new social field, and this results in new daily practices and habitus. The concept of NGO was new for many of the students because, in Syria, organisations and associations are supported by the regime and Syrian state, so cooperation and making decisions freely, two dominant features of cooperational places, are new ideas for many of the students. Several students were involved in an organisation that aims to find solutions for socioeconomic problems in Turkey. For instance, the students drew on their own experiences to help identify migration-based problems and solutions. Moreover, helping others is a way to try to decrease their own traumas and problems.

Rama volunteers in a Turkish organisation and stated that:

> 'I can do something for the people in my country. We have suffered more. Our children have suffered. I work voluntarily for them. We try to create a bridge from heart to heart. There are lots of things to do. Not only for my people but also for Turkish people. The great happiness is making someone happy and seeing the happiness [in] their eyes.' (Rama, woman, 20, undergraduate student)

Since Syrian students are active both in Syrian and Turkish organisations, I see them as meaningful places of interaction and encounter. These cooperational spaces are also the place of charitable activities and provide opportunities for future and transnational connections. In this regard, as new places, they are functional both for the present and the future through producing relations between migrants and people from other countries, all for a common purpose.

Abdulhey expressed how volunteering at an NGO made it possible to have national and international connections:

> 'I go to foreign events, I am social. I [am] generally part of NGOs of voluntary actions. For instance, Istanbul N&I. They have voluntary programmes. There are lots of Turkish and foreign people there. I met a friend of my friend in Çay (tea) talks for people from different countries. She works as a lawyer. She helped me a lot and she became my Turkish sister. She supported me. She [is] always there. If she has a problem also I [am] always there. We also support other foreign students together.' (Abdulhey, man, 21, undergraduate student)

I see this attempt as a new habitus in their lives. However, while this is a new activity, there is a close relationship between Islamic tradition and charity activities. According to Bourdieu, habitus is, among other things, an acquired disposition towards attitudes and behavioural patterns that generates and determines all the social actions of an individual (Bourdieu, 1984, pp 277–354). Charity and volunteering are habitualised dispositions, characterised by social upbringing and religious and cultural heritage. These heritages may be explicitly religious – such as *Zakat-ul-Fitr* or *Qurbani* – but may also be less clearly religious, such as the more mundane acts of giving to charity on a day-to-day basis to help others.

As a result, cooperational space provides a new habitus for them, while it still has religious and cultural implications in the lives of the students. These spaces do not only let different groups come together and mix; they also produce national and international connections.

Open spaces

Education, the most important space, provides a door for negotiation and better living standards by helping the participants to find good jobs and understand the logic behind the relations in the host country through their student identity.

It was my friend, who actively worked for Syrians and had communication with many of them, who helped me to meet Meryem. Meryem had lost one leg in the war. She had changed cities three times and had eventually come to Istanbul, where she attended her courses despite her prosthetic leg and studied for the university entrance exam. I quickly contacted Meryem. As soon as I entered her home, a girl appeared, steady on her feet.

Meryem stressed the importance of education:

> 'I am studying for the university entrance exam every day intensively because I need to have a professional job. I have to stand firm on my feet for my life, for my future. Even if my situation had been different, I would still like to receive training. As a girl who changed her country, I have to empower myself in every way. Uneducated people know nothing about life. I don't want to be like that.' (Meryem, woman, 21, YOS student)

By differentiating themselves from other immigrants and uneducated people, Meryem and other educated young immigrants believe that education makes them stronger individuals in society. Hence, education is seen as a tool that provides inclusion for both the present and the future. Moreover, educational places turn into centres where dialogue is possible, and differences come together in an open space. This is because education is not only crucial for the production of cultural capital, which is possible with qualifications, but also social capital, defined by Bourdieu as 'the aggregate of the actual or potential resources, the possession of a durable network of more or less institutionalised relationships of mutual acquaintance and recognition' (1984, p 248).

Social functions of the spaces

The spaces analysed thus far are attributed with different meanings by Syrian students, and these meanings illustrate spaces with inclusionary and exclusionary functions in terms of relations with Turkish society. While

Table 9.1: Social functions of spaces

Exclusion	Inclusion
Segregated spaces: Fatih, Esenler, Bağcılar, Zeytinburnu	Comfort zones: Üsküdar, Beşiktaş, Şişli.
Judicial spaces: public transportation, cafes, restaurants	Cooperational space: NGOs
Private spaces: homes	Open spaces: education

they feel a part of Turkish society in inclusionary spaces, in exclusionary spaces they feel isolated, labelled and outside the relations of everyday life. Although these students flow between different spaces, I have categorised these spaces with their functions in Table 9.1.

Exclusion spaces

I categorised segregated spaces, judicial spaces and private spaces as exclusion spaces. The relations between the migrants and native Turks within these spaces can produce feelings of exclusion and discrimination. However, the types and level of exclusion vary between each space. Through negative and stigmatising representations, segregated spaces become exclusionary spaces. Living in them can produce feelings of exclusion, and many Syrian students see leaving segregated spaces as the long-term solution. Judicial spaces are different from segregated spaces because they are based on temporary power relations within public spaces, such as public transport, cafes, restaurants or any other place where physical contact is possible. Different from segregated spaces, this is not about associating a place with Syrian identity, rather it is about how Syrian identities are treated and often excluded in shared and public spaces of the city. Although it is also an exclusion space, I see the function of private spaces as different from the previous two spaces discussed. Segregated and judicial spaces are public spaces, while private spaces such as houses work as spaces of protection and resistance against the exclusion of Syrian identities in public spaces. However, while providing protection, a private space also increases exclusion – to some extent – as it prevents inclusionary encounters. The houses can turn into an isolation area, where there is no interaction with local Turks.

Inclusion spaces

Despite the spatial exclusion of Syrian youth, they also experience inclusion through encounters with native people in shared places. These places are categorised as comfort zones, cooperational spaces and open spaces. While all these have inclusive functions, they affect different dimensions of the migrant's life in terms of education, work-life, free time activities, and so on. Cooperational spaces bring different people together for a shared purpose, and this positively feeds into a sense of social togetherness within NGOs and other charity organisations. Moreover, they have inclusive functions through engendering relations between migrants and people from other countries. Comfort zones refer to the everyday places where Syrian students socialise or live within mixed groups without stigmatisation of their migrant identities. These comfort zones are heterogenous and multicultural parts of Istanbul, which are directly functional for students' socialisation. Open spaces are directly related to their student identity. As students, they try to provide a life in Turkey for the future with their educational tools and also come together with different groups in education centres.

Conclusion

In this qualitative research with participant observation and in-depth interviews, I have explored how the everyday geographies and encounters of Syrian students produce a sense of place in Istanbul. Migrants do not only select a place to live that matches their experiences directly; rather places are made through repeated everyday actions and encounters. In this regard, the dynamic nature of place and performative dimension of belonging are key for understanding the place-making processes of Syrian students. However, place-making and producing a sense of place directly relate to experiences of exclusion and inclusion. Feelings of exclusion in 'segregated', 'judicial' and 'private' spaces and also inclusion in 'comfort zones', 'cooperational' and 'open' spaces are shaped by everyday encounters. As a result, the performativity of Syrian students in Istanbul is at the heart of place-making processes and experiences of inclusion and exclusion.

References

Ahmed, S. (2009) *Seen and Not Heard: Voices of Young British Muslims*, Leicester: Policy Research Center.

Amin, A. (2002) 'Ethnicity and the multicultural city: Living with diversity: environment and planning', *Economy and Space*, 34(6): 959–980.

Amin, A. (2006) 'The good city', *Urban Studies*, 43(5–6): 1009–1023.

Anderson, K. (1991) *Vancouver's Chinatown: Racial Discourse in Canada, 1875–1980*, Montreal: McGill/Queen's University Press.

Bourdieu, P. (1984) *Distinction: A Social Critique of the Judgement of Taste*, London: Routledge and Kegan Paul.

Cole, N.L. (2019) 'Goffman's Front Stage and Back Stage Behavior', *ThoughtCo*, 14 July, available from: www.thoughtco.com/goffmans-front-stage-and-back-stage-behavior-4087971

Cresswell, T. (1996) *In Place/Out of Place: Geography, Ideology and Transgression*, Minneapolis: University of Minnesota Press.

Dwyer, C. (1998) 'Challenging dominant representations of young British Muslim women', in T. Skelton and G. Valentine (eds) *Cool Places: Geographies of Youth Culture*, London: Routledge, pp 50–65.

Easthope, H. (2009) 'Fixed identities in a mobile world? The relationship between mobility, place, and identity', *Identities: Global Studies in Culture and Power*, 16(1): 61–82.

Elias, N. and Scotson, J.L. (1994) *The Established and the Outsiders*, London: SAGE.

Erdoğan, M. (2018) *Suriyeliler Barometresi. Suriyeliler İle Uyum İçinde Yaşamanın Çerçevesi*, İstanbul: İstanbul Bilgi Üniversitesi Yayınları.

Ergun, A. and Erdemir, A. (2010) 'Negotiating insider and outsider identities in the field: "insider" in a foreign land; "outsider" in one's own land', *Field Methods*, 22(1): 16–38.

Evans, B. (2008) 'Geographies of youth/young people', Geography Compass, 2(5): 1659–1680.

Goffman, E. (1959) *The Presentation of Self in Everyday Life*, New York: Doubleday Anchor Books.

Hamsici, M. (2019) 'Türkiye'de kaç Suriyeli var, en çok Suriyeli nüfusu hangi şehirde yaşıyor?', available from: www.bbc.com/turkce/haberler-turkiye-49150143

Harunoğulları, M., Süzülmüş, S. and Polat, Y. (2019) 'Türkiye'deki Suriyeli Üniversite Öğrencileri İle İlgili Bir Durum Tespiti: Osmaniye Korkut Ata Üniversitesi Örneği', *Afyon Kocatepe Üniversitesi Sosyal Bilimler Dergisi*, 21(3): 816–837.

Huizinga, R.P. and van Hoven, B. (2018) 'Everyday geographies of belonging: Syrian refugee experiences in the Northern Netherlands', *Geoforum*, 96: 309–317.

Massey, D. (2005) *Space*, London: Routledge.

O'Reilly, K. (2012) *Ethnographic Methods*, New York: Routledge.

Phillips, D. (2006) 'Parallel lives? challenging discourses of British Muslim self-segregation', *Transactions of the Institute of British Geographers*, 24: 25–40.

Thrift, N. (2005) 'But malice aforethought: cities and the natural history of hatred', *Transactions of the Institute of British Geographers*, 30: 133–150.

Valentine, G. (2008) 'Living with difference: reflections on geographies of encounter', *Progress in Human Geography*, 32(3): 323–337.

Wilson, H.F. (2017) 'On geography and encounter: bodies, borders, and difference', *Progress in Human Geography*, 41(4): 451–471.

10

'You're Judged a Lot': Australian Sudanese and South Sudanese Youths' Perspectives on Their Experiences in Public Spaces

Luke Macaulay

Introduction

This chapter explores Australian Sudanese and South Sudanese youths' perspectives on their experiences within public spaces in the city of Melbourne. Australia has large Sudanese and South Sudanese communities, with the city of Melbourne being 'home to the largest number of Sudan- or South Sudan-born residents' (Robinson, 2013, p 22). Since the early 2000s, approximately 50,000 people from sub-Saharan African nations have been settled in Australia under the country's Humanitarian Entrant Programme for refugees (DSS, 2016; Baak, 2019). It is important to note that for many of these individuals at their time of birth (and later at their time of entry into Australia), South Sudan was not recognised as a nation state. It has since become the world's youngest nation state, officially gaining independence in 2011. Of these 50,000 individuals, more than half identified their country of birth as Sudan or South Sudan (DSS, 2016; Baak, 2019). In Australia, many young people from these communities are socially and educationally thriving (Harris et al, 2013; Santoro and Wilkinson, 2016). However, others experience a variety of social, political, educational and familial challenges throughout the youth years (Abur and Spaaij, 2016; Deng, 2016). Chief among these challenges are the influence and consequences of negative racialised public and political attention experienced by these youth, which frames these young people as dangerous 'outsiders' (Benier et al, 2018; Macaulay and Deppeler, 2020b).

To better understand the broader social and political context of this negative racialised attention, it is important to contextualise this attention within Australia's broader settlement and migration history. As a relatively young nation state, Australia has a contentious colonial history, with a denial of traditional Indigenous ownership of land (Due, 2008). Additionally, under Australia's Immigration Restriction Act 1901 (colloquially known as the 'white Australia policy' and formally removed from government in 1973), patterns of migration were heavily regulated and 'restricted any legal non-white immigration' (Benier et al, 2021, p 224). Against the backdrop of the country's colonial and migration history, 'Australian identity' has been socially and political positioned as being those from Anglo-Celtic (and similar European) backgrounds (Ahluwalia, 2001; Macaulay and Deppeler, 2020b). Therefore, it has been argued that through an ongoing 'colonial objective to make Australia a white country and for white people' (Majavu, 2017, p 6), Australian communities with sub-Saharan African heritage are often cast as 'Black others' in 'White Australia'.

For Australian Sudanese and South Sudanese youth, significant lived experiences of being cast as 'Black others' within 'White Australia' have previously been argued to be heightened within public spaces (Benier et al, 2018; Baak et al, 2019). I have previously defined public space as 'occupiable space that exists outside of the private sphere and at the same time is differentiated from occupiable institutional fields that have organisational mandates and that individuals need approval to enter (for example, workplaces, schools)' (Macaulay, 2020b, p 203). Additionally, Hénaff and Strong (2001) indicate that public space is 'created by and for humans ... [and] is always contestable precisely because whereas there are criteria that control admission to its purview, the right to enact and enforce those criteria is always in question' (p 4). As such, a range of variables linked to social norms and power can mediate who belongs within these spaces. In Australia, those who occupy public spaces and are 'visibly different' from Australia's hegemonic 'White' norms are argued to be a challenge to those norms (Majavu, 2017, 2020). Mapedzahama and Kwansah-Aidoo (2017) articulate that in Australia the presence of Blackness within White spaces can be 'an ontological and epistemological disturbance to whiteness' (pp 10–11). As such, it has been reported that within public spaces it is not uncommon for Australian Sudanese and South Sudanese youth to experience racial vilification from certain members of the broader Australian community, as well as receiving heightened attention from law enforcement (Benier et al, 2018; Baak et al, 2019).

There is ongoing concern regarding the future implications of negative public and political attention, perpetuated by racialised histories and discourses, experienced by Australian Sudanese and South Sudanese youth (Benier et al, 2018; Macaulay and Deppeler, 2020b). For example, these discourses may result in fear for safety, social and educational disengagement, reduced opportunities and a poor sense of belonging (Abur and Spaaij, 2016; Benier et al, 2018; Han and Budarick, 2018). Similarly, in the US context, it has been identified that racialised and discriminatory public and political discourses can have detrimental impacts on youth mental health and hinder a smooth transition to adulthood (Kogan et al, 2015). Subsequently, the associated consequences of this type of attention have the potential to impede these youths' future social and economic prosperity and wellbeing in their adult years (Macaulay and Deppeler, 2020b).

Method

The findings that are presented and discussed in this chapter were drawn from a larger qualitative study that explored Australian Sudanese and South Sudanese youths' experiences and perspectives on becoming adults. The data collection phase of the research (late 2017–early 2018) was at a time when these youth were experiencing an intensification of negative racialised public and political attention. Majavu (2020) highlights that the common trope in Australia of conflating 'Blackness' with 'criminality' was heavily used throughout this time, when narratives of 'African gangs' became commonplace in public and political discourses (Majavu, 2020).

Utilising a multi-site case design (Bogdan and Biklen, 2007), participants were recruited from two Melbourne-based community organisations. Community organisation one (CO.1) works with Victorian Sudanese communities and offers a youth programme for young people in their final years of secondary school to support them throughout this time in their education. Community organisation two (CO.2) works with Victorian South Sudanese communities and offers a youth programme for recent school-leavers to support them in their initial years of post-secondary education. Notably, CO.1 is run and led by individuals from Jewish Australian backgrounds, whereas CO.2 is run and led by community leaders from Australian South Sudanese backgrounds. Inclusion criteria was that participants were currently or had been recently involved in a youth programme offered by CO.1 or CO.2. As advised by community leaders, participants' ages were not gathered. For some members from these communities, there is the possibility that their ages were assigned in refugee camps via medical assessment. These assigned ages can be contestable and linked to trauma. Therefore, the designator 'youth' was tacitly self-assigned by participants via their self-referral into the study from a youth programme. Twelve participants in total were recruited into the study (seven young women and five young men).

Data were collected through interview strategies. All participants engaged in an individual interview, and those recruited from CO.1 additionally engaged in a single focus group interview. All participants were given the option to participate in a focus group interview, and only those from CO.1 took this option. When presenting examples of data, data collected from the focus group will appear with the letters FG after participants' pseudonyms. Please note, participants chose their own pseudonyms. All interviews were audio-recorded, and audio data were transcribed. Transcripts were analysed using voice-centred relational methodology strategies (VCRM). This approach places the voices of the participants at the centre of the analysis and explores how these voices are in relationship and influenced by the self, others and wider social/political systems and structures (Brown and Gilligan, 1991). This approach has been demonstrated as being effective when working with communities whose voices may be marginalised in society (Gilligan et al, 2003). Given the social and political context of this research, such an approach was deemed suitable.

In line with the four VCRM perspectives proposed by Brown and Gilligan (1991), transcripts were analysed from the following perspectives:

1. What is the story of who is speaking (is there any overarching plot/narrative)?
2. In what body (how does the individual position themselves within the plot/narrative)?
3. Telling what story about relationships (how does the individual position others within the plot/narrative)?
4. In which societal and cultural framework (in consideration of the former perspectives, is there a societal/cultural framework in which the plot/narrative appears to be positioned)?

Throughout the perspectives of analysis, detailed researcher notes were compiled and subsequently discussed with participants, colleagues and community leaders, regarding interpretations of findings. For examples of how transcripts were analysed using these perspectives, see Macaulay (2020a) and Macaulay and Deppeler (2020b).

As argued by Gilligan and Eddy (2017) and Gilligan et al (2003), the voice can be multilayered. To better understand the multiple layers of participants' voices within their narratives, *pronoun poems* were produced. This was done by focusing on three layers of participants' usage of pronouns:

1. using a first-person voice to present a personal experience (for example, "When *I* am in public, *I* ...");
2. using a collective second-person voice to present a personal experience (for example, "When *you* are in public, *you* ..."); and
3. using quotes or mimicry of others to present a personal experience (for example, "My friends are always saying, '*When you are in public, you* ...'").

Importantly, cultural ontologies and epistemologies can influence how individuals use pronouns in speech to convey meaning (Krog, 2011; Baak, 2016). In consultation with community leaders, certain African philosophies (for example, *cieng*) were considered when understanding *pronoun poems*. *Pronoun poems* were produced via underscoring pronouns within single sections of participant transcripts and placing these on individual lines along with relevant surrounding verbs and/or important words, creating a stanza. For example:

> 'One time I sat next to an elderly lady in a tram, and she moved – picked up her bag and moved to a different seat. I mean, this is all media things. Does she know me? No.' (Joseph)
>
> *Pronoun poem*
> I sat next to an elderly lady in a tram
> She moved
> Picked up her bag and moved to a different seat
> I mean, this is all media things
> Does she know me? No.

Participants were given the opportunity to review their poems, to give permission for their words to be used in this way, and to suggest any changes and/or omissions they felt were needed.

Findings in this chapter are presented thematically. *Pronoun poems* were thematically analysed (Braun and Clarke, 2006). The rationale to focus on *pronoun poems* for thematic analysis was that these poems provided a clear account of how participants situated their voices within their narratives. Themes were identified via the open coding of *pronoun poems*, which were clustered into categories to identify any overarching themes. A key overarching theme was identified, which therein contained three sub-themes.

Findings

It was reported by participants that their experiences in public spaces are strongly influenced by a sense of 'visible difference'. Previous scholars have discussed the notion of visibility in public spaces along the lines of 'recognition' and 'control' (Brighenti, 2007; De Backer, 2019). In this sense, recognition refers to 'acts of resistance and empowerment by minority groups against the mainstream, for instance, how they claim a space to make themselves visible' (De Backer, 2019, p 309). Conversely, control refers to the processes whereby one's visibility in public spaces places the individual under an increased amount of surveillance, particularly at the individual level (self-surveillance) (Brighenti, 2007). De Backer (2019) has previously argued that these concepts of visibility in public spaces are not mutually exclusive and can intersect and overlap. However, given the context that this research was conducted in, where participants were experiencing substantial negative racialised public and political attention, a sense of control was presented as being the primary perspective regarding their visibility in public spaces. These findings are discussed under the identified overarching theme of *visible difference*, which therein contained the following sub-themes: *racial identity*, *group identity* and *racial profiling*. In line with participants' narratives being central to this research, Yuval-Davis's (2010) conceptualisation of identity will be adopted in this context as being 'narratives, stories that people tell themselves about who they are, who they are not, as well as who and how they would like to/should be' (p 266).

Racial identity

Several participants explicitly referenced their 'skin colour' as homogenising their identity under the gaze of others in public spaces. The homogenisation of the identity of Australian Sudanese/South Sudanese communities as 'Black others' within 'White Australia' is an example of 'racial identity' being ascribed as an individual's 'master status' (Hughes, 1945; Becker, 1963; Giddens, 2006). Giddens (2006) describes a 'master status' as 'the status or statuses that generally take priority over other indicators of social standing and determine a person's overall position in society' (p 1024). For several participants, these homogenising effects discounted the individuality of them as people. For example, as stated by Mary, 'People won't even know you, but they'll just have a perception of you because of the colour of your skin.' This sentiment is similarly presented by Titirum in the following *pronoun poem*:

> *Judge Me*
> Walking down the street, if someone looks at me
> They don't judge me for who I am
> They judge me for my skin colour. (Titirum)

Within this *pronoun poem*, Titirum places himself at the centre through his exclusive use of a first-person voice. However, Titirum speaks broadly when referring to the 'other' within this poem ('They don't judge me for who I am'). Within this instance, Titirum is not referring to a specific person. Rather, it would appear that Titirum is referring to a wider category of people, which given the context, could be interpreted as referring to a broader Australian majority. Given the framing of the 'I' and 'they', it appears that Titirum does not situate himself in the broader category that the 'they' represents.

Yasmin offered a similar contention to Titirum in her *pronoun poem* entitled 'Your Colour'; however, Yasmin offered greater detail and spoke in a much more collective voice than Titirum:

> *Your Colour*
> I think
> You're judged a lot
> You're racially profiled
> People are prejudiced because they see you in a certain way
> You're restricted from living every day
> You're going out and everybody just sees you as this bad person
> It doesn't really give you motivation to do things with your life
> It's uncomfortable to be in public places, especially with your friends
> I think
> Just as a Black person in general
> You always have to look at your colour before anything
> Your colour will always be something you're going to think about. (Yasmin)

Like Titirum, Yasmin presents that she is judged in public spaces, based on the visibility of being a 'Black person'. Importantly, Yasmin draws links to these experiences with the influence they have on other aspects of her life. For example, Yasmin indicates these experiences to be restricting as well as impacting her goals and motivation. It is important to explicitly highlight the influence of social and political context in Yasmin's *pronoun poem*. Yasmin states, 'You're going out and everybody just sees you as this bad person,' which is a statement linked to visibility as influenced by racial identity. It is important to note that perceptions of links between being a 'bad person' and being a 'black person' are in this context constructed by negative racialised public and political discourses that are perpetuated by media and political rhetoric.

Unlike Titirum in his *pronoun poem*, in Yasmin's *pronoun poem* she utilises a collective second-person voice to articulate her experiences ('<u>You're</u> judged a lot'; '<u>You're</u> racially profiled'). The use of '<u>you</u>' in this way places Yasmin as being a member of a broader collective community. In other words, by not using a first-person voice (for example, '<u>I'm</u> judged a lot'), Yasmin does not just place herself in the centre of her narrative. For those from individualistic cultural backgrounds, the use of the first-person '<u>I</u>' versus the second-person '<u>you</u>' being used to discuss personal experiences can be confusing. For example, the latter can be mistakenly interpreted as an evasion of accountability of the lived experiences being discussed (Krog et al, 2009; Baak, 2016). However, the influence of relational ontologies for those from collectivistic backgrounds renders the use of the second-person 'you' in this context as Yasmin's experiences being presented as part of a collective (Krog et al, 2009; Baak, 2016). Therefore, Yasmin's experiences are articulated as not just being hers; these experiences are shared by others within her collective community. Further, these experiences are presented to be exacerbated in public spaces when there is an increased visibility of that collective, causing a sense of discomfort for her in public: 'It's uncomfortable to be in public places, especially with your friends.'

Group identity

As indicated previously, experiences of the homogenisation of identity along lines of race were reported to be exacerbated when in groups in public spaces. Throughout the time this research was conducted, the phrase 'African gangs' was extremely common in public and political discourse. As stated by Benier et al (2021), 'many instances of youth disorder committed by someone of colour were related to "African gangs" and this led to increased discrimination and overt expressions of hostility levelled towards people of African appearance' (p 222). As discussed in the previous section, when in public this was presented as leading to an erasure of individual identity for participants in this study via their identities being homogenised as belonging to a problematic collective identity based on visible difference. These processes made socialising in groups difficult. For example, see Daniel's *pronoun poem*:

> *Walk Together*
> According to our culture, we walk together, five or six together
> We can socialise
> Just across the road, you can see people moving in a group
> When they move in a group
> Because of their visibility
> People say, 'Oh, these people is a gang.' (Daniel)

In Daniel's *pronoun poem*, for the most part, he speaks in collective voice. This collective voice is a reflection of the collective social practices that Daniel is articulating. As he expresses, his is a collective culture where it is a cultural norm to socialise in groups in public spaces. However, 'because of ... visibility', this collective presence in public spaces is interpreted by some through a negative lens reflective of media and political representations.

However, of importance is the last line of Daniel's *pronoun poem*. In this line, Daniel employs the use of mimicry to discuss a group of young people across the road from where his interview is taking place and states, 'Oh, these people is a gang.' In this instance, Daniel is mimicking a voice of a collective group he refers to as 'people' (for example, 'People say ...'). Given the use of mimicry, it could be interpreted that the voice he is mimicking does not represent his collective identity. In this instance, Daniel presents his interpretation of how his collective visibility is interpreted by 'other people/s', which could result in increased instances of self-awareness and surveillance in public spaces.

Building on Daniel's place-based example, in which he points across the road, it is important to note that this interview occurred in a neighbourhood that was commonly referred to in the media regarding representations of 'African gangs'. As articulated by Mohammed in the focus group interview, "Now if you say Sudanese in [name of suburb], right, straight away someone is going to think criminal." This comment was directly followed up by Yasmin who said, "or, there is police everywhere", to which Mohammed responded, "Yeah, all the time now." For many participants in this study, this is the neighbourhood where they live. Their experiences in public spaces within their own neighbourhood were presented as being underpinned by a control of their group identity. As articulated by Yasmin in the following *pronoun poem*:

> *Watching You*
> You can already tell
> When you're out
> Especially if you're in a group
> There is police there
> The police are going to be watching you. (Yasmin, FG)

Within this *pronoun poem* Yasmin speaks in a second-person collective voice to convey personal experiences ('You can already tell ... When you're out'). This can be interpreted as Yasmin placing her voice within a wider collective community and/or using her voice in this way to speak with and on behalf of her peers, given this came from the focus group interview. Yasmin presents a clear sense of being under surveillance in her neighbourhood as being under the gaze of police. This articulation aligns with Brighenti's (2007) conceptualisation of control vis-à-vis visibility as well as Foucauldian (1977) panopticism. In this sense, Yasmin presents a clear and explicit account of being watched as a result of her collective identity, which may have an impact on how she conducts herself under this gaze.

Racial profiling

When in public spaces, several participants indicated that they experience negative interactions with authority (for example, police, ticket inspectors on public transport), which they linked to processes of racial profiling. These experiences presented by participants reflect findings in other studies that report that being stopped by police is a common occurrence for African Australian youth (Benier et al, 2018; Baak et al, 2019). Racial profiling can be described as a process in which 'police stop, question, search or detain a person because of their race' (Police Accountability Project, 2021, para 1). For example, as explained by Titirum, "The police right now, they're targeting everyone, everyone of African background. If they see you … you are number one suspect." Of significance is Titirum's articulation of the police gaze (for example, "If they see you"), which highlights a sense of visibility linked to racial profiling. Titirum further expressed accounts of these experiences in the following *pronoun poem*:

> *Routine Check*
> I got pulled up by police
> I wasn't driving, I was walking
> They ask me, 'Do you have an ID?'
> They go like, 'What's your name?'
> I was walking and they just pull over next to me
> I'm like 'What for, what do you need my name for?'
> They go, 'We're checking, doing routine check'
> I said, 'You see that fellow right there, you have not checked his name.' (Titirum)

Titirum places himself at the centre of this *pronoun poem* and moves between his own voice and mimicking the voices of the police. Titirum is explicit that he is being targeted in this anecdote when compared with other members of the community ('You see that fellow right there, you have not checked his name'). Furthermore, this type of policing is a form of control that is not explicitly linked to a crime being committed. This type of policing is 'based on risk assessment, rather than on the identification of specific criminal behaviour' (Coleman and McCahill, 2011, p 69). This has been previously highlighted by Baak et al (2019) as being a common experience regarding police interactions for African Australian youth.

Joseph similarly described experiences of interactions with police in the following *pronoun poem* and makes explicit links between these interactions and visible racial identity.

> *Same Scenario, Different Sort of Colour*
> The police, the way they talk to you
> I shake my head
> I have seen ticket inspectors and the police
> The way they speak to someone from the mainstream
> The way they speak to our youth

> You can see clearly there is no trust or respect
> Who's supposed to show respect
> You are a professional
> You need to show that respect
> Just the way they respect the mainstream
> I have seen them approaching them looking very polite
> But the same scenario, the same young kids, different sort of colour, it's different. (Joseph)

In this *pronoun poem*, Joseph highlights how police and ticket inspectors (who check the validity of tickets on public transport) engage in racial profiling of youth. These instances are presented as being indicative of low levels of trust and respect between youth from his community and police/ticket inspectors. For Joseph, this is linked to racial identity, in which youth from the 'mainstream' are not placed under the same levels of control. Of interest is Joseph's use of 'mainstream' in this context. Later in the poem, Joseph is explicit in how this links to racial identity ('the same scenario, the same young kids, different sort of colour, it's different'), and, as such, "mainstream" can be interpreted as being of a 'White' identity. By virtue of these comments, Joseph highlighted the power differentials between 'White' and 'Black' identity in public spaces in Australia. While discussing similar experiences (in this case having her ticket inspected on public transport), Ruby challenged and questioned the underpinnings of these power differentials. She asked, "Why can't you ask the person that walks right in front of you that is the same age as me and is White? What's the difference between them and me?" Such examples are indicative of how these participants are aware of their visibility in public spaces and how this is linked to notions of hegemonic 'Whiteness' in Australia. Mapedzahama and Kwansah-Aidoo (2017) previously have indicated that an experience of this kind in the 'predominately white Australian context is burdensome' (p 11). These experiences may lead to increased levels of self-surveillance in public spaces, which have the potential to impact these youths' overall sense of identity relative to their belonging in Australia.

Conclusion

Participants' sense of visibility within public spaces was reported to significantly impact how they experienced public spaces and their interactions with others therein. Against the backdrop of hegemonic 'White' norms regarding Australian identity, participants' visible difference relative to these norms placed them under heightened levels of control and surveillance. This has the potential to have a detrimental influence on their overall sense of belonging and how they construct their identities as African Australian youth. For example, utilising a VCRM approach, participants' presentations of their identities through their narratives indicated that the positionality of these identities was marginalised as 'other', reducing a sense of belonging in the spaces they occupy. Within her theory of the 'politics of belonging', Yuval-Davis (2006) defines belonging as 'emotional attachments' and 'feeling at home' (p 197). Yuval-Davis (2006) articulates that within this sense of belonging, an individual's social locations (ethnicity, socioeconomic status, and so on) do not influence their belonging. Rather, it is through the politicisation of social locations that one's sense of belonging is impacted.

Negative racialised public and political attention experienced by participants is a prime example of the politicisation of their identities, which appears to have had an impact on their overall experiences in public spaces. Subsequently, this may have the capacity to influence their overall sense of belonging as Australians. Of concern is the way that these experiences may influence these youths' future social and economic prosperity moving into the adult years. For example, previous research has indicated that negative racialised experiences in public for African Australian youth can leave these youth vulnerable to social and education disengagement (Benier et al, 2018; Han and Budarick, 2018). Therefore, disengagement of this nature may have the capacity to reify and reproduce inequitable social conditions catalysed via negative public and political discourses. Subsequently, opportunities for future success may be reduced.

While all participants in this study came to Australia from refugee backgrounds, at the time of this research they were all Australian citizens. As such, within public discourses, some commentators have questioned the need to provide information such as race or place of birth, in media reporting (Nyuon, 2018). For example, what is the necessity of drawing attention to identifiers such as 'Sudanese' or 'of African appearance' when reporting on issues pertaining to youth crime, particularly when many of these young people are Australian citizens? Previous research has indicated clear links between this type of reporting and increased instances of negative racialised experiences in public spaces, where everyday racism is normalised, and racists feel emboldened to vilify African Australian youth (Benier et al, 2018; Han and Budarick, 2018; Macaulay and Deppeler, 2020b).

Building on the findings presented and discussed in this chapter, there are several areas identified for future research. As mentioned earlier, the context of this research was at a time when these youth were under significant amounts of racialised public and political scrutiny. It could be argued that this context significantly contributed to a sense of control being the primary lens through which participants present their experiences in public spaces regarding their visibility (Brighenti, 2007). While acts of recognition (that is, resistance) were not notably present in the data regarding experiences in public spaces, I have elsewhere presented acts of recognition performed by this cohort of youth in resistance to negative narratives throughout their transition to adulthood (Macaulay and Deppeler, 2020a). This resistance was primarily manifested via the emphasis placed on being role models for those younger than them within their communities. Thus, it is recommended that an area for future research is to explicitly explore experiences of resistance performed by these youth within their day-to-day lived experiences of public space.

Additionally, of significance were gender-related differences between participants' perspectives or, to be more specific, the lack thereof. Previous research has highlighted that gender can be a contributing factor regarding how African Australian youth experience public spaces (RHRC, 2007; Benier et al, 2018). Further, similar contentions have been made relative to other global contexts (see, for example, De Backer, 2019). However, there were no notable differences between young men and women in this study regarding their experiences of visible difference in public spaces and how this influenced their perceptions of control and surveillance. This is not to say that there are no differences in this regard, rather, no notable differences were evident in the data. Elsewhere, I have discussed gender-related differences for this cohort of youth within their relationships with their parents in the private sphere, which have implications for barriers to entering the public sphere, yet this did not extend to a discussion of experiences once actually in public (Macaulay, 2020a). The nuances of gender-related differences in public spaces for this cohort could be explored in depth in future research.

References

Abur, W. and Spaaij, R. (2016) 'Settlement and employment experiences of South Sudanese people from refugee backgrounds in Melbourne, Australia', *Australasian Review of African Studies*, 37(2): 107–128.

Ahluwalia, P. (2001) 'When does a settler become a native? Citizenship and identity in a settler society', *Pretexts: Literary and Cultural Studies*, 10(1): 63–73.

Baak, M. (2016) *Negotiating Belongings: Stories of Forced Migration of Dinka Women from South Sudan*, Rotterdam: Sense Publishers.

Baak, M. (2019) 'Racism and othering for South Sudanese heritage students in Australian schools: is inclusion possible?', *International Journal of Inclusive Education*, 23(2): 125–141.

Baak, M., Summers, R., Masocha, S., Tedmanson, D., Gale, P., Pieters, J. and Kuac, A. (2019) 'Surveillance, belonging and community spaces for young people from refugee backgrounds in Australia', in S. Habib and M.R.M. Ward (eds) *Youth, Place and Theories of Belonging*, London: Routledge, pp 25–38.

Becker, H.S. (1963) *Outsiders: Studies in the Sociology of Deviance*, London: Free Press of Glencoe.

Benier, K., Blaustein, J., Johns, D. and Maher, S. (2018) *'Don't Drag Me Into This': Growing up South Sudanese in Victoria after the 2016 Moomba 'Riot'*, full report, Melbourne: Centre for Multicultural Youth.

Benier, K., Wickes, R. and Moran, C. (2021) '"African gangs" in Australia: perceptions of race and crime in urban neighbourhoods', *Australian & New Zealand Journal of Criminology*, 54(2): 220–238.

Bogdan, R. and Biklen, S. (2007) *Qualitative Research for Education: An Introduction to Theory and Methods*, Boston, MA: Pearson.

Braun, V. and Clarke, V. (2006) 'Using thematic analysis in psychology', *Qualitative Research in Psychology*, 3(2): 77–101.

Brighenti, A.M. (2007) 'Visibility: a category for the social sciences', *Current Sociology*, 55(3): 323–342.

Brown, L.M. and Gilligan, C. (1991) 'Listening for voice in narratives of relationship', *New Directions for Child Development*, 54: 43–62.

Coleman, R. and McCahill, M. (2011) *Surveillance and Crime*, London: SAGE.

De Backer, M. (2019) 'Regimes of visibility: hanging out in Brussels' public spaces', *Space and Culture*, 22(3): 208–320.

Deng, S.A. (2016) *South Sudanese Youth Acculturation and Intergenerational Challenges*, paper presented at the 39th African Studies Association of Australasia and the Pacific (AFSAAP), December.

DSS (Department of Social Services) (2016) *Settlement Report: Settlers by Calendar Year of Arrival, Arrival Dates 1/1/01–1/1/16, Migration Stream: Humanitarian, Country of Birth: Republic of South Sudan; Sudan*, Canberra: Australian Government Department of Immigration and Citizenship.

Due, C. (2008) '"Who are strangers?": "absorbing" Sudanese refugees into a white Australia', *ACRAWSA e-journal*, 4(1): 1–13.

Foucault, M. (1977) *Discipline and Punish*, translated by A. Sheridan, New York: Pantheon Books.

Giddens, A. (2006) *Sociology*, Cambridge: Polity Press.

Gilligan, C. and Eddy, J. (2017) 'Listening as a path to psychological discovery: an introduction to the listening guide', *Perspectives on Medical Education*, 6(2): 76–81.

Gilligan, C., Spencer, R., Weinberg, M.K. and Bertsch, T. (2003) 'On the listening guide: a voice-centred relational method', in J.E. Rhodes, L. Yardley and P.M. Camic (eds) *Qualitative Research in Psychology: Expanding Perspectives in Methodology and Design*, Washington, DC: American Psychological Association, pp 157–172.

Han, G.S. and Budarick, J. (2018) 'Overcoming the new kids on the block syndrome: the media "endorsement" on discrimination against African-Australians', *Continuum*, 32(2): 213–223.

Harris, A., Ngum Chi Watts, M.C. and Spark, C. (2013) ' "The barriers that only you can see": African Australian women thriving in tertiary education despite the odds', *Multidisciplinary Journal of Gender Studies*, 2(2): 182–202.

Hénaff, M. and Strong, T.B. (2001) 'Introduction: the conditions of public space: vision, speech, and theatricality', in M. Hénaff and T.B. Strong (eds) *Public Space and Democracy*, Minneapolis, MI: University of Minnesota Press, pp 1–32.

Hughes, E.C. (1945) 'Dilemmas and contradictions of status', *American Journal of Sociology*, 50(5): 353–359.

Kogan, S.M., Yu, T., Allen, K.A. and Brody, G.H. (2015) 'Racial microstressors, racial self-concept, and depressive symptoms among male African Americans during the transition to adulthood', *Journal of Youth and Adolescence*, 44(4): 898–909.

Krog, A. (2011) 'In the name of human rights: I say (how) you (should) speak (before I listen)', in N.K. Denzin and Y.S. Lincoln (eds) *The SAGE Handbook of Qualitative Research*, London: SAGE, pp 381–386.

Krog, A., Mpolweni-Zantsi, N.L. and Ratele, K. (2009) *There was this Goat: Investigating the Truth Commission Testimony of Notrose Nobomvu Konile*, Scottsville: University of KwaZulu-Natal Press.

Macaulay, L. (2020a) 'Australian Sudanese and South Sudanese youths' perspectives on the youth/parent relationship and its influence on the transition to adulthood', *Young: Nordic Journal of Youth Research*, 29(2): 137–156.

Macaulay, L. (2020b) *The Transition to Adulthood: Experiences and Perspectives of Australian Sudanese and South Sudanese Youth in Melbourne, Australia*, unpublished doctoral dissertation, Monash University, Melbourne, Australia.

Macaulay, L. and Deppeler, J. (2020a) ' "Eighteen just makes you a person with certain privileges": the perspectives of Australian Sudanese and South Sudanese youths regarding the transition to adulthood', *Identities: Global Studies in Culture and Power*, 29(2): 1–20. doi:10.1080/1070289X.2020.1844517

Macaulay, L. and Deppeler, J. (2020b) 'Perspectives on negative media representations of Australian Sudanese and South Sudanese youths', *Journal of Intercultural Studies*, 4(2). doi:10.1080/07256868.2020.1724908

Majavu, M. (2017) *Uncommodified Blackness: The African Male Experience in Australia and New Zealand*, Cham: Palgrave Macmillan.

Majavu, M. (2020) 'The "African gangs" narrative: associating blackness with criminality and other anti-Black racist tropes in Australia', *African and Black Diaspora: An International Journal*, 13(1): 27–39.

Mapedzahama, V. and Kwansah-Aidoo, K. (2017) 'Blackness as burden? The lived experience of Black Africans in Australia', *SAGE Open*, 7(3): 1–13.

Nyuon, N. (2018) 'Why do the media demonise African Australians?', *The Age*, 11 July, available from: www.theage.com.au/national/victoria/why-do-the-media-demonise-african-australians-20180710-p4zqoh.html

Police Accountability Project (2021) *Racial Profiling*, available from: www.policeaccountability.org.au/issues-and-cases/racial-profiling

RHRC (Refugee Health Research Centre) (2007) 'Good starts for refugee youth, broadsheet #2', *Promoting Partnerships with Police*, Melbourne: RHRC.

Robinson, J. (2013) 'People of Sudanese heritage living in Australia: implications of demography for individual and community resilience', in J. Marlowe, A. Harris and T. Lyons (eds) *South Sudanese Diaspora in Australia and New Zealand: Reconciling the Past with the Present*, Newcastle upon Tyne: Cambridge Scholars, pp 12–47.

Santoro, N. and Wilkinson, J. (2016) 'Sudanese young people building capital in rural Australia: the role of mothers and community', *Ethnography and Education*, 11(1): 107–120.

Yuval-Davis, N. (2006) 'Belonging and the politics of belonging', *Patterns of Prejudice*, 40(3): 197–214.

Yuval-Davis, N. (2010) 'Theorizing identity: beyond the "us" and "them" dichotomy', *Patterns of Prejudice*, 44(3): 261–280.

11

Hair Salons as 'Private-Public Spaces': Exploring the Experiences of Young Migrant Women in an Urban Township in South Africa

Rebecca Walker and Glynis Clacherty

Introduction

Despite a growing body of literature dealing with gender and migration, as well as children on the move, few studies focus on the intersection of gender, age and migration and more specifically the experiences of girls on the move (Save the Children, 2020a). The lack of awareness and understanding of girls and young women who migrate, their experiences en route and their arrival, mean that generalised notions of 'vulnerable children' as victims of smuggling or trafficking fill the gap (O'Connell Davidson and Farrow, 2007; Walker et al, 2020). In South Africa, approximately 33.5 per cent of all female African migrants are under 25 (based on the limited data available) (Statistics South Africa, 2015) and the majority are between 16 and 25 (Save the Children UK, 2007). The multiple vulnerabilities faced by girls and young women on the move in South Africa are clear, particularly given the context of increasing xenophobia, extremely high rates of gender-based violence and escalating levels of unemployment. However, this cannot tell the whole story of youth and migration in South Africa and, in fact, overshadows the role of decision-making, strategising and negotiation of private, public and – central here – 'private-public spaces' that young women and girls employ in order to survive.

Based on research conducted by the authors as part of a larger study (Save the Children, 2020) commissioned by the International Organisation, Save the Children, to better understand the migration experiences of young women and girls in Southern Africa, Latin America and Europe, this chapter explores these forms of survival. The Save the Children study aimed to address a gap in their global Children on the Move intervention programme around policy and programmatic interventions for girls and young women and to advocate generally for increased understanding of their migration experiences. Drawing from the findings from our participatory research conducted in one of the Southern African sites, we focus on the experiences of 16 girls aged between 15 and 17 and six young women aged from 20 to 22 from Mozambique and living in Thembisa, a township on the outskirts of Johannesburg, South Africa (Save the Children, 2020). The distinction made here between girls and young women is based on the legal definition of children in South Africa. The Children's Act No 38, 2005 defines a child as a person 'under the age of 18 years'. For the purposes of this chapter, we refer to participants as 'young women' thus reflecting the fact that a 15-year-old girl's experiences can vastly differ from those of a five-year old and therefore the term 'girl' can be misleading and frame specific assumptions. A number of the girls and young women were also mothers and parenting alone. Locating the research within the intimate spaces of small hairdressing salons, where the young women spend their days congregating and sharing experiences and advice, we show that these 'private-public spaces' become spaces in which friendships are built, connections and threads of trust developed, and advice for staying safe shared. We use the term 'private-public spaces' here to refer to spaces like hair salons; they can be open to anyone, located on a busy, open street, shaped by the anticipation of encounters (and thus income) and an awareness of being visible, while also providing a space that offers personal connections, intimacy and social, emotional and practical support. Here, among the braids and smell of hair oils, girls and young women can quietly share their desires, fears, aspirations and realities of looking for better futures in a context where the lack of documentation, limited access to health and education, and xenophobic and gender-based violence pose constant threats.

The chapter is structured into four sections. The first considers the hidden spaces of the urban context that the young women inhabit. The second describes how these hidden spaces have become spaces of fear for young women migrants due to xenophobia, gender-based violence and poverty. In the third section, we locate our research in the private-public spaces of hair salons, exploring how the young women and, in turn, the researchers negotiated these spaces to find networks of intimacy and support. Finally, looking at how the intersecting experiences of being migrants, young women and mothers render the young women invisible, we argue for greater focus on the realities and needs of migrant youth and especially girls as they move across borders, and base their survival on spaces that simultaneously expose and provide protection from the precarious experiences of everyday life in South Africa.

The urban context and hidden spaces

The focus of this chapter is Thembisa, a sprawling township on the northern outskirts of the city of Johannesburg, South Africa. Established in 1957 as part of the resettlement of people under the apartheid regime, the area is centrally placed between the industrial areas of the cities of Pretoria and Johannesburg. This makes it a common 'landing place' for many migrants who come to South Africa in search of work. Migrants from Mozambique, Zimbabwe and Malawi live alongside South Africans in the new housing, built under the democratic government, old apartheid-style four-room houses and the informal houses that proliferate around the edge of the township and in the backyards of formal houses. A large population of Mozambicans live in the area (Muanamoha et al, 2010), many having been there for three generations, their grandfathers coming to work on the mines in the 1950s followed by their children to work in the growing industrial complex between the two large cities.

Through previous work with unaccompanied migrant women and children in Johannesburg, the authors identified Thembisa as a site where many young women who crossed the border from Mozambique informally, settle (Walker and Clacherty, 2015; Clacherty, 2019). Drawn by a sense of familiarity gathered from family members or friends who had migrated before them, young women make their way from the border areas to this township. They now live mostly with peers or boyfriends/partners in rented, informally built rooms in backyards. The young women in our study, like many Mozambicans who preceded them, had all chosen to leave Mozambique in search of work in South Africa.

Despite the realities of xenophobic violence, endemic gender-based violence and high levels of unemployment and poverty, South Africa continues to be regarded as a country of opportunity and hope, with Johannesburg as the 'city of gold' in which money can be made and lives, both in the host country and back home, improved (Fauvelle-Aymar, 2014; Jinnah and Cazarin, 2015; Walker et al, 2017). This image is bolstered by the tales told by young and older return migrants, arriving back in Mozambique talking of riches and opportunities, which belie the realities of a tough and brutal life in South Africa (Hassim et al, 2008).

Yet the choice to migrate described by the young women is more complex than simply 'coming to the city from the village to find work'. While they acknowledge that they knew that the stories of returning migrants were often embellished and had heard about the risks of xenophobic violence, they also felt that they had very limited choice. If they were to make something of their lives, then migration seemed the best solution. Two of the young women described their situations and decisions in the following ways:

'Because there's no work in Maputo. If … if it was possible to work in Maputo, I would stay there with my kids – my old mother looks after them. If you could find me a job in Maputo, I wouldn't come here anymore.' (Young woman 1)

'I was just sitting there. I decided at least to try and get work here. To pay for my two children.' (Young woman 2)

Such statements do not suggest rash, unplanned decisions but show that a lack of opportunities for work and the increasing responsibilities at home meant that the young women were forced to make a plan. These realities are in keeping with some of the recent work exploring the motivations and experiences of young migrants seeking better lives across Southern Africa (Hertrich et al, 2012; Clacherty, 2015; de Regt, 2016; Mahati and Palmary, 2017; Walker et al, 2020). It also shows the limitations of approaches that view young people on the move as only vulnerable and lacking in agency. Reflecting Kihato's (2013) seminal work with migrant women in Johannesburg, through which she shows how women can be vulnerable and resilient as they create lives in the city, the stories in this chapter go on to show how the young women can also occupy these complex and sometimes contradictory spaces. They can be scared and fearful but also strategic and savvy; they can be (hyper-)visible as migrants and rendered invisible as mothers. It is these multiple and layered identities of the young women that fall outside of the social and political norms – resulting in their needs being misunderstood or, simply, not recognised.

In our report for Save the Children, we describe the enforced 'invisibility' of girls and young women on the move through the notion of the 'triple anomaly' that young women migrants pose to hegemonic social orders (Save the Children, 2020). As migrants, they are 'out of place' in the system of the nation state; as females they are outside the private domestic domain assigned to them as their 'natural' place (Hertrich et al, 2012; O'Neil et al, 2016); and as children they are out of place as they are 'unprotected' by the institution of the family and no longer living within the 'innocence' of childhood (Burman, 1994; Beazley, 2002; O'Connell Davidson and Farrow, 2007). Such a view resonates with Beazley's description of street girls in Indonesia, whom she suggests are 'seen to be "out of place" through committing a "social violation", by transgressing that which is considered to be appropriate behaviour' (Beazley, 2002, p 1666).

These ideas of migration, of gender, of the family and of home, while complex and contested, also clearly shape much of what is understood of girls on the move in terms of their vulnerabilities and needs (Temin et al, 2013; Walker and Vearey, 2019). Yet the 'triple anomaly' of not belonging to a nation, the private space of home and the innocence of childhood not only sustains the 'invisibility' of migrant young women in public spaces but, importantly, as our research shows, renders them vulnerable in ways that are different and more complex than often considered.

Securitised migration and spaces of fear

Arriving in South Africa, the young women find themselves in highly precarious situations shaped primarily by their lack of documentation, which essentially means they are 'illegal immigrants' in the eyes of the state (Sloth-Nielsen and Ackermann, 2016). For many migrants, especially from the rest of Africa, the challenges of accessing documentation in order to regularise one's stay in South Africa are manifold. Entangled in a web of corruption, lack of political will and xenophobic policies designed to make migrants feel unwelcome (Amit, 2015; Landau and Pampalone, 2018; Gandar, 2019), the consequences of not having documentation are far reaching. They include being unable to secure formal employment, facing barriers when accessing healthcare and education for their children as well as other forms of support, and the ongoing threat of arrest, detention and deportation (Lefko-Everett, 2007a; Kihato, 2009; Walker et al, 2017; Mbiyozo, 2018).

For the young women from Mozambique, not having documents means surviving as 'illegal' in a country characterised by xenophobic attitudes and behaviour that often lead to extreme forms of violence (Hassim et al, 2008; Misago, 2017; Walker, 2018). As the following interview excerpt suggests, young women live in fear of being arrested. They are forced to try to remain invisible while also needing to survive, earn money and support themselves and their children:

Older woman:	There is another girl who lives near here, but she did not want to come and talk to you. She's afraid of being arrested.
Researcher:	Does it happen that girls get arrested?
Girl 1:	Some people [South Africans] tell the police that people which [*sic*] live nearby [have no documents]. … They arrest you then they investigate, wanting to find out: Who did you come with? How did you come? They take you to the nearest police station. If you have money, you pay them; if you don't have [money] they take you [arrest you].
Girl 2:	My friend, ah, they kept her in the cells for two weeks.
Older woman:	Sometimes they arrest you when you are living with your husband. He went to work when he comes from there, he misses you. You're gone, and he has no money to pay so that they will release you.

Girl 1:   I am afraid of that, so I stay in the house and don't go out alone.

Many found themselves relying on informal work to get by, reflecting global research that shows that young women migrants typically work in the informal, unregulated sector as vendors, car washers, fetching firewood or doing part-time domestic work (Beazley, 2002; O'Neil et al, 2016). This kind of work is also located in 'hidden spaces' (Vearey, 2010): spaces that enable opportunities to informally earn a living while ensuring that irregular migrants stay below the radar and hidden from police, immigration officers and other potentially threatening state actors (Palmary et al, 2014). Elsewhere, this is described by Oliveira and Walker as 'striking a balance between being visible enough to gain a footing in the city, and invisible enough to elude persecution and harassment' (Oliveira and Walker, 2019, p 14).

Negotiating such spaces also influenced our research approach. For example, the previous interview excerpt illustrates how some of the young women were too scared to be out in the open and talk to us – or the Mozambican field researcher we worked with. This was due to the attention that talking with strangers could attract, as well as a more general fear of being visible as undocumented, migrant young women.

While we discuss this further in the later research approach section, suffice it to say that knowing there was fear among the participants meant that we needed to think more about how we created a connection and did not increase risks for the participants or that they did not feel unsafe or threatened in any way.

These spaces of fear need to be located within the broader context of the securitisation of migration in South Africa, which makes life for migrants tougher and riskier. In spite of its progressive, human-rights-based constitution, South Africa, like many other places across the globe, is instituting an increasingly restrictive and exclusionary immigration regime (Misago, 2017; Misago and Landau, 2018). Justified through unsubstantiated and xenophobic claims about migrants burdening the state, taking jobs from locals and driving up levels of crime, moves by the South African government to securitise migration and restrict access to basic services are part of a broader global shift to prevent the movement of certain kinds of migrants (Vearey, 2017; Walker and Vearey, 2019) (see, for example, the proposed changes to the 2002 Immigration Act laid out in the Department of Home Affairs White Paper on Immigration [2017]; Walker and Vearey, 2019). Anti-migration policies and, in particular, the search by police for undocumented migrants in urban areas, create fear and violence and hugely impact on the everyday lives of girls and young women once they arrive in South Africa (Amit, 2015; Walker et al, 2017; Gandar, 2019).

Research in a hair salon: private-public spaces

In response to the need for 'invisibility', the young women in Thembisa had to seek out spaces where they felt safe. We discovered one of these spaces as we undertook our research in the area. In Thembisa, Mozambican women are recognised as experts in hair braiding. With easy access to cheap hair extensions from China through Maputo (the capital of Mozambique) and then into South Africa, older Mozambican women have been able to set up their own hair salons in small, informally built zinc structures along every 'shopping' street in Thembisa. This is where young Mozambican women can be found congregating and chatting on a daily basis.

These safe spaces became visible to us through the work of the young, female, Mozambican field researcher in her early thirties, whom we had tasked with finding young women and then leading some arts-based research workshops. The young researcher had previously lived in Thembisa as an informal migrant (although she had now moved back to Mozambique) and so sought out young women in the spaces where she knew girls and young women could be found at work. These included the bus station and marketplace where they sold vegetables. However, she soon realised that none of them would agree to attend a workshop or allow her to interview them in these public spaces. As already noted, this was due to the fear of drawing attention to themselves through being seen talking to a stranger. Even though the researcher had lived in the same area a number of years before, she would still have been perceived as a stranger by locals – something that concerned the girls and made them unwilling to talk openly in these spaces.

Over time, as she sat with these young women, she became aware that there was another space where many young women from Mozambique could be found, which, although public, was also considered private and therefore 'safe': the small hair salons (see Figure 11.1).

This was where we based our research, in these small, public-private intimate spaces. The researcher made friends with the owners and asked if she could talk to the young women who gathered there and invite groups of three or four girls she had met in the market to meet and talk there. As the owners braided the hair of a client, she talked quietly to the young women. If space allowed, this would be to the side of the room, or, if not, they would sit just behind the salon away from the gaze of passers-by. In this way, the young women could talk to the researcher more comfortably, confident that they were in a safe space close to an older woman they knew and trusted.

The ways in which the young women opened up and shared stories in the hair salons revealed how they had sought out and negotiated spaces that allowed them to participate in an everyday activity while remaining invisible to local South African residents and to police harassment. Resonating with how Beazley (2002) describes the way that street girls in Indonesia develop

Figure 11.1: One of the hair salons where the young women gathered

Source: Suzy Bernstein

informal networks and discourse in their everyday lives as both 'survival strategies and as strategies of resistance', the young women in the salons also learned to strategise by navigating fluid and risky spaces and finding specific ways in which they could feel safe® and protected. Similarly, Street and Coleman (2012) suggest that hospitals can also reflect public-private spaces as 'simultaneously bounded and permeable ... both sites of social control and spaces where alternative and transgressive social order emerge and are contested' (p 5). Meanwhile, Kihato locates the everyday lives and struggles of migrant women in Johannesburg within an entanglement of intimate private spaces and public urban spaces, both spaces permeated by threats of violence and forcing a careful balance and negotiation in order to survive (Kihato, 2007, 2013). Reflecting on Kihato's nuanced analysis of migrant women's lives as they seek to make a living and find a space to belong within the city, Bianisa thus highlights the extent of the 'liminal city which engenders liminal lives' (Binaisa, 2015).

For the young women in Thembisa, the hair salons were easily accessible, as there was always one nearby. They were also uniquely Mozambican spaces – based on the tradition of hair-braiding from home; a walk through a Mozambican city, town or village reveals women somewhere on a street corner or under a tree chatting as a friend's hair is braided. That the salons were owned by older Mozambican women who had mostly moved to

Thembisa when they, too, were younger women of 17 or 18 meant that they could share experiences and knowledge that helped the girls negotiate the complexities of their new lives. As one young woman described: "Marlena here [pointing to a woman in her thirties who works in the salon] she knows us as she is from Maputo too. She advises us."

Research approach

The research approach was based on an adapted arts-based approach, which we knew from past experience would allow time for reflection and therefore deeper and richer discussion (Clacherty, 2019). It is useful to reflect briefly on this approach, as it not only illustrates what stories were shared but, critically, how they were shared in public-private spaces where the young women had grown to feel more comfortable and confident and could risk visibility with others and, to an extent, with the researchers (see Figure 11.2).

We began by asking the young women to draw their homes and families at home and used these drawings to discuss why they had left home. Sitting squashed together on the arm of an old sofa, and balancing paper on their laps, the young women sketched simple drawings. They also drew their journeys from their hometowns and villages and told us the details of how they crossed the border and how they made sure that they were safe on

Figure 11.2: Inside the hair salon. The hair extensions can be seen hanging on the wall.

Source: Suzy Bernstein

Figure 11.3: A cut-out doll used to tell stories

Source: James Clacherty

their journey. Usually 'keeping safe' entailed asking advice of older women who were already in South Africa or those at home who knew the route through their own past experience. Then they told us about their lives now in Thembisa.

Given the contexts in which the girls lived and the stories being told, the research also needed to be careful, ethical and based on the principle of least harm in the way that activities and questions were structured and presented. This was in line with Save the Children's Safeguarding Policy (Save the Children, 2018) and with the endorsement of the University of the Witwatersrand, Johannesburg Human Research Ethics Committee (Non-Medical). One strategy developed was to use a cut-out girl, which the participant girls and young women used to describe their own, often very difficult, experiences (Figure 11.3). We presented the girl as 'a Mozambican girl living in Thembisa' and asked how she earned money, for example. This meant that the young women could talk about issues such as transactional sex without owning the activity themselves and allowing some distance between the story and their lives.

The discussions were held in a mixture of Portuguese, Xitsonga or Xitswa, the languages the women knew best. We used a small tape recorder after explaining that recordings would be used only by the researchers and that no names would be used in reports. The recordings were subsequently transcribed, translated into English and analysed using an 'experience-centred approach' (Andrews et al, 2008). Through this approach, we saw the narratives as a 'means of human sense-making' (Andrews et al, 2008, p 43). In other words, the stories the young women told us helped us understand how they had made sense of their experiences as they left home, journeyed and arrived, and how they coped now; they were more than mere descriptions.

Migrants, young women and mothers: invisible spaces

One of the key findings from the Save the Children Southern African 'Girls on the Move' research study (2020) was that many of the young women migrants were mothers – another space in which young women migrants are invisible. Commonly, literature on migrant mothers explores motherhood within the context of migrating and leaving children behind – thus mothering from a distance (Mazzucato et al, 2015; Tyldum, 2015; Walker et al, 2017; Walker, 2018). While little attention is paid to migrant women as mothers when on the move and in their host countries, a focus on young migrant mothers especially under the age of 18 is almost completely absent. Given the high levels of teenage pregnancy in South Africa, much research speaks to this issue and considers how to support teenage mothers and keep young mothers in school (Jewkes et al, 2009; Taylor et al, 2014). Yet there is little that addresses migrant girls specifically or separates out their experiences and unique vulnerabilities. The fact that young migrant mothers challenge the stereotypes of girls on the move makes them invisible in policy and programme interventions too, as the summary report of the Save the Children Global Study on Girls on the Move points out (Save the Children, 2020. 'The vulnerability of girls who become mothers during the course of their migration journeys, and the way in which motherhood and the 'burden' of care can increase girls' invisibility and risk-taking, is clear in the narratives of girls on the move in Southern Africa' (Save the Children, 2020, p 22).

The international non-governmental organisation understanding of an 'unaccompanied child' does not include motherhood (Uppard and Birnbaum, 2016). Motherhood moves young women away from being seen as a 'child' and relatedly as 'innocent', thereby removing them from any options of support that they may gain from protective policy or programming for 'unaccompanied children' or 'vulnerable girls' (Mahati and Palmary, 2017).

We found women as young as 16 with children in Thembisa, and the topic of children and how to cope as a mother frequently shaped discussions in the salons. The young women talked about how hard it was to mother in a context of deep poverty and isolation from family support: conversations that reflected experiences that Walker has described as the 'burden of care' for migrant mothers (Walker, 2018). Exploring the experiences of refugee women who are single mothers in inner-city Johannesburg, Walker captures the ways in which the struggles of daily life as a migrant and a woman are compounded by having children.

> This is not just a burden in terms of the difficulties of having to provide – it's about feelings and desires and desperation and distress. What emerges most palpably in our group discussions is the absolute exhaustion of having to care, the challenges of facing daily struggles with additional worries about food, money and rent. (Walker, 2018, p 351)

At home in Mozambique, the young women had social networks of support that they could fall back on when things became desperate and they could not provide food for their children. Yet in South Africa, they complained that people did not care: "Here it's bad because you can go to bed hungry, while in Mozambique you can ask for a plate of food at least to give a child. While here, people can eat in front of you. They don't care." This made the struggle for young women who strived to be 'good' mothers all the harder; they sought out help to have their children immunised, they made sure that the children were warm as we sat talking in the evening air, they used whatever money they had to buy food and nappies. One young woman described how sad she was that she could not give her little boy a birthday cake: "For me it's complicated because, for example, yesterday it was my son's birthday, so I didn't have even a R6 (USD0.40) cake for my child. So, it's complicated, I wish I could be like other mothers that sing happy birthday to their children." We also observed discussions around the health of children, some of whom were with their mothers in the salon at they chatted.

In spite of the fact that protective legislations, policies and international declarations exist in South Africa to ensure access to primary healthcare for all, including migrants (Crush and Tawodzera, 2011; Walls et al, 2016), the xenophobic attitudes of South African government health service staff make accessing healthcare very difficult for migrants. These difficulties are well documented (Chekero and Ross, 2017; Makandwa and Vearey, 2017), but of particular relevance to the young women in Thembisa is the research that highlights how migrant women face difficulty in accessing maternal healthcare (Chekero and Ross, 2017). A 2009 Human Rights Watch report recorded cases of migrants turned away, even in emergencies such as rape; there were also reports of harassment, charging illegal user fees and calling the police to report 'illegal migrants' (Human Rights Watch, 2009). This meant that the young women had to take great care in deciding where to seek health services for themselves and their children, often finding that those options were extremely limited or did not even exist.

On discussing these issues, the group of women in the hair salon discovered that there was a particular primary health clinic in the area that had friendly nurses who did not ask for documents before treating non-nationals or their children. This became the clinic they all attended for immunisations for their children and to access contraceptives and meet other health needs for themselves. This strategy of sharing information thus enabled the young women to negotiate challenges they faced living in South Africa through a network of support and advice that extended from the safety of the public-private space of the salon into the riskier spaces of healthcare facilities. Beazley coins the term 'geographies of resistance' to describe how street girls in Indonesia negotiated social and personal spaces to create 'their own gendered sense of place on the street' (Beazley, 2002, p 1666), and the women in the hair salon too crafted spaces that offered intimacy and care amid a context of rejection and risk.

Support systems: spaces of relative safety and partial justice

While working with the young women in the hair salons, we observed that they often talked to each other and the older women in the salon about ways to earn money. This was an ever-present and pressing worry for them. Many of them had started trying to earn, based on what they heard from people returning to their home areas, who had attempted to run their own businesses in South Africa. "So, I tried to sell. ... I cooked chicken feet, sold tomatoes and other things. I tried to cook, like, but things were not working out." Such an endeavour was difficult, however, as beyond the competition on the streets among those vying for survival in the opportunistic 'hidden spaces' (Vearey, 2010), there was also the need for start-up capital, support and stability to keep going. This meant that the young woman had to figure out what could work for them, often turning to what are referred to as 'piece jobs', which are small part-time jobs, which included washing and cleaning for neighbours. The young woman quoted here, for example, worked out a system with three other girls, which allowed them to take turns to work while those not working would care for all the children. The importance of this system is not only that it allowed the young women to earn a living and provide for their children but that it was a support system developed and worked out in the space of the hair salon. The nature of the private-public space meant that they could congregate to share ideas and problem-solve while also feeling a part of a community or, at least, less isolated than they would be when hidden in private spaces.

Drawing on a case study of land occupation and informal settlements in Brazil, Amin provides a similar example of shared experiences of poverty, loss and risk in the creation of solidarities among the poor. Amin demonstrates how the actions of the poor to co-construct access to basic needs, such as water, electricity and shelter, creates visible and invisible infrastructure, which is 'deeply implicated in not only the making and unmaking of individual lives, but also in the experience of community, solidarity and struggle for recognition' (Amin, 2014, p 137).

For the young women, too, beyond a space of sharing information and advice, the hair salons also offered a space of solidarity, where they could find a sense of safety within a wider context of violence. The young women told us about the many other spaces they moved through that were unsafe, including the backyard rooms they lived in and shared with men. Kihato similarly depicts the violence that pervades the private sphere of migrant women's homes and, in doing so, questions the absence of the private from the public spaces of the city in much of the literature on African cities. Insisting that the intimate space of the 'home' is irrevocably intertwined with the public urban space, Kihato highlights the need to recognise the continued and permeating presence of violence in the lives of migrant women at the hands of men (Kihato, 2013).

For the young Mozambican women, some of these relationships with men were formed at home in Mozambique and had precipitated them following the men to South Africa. Others were formed once they arrived. These relationships were often linked to economic need (particularly if the young women had children), as young men were more likely than young women to obtain jobs in the local factories. These relationships held complexities, however, many of which were related to the women being migrants. They were isolated in Thembisa from the protection of family and community that they had in Mozambique as described here: "Men when they get here, they become rough because they can mistreat you. They know you have nowhere to go. But in Mozambique they know you have relatives, you have neighbours that care, so it's different, yes." Through discussing these issues with each other in the hair salons, the young women could reinforce the bonds of support and create their own social worlds through friendships shaped by the intimate public-private spaces they occupied (Beazley, 2002).

We realised, however, that the discussions in the hair salons were more than safe spaces where they could seek out comfort and information. They were also places where they could discuss future plans and dreams. Tereasa, one of the young women, described her plans of finding domestic work so that she could earn enough money to rent a place for herself and her son:

> 'We talk about our plans [here at the salon]. I am thinking to try to get a job at that place where they are building new houses. They call girls to come clean the houses [once they are built]. That is a full-time job. Then I can move to my own room with my son.'

Mann's (2010) work in the city of Dar es Salaam shows that one of the ways unaccompanied migrant boys cope with the challenges of everyday life is to hold a quest to 'find a life' or 'make a future' before them, as they journey through the injustices of their everyday lives. Mann suggests that, alongside helping the boys cope with the loss in their past lives, this process of imagining a future allows them to face the reality of not (and perhaps never) belonging. The discussion about future plans and dreams in the hair salons suggests that this was one of the spaces where the young women could articulate the same 'quest'. In the same way that Huang and Yeoh describe women as negotiating spatiality 'as a strategy of resistance … to breach the boundaries imposed on them' (Huang and Yeoh, 1996, p 107) we suggest that meeting in the hair salons was a form of resistance to the injustices of their everyday lives for the young women (Beazley, 2002).

Walker (2013), in work with women living through war in eastern Sri Lanka, describes how women seek out normality as an act of resistance to the violence around them. Through small daily tasks and actions, like chatting with friends, cooking, sewing and washing clothes, women create small safe places for themselves. Walker relates this seeking out of normality to de Certeau's idea of the 'tactic', which is a creative response to the overwhelming of the weak by the strong, 'whether the strength be that of powerful people or the violence of things or of an imposed order' (de Certeau, 2011, p xix). In this sense, the chatting in the salon is a tactic to resist the violence of the imposed order. Meeting in the hair salons gave the young women from Mozambique a safe place where they could resist and also take a breath and gather the strength they needed to cope with the everyday injustices they encountered in their new lives.

Conclusion

The young women we worked with in Thembisa struggle on a daily basis. They struggle as migrants, as young women and as mothers, and with what these intersecting categories and identities mean. However, what is clear is that, through this largely invisible struggle, the young women have also sought spaces that can offer them relative safety and, to some extent, hope. As Walker notes in reference to the burden of motherhood and the frequent desire she witnessed among migrant mothers to 'give up', and that many find a way to manage. Week after week they come back to the research group, often saying, "We are still trying. We are still here" (Walker, 2018).

For the Mozambican women, these efforts to keep trying are tied to the particular public-personal spaces. They are spaces that allow them to feel like they have a foothold in the everyday life of Thembisa by entering a public hair salon, which offers services such as information but at the same time offers an intimacy that detaches them from the risk and vulnerabilities they face in the broader context.

The important contribution this research made at a programming level was that it explained why Save the Children staff so often failed to find young women migrants in their work in the urban centres of Southern Africa: "We know they [migrant girls] are out there … but they are so hard to find, to see them" (Save the Children, Children on the Move project co-ordinator, Zambia). What this illustrates is the value of ethnographic research such as this for developing support for this largely invisible group of migrants. It also illustrates how understanding endogenous supports and spaces, rather than creating new 'drop-in centres' or 'youth-friendly spaces' (the usual non-governmental organisation response to supporting unaccompanied children) can make support programmes more rooted in reality and therefore more sustainable and effective (Wessells, 2015). The 'Children on the Move' team at Save the Children South Africa provide a strong example of the way that programming can be built from spatially aware ethnographic research. Drawing from the key findings of our research with girls and young women, Save the Children has begun to explore piloting a project that works with a local community outreach worker employed by Save the Children in Thembisa. The community worker will begin by reaching out to the women who own the hair salons with the aim of providing them with information about sexual and reproductive health and child health, which they can then share with the young women. While this approach will need to be sensitive to the salon dynamics – especially to ensuring that there is no disruption to the existing support systems between the salon owners and the girls (Wessells, 2018) – it demonstrates how a support programme can develop from what is already in place rather than offering something new and unfamiliar. It is hoped that over time the hair salons will become a site for young women to access other support services such as vocational training and childcare.

This chapter has shown that acknowledging the existence and role of the different private-public spaces that exist in the lives of migrant young women is critical to understanding their complex and fluid realities through a spatial understanding of migration. The example of the hair salons and the networks and support systems that are developed also illustrates the importance of understanding the spaces that girls and young women traverse and occupy from their perspective and in relation to the challenges and vulnerabilities they face as migrants (often undocumented) and as mothers. Drawing on these kinds of examples can help not only in better understanding everyday realities but also in allowing and supporting young people to access the justice they deserve.

References

Amin, A. (2014) 'Lively infrastructure', *Theory, Culture & Society*, 31(7–8): 137–161.

Amit, R. (2015) *Queue Here for Corruption: Measuring Irregularities in South Africa's Asylum System*, Pretoria: Lawyers for Human Rights, available from: www.lhr.org.za/publications/queue-here-corruption-measuring-irregularities-south-africa%E2%80%99s-asylum-system

Andrews, M., Squire, C. and Tamboukou, M. (2008) *Doing Narrative Research*, Oxford: Oxford University Press.

Beazley, H. (2002) '"Vagrants wearing make-up": negotiating spaces on the streets of Yogyakarta, Indonesia', *Urban Studies*, 39(9): 1665–1683.

Binaisa, N. (2015) 'Review: migrant women of Johannesburg: life in an in-between city', UrbanAfrica.Net, available from: www.urbanafrica.net/review/review-migrant-women-johannesburg-life-city/

Burman, E. (1994) 'Innocents abroad: western fantasies of childhood and the iconography of emergencies', *Disasters*, 18(3): 238–253.

Chekero, T. and Ross, F.C. (2017) '"On paper" and "having papers": migrants navigating medical xenophobia and obstetric rights in South Africa', *Somatosphere*, 41(1): 41–54.

Clacherty, G. (2015) 'The suitcase project: working with unaccompanied child refugees in new ways', in I. Palmary, B. Hamber and L. Nunez (eds) *Healing and Change in the City of Gold*, Cham: Springer International Publishing, pp 13–30.

Clacherty, G. (2019) 'Art-based, narrative research with unaccompanied migrant children living in Johannesburg, South Africa', *Journal of Borderlands Studies*, 36(4): 547–563.

Crush, J. and Tawodzera, G. (2011) *Medical Xenophobia: Zimbabwean Access to Health Services in South Africa*, Migration Policy Series 54, Waterloo: ON.

de Certeau, M. (2011) *The Practice of Everyday Life by Michel de Certeau* (3rd edn), Berkeley: University of California Press.

de Regt, M. (2016) *Time to Look at Girls: Adolescent Girls' Migration in Ethiopia*, available from: https://research.vu.nl/ws/portalfiles/portal/16412107/Final_report_Adolescent_Girls_Migration_in_Ethiopia_May_2016.pdf

Fauvelle-Aymar, C. (2014) *Migration and Employment in South Africa: An Econometric Analysis of Domestic and International Migrants*, Johannesburg: University of the Witwatersrand, available from: www.miworc.org.za/docs/MiWORC-Report-6.pdf

Gandar, S. (2019) *'They Treated Me as If I Was Nothing': Research Report on the Gendered Impact of the Decision to Close the Cape Town Refugee Reception Office*, available from https://genderjustice.org.za/publication/they-treated-me-as-if-i-was-nothing/

Hassim, S., Kupe, T. and Worby, E. (eds) (2008) *Go Home or Die Here: Violence, Xenophobia and the Reinvention of Difference in South Africa*, Johannesburg: Wits University Press.

Hertrich, V., Lesclingand, M., Jacquemin, M. and Stephan, A. (2012) 'Girls' labour migration in rural Mali', working paper prepared for the project, 'Adolescent Girls' Migration', New York: Population Council, available from: www.researchgate.net/profile/Veronique_Hertrich/publication/280683155_Girls'_labour_migration_in_rural_Mali/links/55c10aee08aed621de153ea0/Girls-labour-migration-in-rural-Mali.pdf

Huang, S. and Yeoh, B.S.A. (1996) 'Gender and urban space in the tropical world', *Singapore Journal of Tropical Geography*, 17(2): 105–112.

Human Rights Watch (2009) *No Healing Here: Violence, Discrimination and Barriers to Health for Migrants in South Africa*, available from: www.hrw.org/report/2009/12/07/no-healing-here/violence-discrimination-and-barriers-health-migrants-south-africa

Jewkes, R., Morrell, R. and Christofides, N. (2009) 'Empowering teenagers to prevent pregnancy: lessons from South Africa', *Culture, Health & Sexuality*, 11(7): 675–688.

Jinnah, Z. and Cazarin, R. (2015) *Making Guests Feel Comfortable: Migrancy and Labour in the Hospitality Sector in South Africa*, MiWORC, Johannesburg: University of the Witwatersrand, available from: www.miworc.org.za/docs/MiWORC-PolicyBrief-6-Migrancy-and-labour-in-hospitality-sector-in-SA.pdf

Kihato, C.W. (2007) 'Invisible lives, inaudible voices? The social conditions of migrant women in Johannesburg', *African Identities*, 5(1): 89–110.

Kihato, C.W. (2009) 'Migration, gender and urbanisation in Johannesburg', thesis, University of South Africa. available from: http://uir.unisa.ac.za/handle/10500/2693

Kihato, C.W. (2013) *Migrant Women of Johannesburg: Everyday Life in an In-Between City*, Cham: Springer.

Landau, L.B. and Pampalone, T. (2018) *I Want to Go Home Forever: Stories of Becoming and Belonging in South Africa's Great Metropolis*, New York: New York University Press.

Lefko-Everett, K. (2007a) *Voices from the Margins: Migrant Women's Experiences in Southern Africa*, Migration Policy Series 46, The Southern African Migration Project, available from: www.africaportal.org/publications/voices-from-the-margins-migrant-womens-experiences-in-southern-africa/

Mahati, S. and Palmary, I. (2017) 'Independent migrant children, humanitarian work and statecraft: mapping the connections in South Africa', in L. O'Dell, C. Brownlow and H. Bertilsdotter-Rosqvist (eds) *Different Childhoods: Non/Normative Development and Transgressive Trajectories*, New York: Routledge, pp 105–118.

Makandwa, T. and Vearey, J. (2017) 'Giving birth in a foreign land: exploring the maternal healthcare experiences of Zimbabwean migrant women living in Johannesburg, South Africa', *Urban Forum*, 28: 75–90.

Mann, G. (2010) '"Finding a life" among undocumented Congolese refugee children in Tanzania', *Children & Society*, 24(4): 261–270.

Mazzucato, V., Cebotari, V., Veale, A., White, A., Grassi, M. and Vivet J. (2015) 'International parental migration and the psychological well-being of children in Ghana, Nigeria, and Angola', *Social Science & Medicine*, 132: 215–224.

Mbiyozo, A-N. (2018) 'Gender and migration in South Africa: talking to women migrants', Southern Africa Report, Institute for Security Studies, available from: https://issafrica.org/research/southern-africa-report/gender-and-migration-in-south-africa-talking-to-women-migrants

Misago, J.-P. (2017) *Xenophobia and Outsider Exclusion: Addressing Frail Social Cohesion in South Africa's Diverse Communities. Synthesis Report*, research report, Johannesburg: ACMS, available from: https://freedomhouse.org/sites/default/files/South_Africa_Community_Social_Cohesion_Profiles_Synthesis%20Report.pdf

Misago, J.-P. and Landau, L. (2018) *Free and Safe Movement in Southern Africa Research to Promote People's Safe and Unencumbered Movement across International Borders*, research report, Johannesburg: ACMS.

Muanamoha, R.C., Maharaj, B. and Preston-Whyte, E. (2010) 'Social networks and undocumented Mozambican migration to South Africa', *Geoforum*, 41(6): 885–896.

O'Connell Davidson, J. and Farrow, C. (2007) 'Child migration and the construction of vulnerability', Save the Children, University of Nottingham, available from: www.academia.edu/1769899/Child_migration_and_the_construction_of_vulnerability

O'Neil, T., Fleury, A. and Foresti, M. (2016) *Women on the Move: Migration, Gender Equality and the 2030 Agenda for Sustainable Development*, London: Overseas Development Institute.

Oliveira, E. and Walker, R. (2019) *Mwangaza Mamas: A Participatory Arts-Based Research Project*, Johannesburg: MoVE and ACMS, University of the Witwatersrand, available from: https://issuu.com/move.methods.visual.explore/docs/mwangaza_mama_ebook

Palmary, I., Hamber, B. and Nunez, L. (2014) *Healing and Change in the City of Gold: Case Studies of Coping and Support in Johannesburg*, Cham: Springer.

Save the Children (2018) *Child Safeguarding Policy: Policies and Procedures*. London: Save the Children, available from: www.savethechildren.org.za/sci-za/files/c9/c9154a3d-4bb9-440d-b499-f9fdb7e2cafd.pdf

Save the Children (2020) *Girls on the Move*, research series, London: Save the Children International, available from: https://resourcecentre.savethechildren.net/node/18292/pdf/girls_on_the_move_southern_africa_final.pdf

Save the Children UK (2007) *Children Crossing Borders Report on Unaccompanied Minors Who Have Travelled to South Africa*, London: Save The Children International, available from: https://resourcecentre.savethechildren.net/node/1487/pdf/1487.pdf

Sloth-Nielsen, J. and Ackermann, M. (2016) 'Unaccompanied and separated foreign children in the care system in the Western Cape: a socio-legal study', *Potchefstroom Electronic Law Journal*, 19: 1–27.

Statistics South Africa (2015) *Census 2011: Migration Dynamics in South Africa*, Pretoria: Stats SA. available from: www.statssa.gov.za/publications/Report-03-01-79/Report-03-01-792011.pdf

Street, A. and Coleman, S. (2012) 'Introduction: real and imagined spaces', *Space and Culture*, 15(1): 4–17.

Taylor, M., Jinabhai, C., Dlamini, S., Sathiparsad, R., Eggers, M.S. and De Vries, H. (2014) 'Effects of a teenage pregnancy prevention program in KwaZulu-Natal, South Africa', *Health Care for Women International*, 35(7–9): 845–858.

Temin, M., Montgomery, M.G., Engebretsen, S. and Berker, K.M. (2013) *Girls on the Move: Adolescent Girls and Migration in the Developing World*, A Girls Count Report on Adolescent Girls, New York: Population Council, available from: www.popcouncil.org/research/girls-on-the-move-adolescent-girls-migration-in-the-developing-world

Tyldum, G. (2015) 'Motherhood, agency and sacrifice in narratives on female migration for care work', *Sociology*, 49(1): 56–71.

Uppard, S. and Birnbaum, L. (2016) *Field Handbook on Unaccompanied and Separated Children*, Inter-Agency Working Group on Unaccompanied and Separated Children, Alliance for Child Protection in Humanitarian Action, available from: https://alliancecpha.org/en/system/tdf/library/attachments/handbook-web-2017-0322.pdf?file=1&type=node&id=31236

Vearey, J. (2010) 'Hidden spaces and urban health: exploring the tactics of rural migrants navigating the city of gold', *Urban Forum*, 21(1): 37–53.

Vearey, J. (2017) 'Urban health in Johannesburg: migration, exclusion and inequality', *Urban Forum*, 28(1): 1–4.

Walker, R. (2013) *Enduring Violence: Everyday Life and Conflict in Eastern Sri Lanka*, Manchester: Manchester University Press.

Walker, R. (2018) 'Migrant mothers and the burden of care: reflections from Johannesburg', *Families, Relationships and Societies*, 7(2): 349–353.

Walker, R. and Clacherty, G. (2015) 'Shaping new spaces: an alternative approach to healing in current shelter interventions for vulnerable women in Johannesburg', in I. Palmary, B. Hamber and L. Núñez (eds) *Healing and Change in the City of Gold: Case Studies of Coping and Support in Johannesburg*, Cham: Springer International Publishing, pp 31–58.

Walker, R. and Vearey, J. (2019) *Gender, Migration and Health in SADC: A Focus on Women and Girls, Policy Brief 1*, policy report, Johannesburg: Sonke Gender Justice.

Walker, R., Vearey, J. and Nencel, N. (2017) 'Negotiating the city: exploring the intersecting vulnerabilities of non-national migrant mothers who sell sex in Johannesburg, South Africa', *Agenda*, 31(1): 91–103.

Walker, R., Mahati, S. and Magaya, I. (2020) Child *Trafficking in South Africa: Exploring the Myths and Realities*, Pretoria: The Centre for Child Law, University of Pretoria, available from: http://centreforchildlaw.co.za/wp-content/uploads/2020/08/WEB-CFCL-Child_Trafficking-Report.pdf

Walls, H.L., Vearey, J., Modisenyane, M., Chetty-Makkan, C.M., Charalambous, S., Smith, R.D. and Hanefeld, J. (2016) 'Understanding healthcare and population mobility in Southern Africa: the case of South Africa', *South African Medical Journal*, 106: 14–15.

Wessells, M.G. (2015) 'Bottom-up approaches to strengthening child protection systems: placing children, families, and communities at the center', *Child Abuse & Neglect*, 43: 8–21.

Wessells, M.G. (2018) *A Guide For Supporting Community-Led-Child Protection Processes*, New York: Child Resilience Alliance, available from: www.socialserviceworkforce.org/system/files/resource/files/Guide-Community-Led-Child-Protection.pdf

12

Emotion and Spatial Belonging: Exploring Young Migrant Men's Emotional Geographies in Cork, Ireland

Mastoureh Fathi

Introduction

Exploring home in migration research has become a vast field that has developed in different directions. An important and interesting aspect of this area is understanding the concept of home from and within dynamics of public spaces, where migrants are physically and emotionally in the presence of others. Public space, in understanding the relationship between emotions and home, is less explored than domestic space, where people construct more private and intimate relationships with objects, close members of family or others, and interior spaces of home. This chapter focuses on 'spatial belonging' as it forms in the *exteriors of domestic homes* for young male migrants who live in Cork, Ireland. The chapter is based on a recent ethnography, Youth-Home, that I conducted with young migrant men on the notion of home. Here, I focus on participants' significant emotions that are involved in relation to the notion of home in Cork. The chapter first draws on recent literature on emotional geographies of home, before moving on to the methodological approach taken in this study and a presentation and discussion of findings.

Emotional geographies of home: a theoretical framework

'Home', as a central concept in sociology and the geography of migration, has developed in different directions (Ahmed et al, 2003; Basu, 2004; Walsh,

2011; Kochan, 2016; Boccagni, 2017; Geurts et al, 2021). In much of this multidisciplinary literature, the concept of home is understood in a wider sense than a house or a dwelling (Mallett, 2004) and is more commonly equated to a place of belonging and familiarity (Ahmed, 1999; Savaş, 2010). It is also linked to a longing for one's 'homeland', where ties to past lives and identification with the 'country of origin' inform practices and feelings after migration (Flynn, 2007). Home also encompasses a variety of 'the sensory world of everyday experience' (Ahmed, 1999, p 341; Vanni Accarigi, 2017). Home is an 'ambiguous site' (Schröder, 2006) that is composed of the interconnection between protective and limiting characteristics at the same time. Mallett (2004) argues that 'home is a place but it is also a space inhabited by family, people, things and belongings – a familiar, if not comfortable, space where particular activities and relationships are "lived"'(Mallett, 2004, p 63). When combined with transnational experiences that include physical detachment of a place, movements and re-attachment to other places, home entails personal and social transformations in emotions (Brickell, 2011; Datta, 2011). Defining home in migration as a complex notion is at the heart of discussions around identity and belonging (Ahmed, 1999;; Basu, 2004; Boccagni, 2017).

In the first part of this chapter, before I discuss the interrelation between emotion and home, I detail my theoretical framework, which is composed of public space and home and emotion. I will use some theories of migrant masculinities to discuss these to highlight gendered identities that are at work in the construction of home and emotion.

Public space and home

Public spaces can constitute home for migrants (van Liempt, 2011; Raffaetá and Duff, 2013; Williamson, 2016). The role of public space in constructing and reformulating community ties is one of the key points in diaspora studies (Werbner, 2000). In diaspora studies, public performances such as religious, ethnic and cultural ceremonies are argued to have the capacity to turn the public arenas in the migration context into spaces for connections that could in turn reinforce national and ethnic identities. For example, the ways that Iranians in the US and, particularly, in Los Angeles, celebrate Persian new year (*Nowruz*) (Ghorashi, 2003) or Catholic Italians perform religious processions in London (Fortier, 2000) are examples of the use of public spaces as places of connection and meaning-making for migrants.

Related to diaspora studies, one of the areas to which human geography has contributed greatly is the micro-meanings that public migrants assign to spaces where deep feelings about other people are experienced. Amin calls them 'spaces of care', while the opposite has been discussed by Valentine (2008). She argues that public spaces can serve as spaces of 'encounters', where only fleeting moments of civility, such as interactions on public transport or in a restaurant, are experienced (Valentine, 2008). Public spaces in Western countries have turned hostile for migrants in recent years, with increasing negative imaging of refugees and migrants in the media, although some still call public spaces 'home' (Lloyd, 2017, p 121). However, I argue that public spaces do not suggest the same level of comfort, security and trust that comes with domestic space. Because of their publicness, these spaces of 'unhome' can be quite intimidating to refugees, which forms one of my recent lines of inquiry (Fathi and Soleimani, 2021).

Increasing racist and xenophobic attacks against migrants in public spaces alienate migrants from the public sphere, and this sense of exclusion, even if the attacks do not happen daily, can implicate an everyday feeling towards the public spaces where migrants live. Exploring these spaces in relation to home is also important in understanding the dynamics of domestic space (Fathi, 2021). Thus, one of the axes of the framework used in this chapter is based on the interrelation of the public space (place-making), the presence of others and the emotions attached (intersubjective shape), and the way in which geographies of home are marked for young refugees and international students.

Places, as Massey (2005, cited in Jupp, 2013, p 533) argues, are a constellation of feelings, resources, potentialities and constraints. Home is the result of continually made memories of past and translocal homes (Ahmed, 1999; Brickell and Datta, 2011) that are spread across borders. It is argued that establishing a new relationship and engaging with activities that make spaces of home meaningful in the short or long term are tightly linked to how 'feelings' are experienced (Blunt and Dowling, 2006; Brickell, 2011). One needs to remember that emotions are not always positive, and emotions about home can be negative, as they are reminiscent of trauma, displacement, separations and uncertainty about the future.

Brooks and Simpson (2012, p 84) argue that migration creates an 'emotional dislocation' due to the geographical distances that it causes between family members; usually the migrant (the person on the move), bears the emotional load of separation (Skrbiš, 2008, p 239) more than those who have stayed put. Ball (2020) looks at emotional dislocation in young migrants and argues that, for them, the sense of instability is the most significant source of ongoing stress. It is important to consider how emotion is linked to the sense of belonging. Yuval-Davis has extensively argued this connection. She explains that it is through the detachment from a place that the sense of belonging to a place is evoked, as the person who is dislocated finds where their allegiances lie mostly when they are exposed to the 'other' (Yuval-Davis, 2006). Even though research shows that identifying with geographical locations alone cannot show the emotional complexities of home in migration (Pink, 2004; Korac, 2009), it is important to know how emotional attachments to spaces form even though temporarily.

Offering a definition of home as a place filled with emotional attachments is challenging and, at times, seemingly impossible. It can turn into an essentialist endeavour that pinpoints migrants' feelings of home to (only) one location, as some have argued (Al-Ali and Koser, 2002). Quite often, migrants engage with transnational activities that show these multiple allegiances. Multiple attachments are discussed in the literature on migrants' practice of sending money to make structural houses in home-countries to reinforce transnational emotional ties (Sandu, 2013; Boccagni and Baldassar, 2015). These scholars stress the importance of materiality and structural homes (houses, dwellings, apartments, and so on) that are tightly linked to migrants' sense of attachment to the homeland and where their 'origins' lie.

Emotions and home

The 'emotional turn in geography' (Smith et al, 2009) and its particular attention to the role of emotions and their interconnections to temporalities and spatialities have become an important aspect of social science research (Bondi et al, 2007). Ryan (2008), drawing on Arlie Hochschild's theorisation of emotions as socially constructed, argues that 'migration is an ongoing emotional journey' (p 301). She investigates how Irish migrant nurses appropriately control and manage their emotions at different stages of migration: the early experiences of migration are those of feeling lonely and homesick, then they have to negotiate transnational family relationships and obligations, and finally the stresses and strains of marriage (p 301). These interconnections between the sense of self and meaning-making of spaces and places become complicated in migration contexts and in the meaning of homes, routes, roots, materialities, practices and identifications.

Once we treat home as multi-scalar (Brickell and Datta, 2011), not bound to the walls of a house, but extending to neighbourhood, towns/cities, nations and transnational experiences (Brickell and Datta, 2011), we can then distinguish the different forms of emotions involved with these scales. For example, are emotions linked to the city where migrants live similar to/different from those of the homes and interiors they create? Research shows that these are different (Walsh, 2012) because they evoke different emotional responses.

The involvement of 'ideas and feelings' and their 'multiscalarity' are the two components that lie at the heart of my discussion of emotions about home, and they need to be unpacked. I argue that home can evoke different forms of emotions and layers of feelings that are related to the various modes of belonging in transnational spaces. The vast variety of existing literature on home confirms Mallett's claims that home is a socio-spatial system that represents fusion between house as a physical unit and household as a social unit (2004, p 68). The physicality (structural materiality) of the house cannot be moved when one migrates; however, as Boccagni (2017) argues, in migration a meaningful 'recollection' and 'aspirations' for another material house are emplaced (2017, p xxiv).

Ambiguous emotions of home

Emotions about home are highly ambiguous and fluctuating. Blunt and Dowling (2006) refer to attending to these ambiguities about home as 'critical geographies of home'. Critical geographies of home interrogate the link between home, power and identity, and shift attention away from the concept of home as a place of living that is devoid of any power structures. What Blunt and Dowling argue is that contradictory emotional narratives about home (both in terms of materiality and concept) refer to a vital aspect of experiences of home that needs contextualisation: the role of power in these interrelations. Contributing to the 'critical geographies of home', Brickell (2011) also connects home to emotional engagements with materialities and the way in which, as researchers, we can 'do' critical geographies of home. She concludes that focusing on unequal power positions in the domestic space is key to critical geographies of home. She particularly encourages us to think critically about the experiences of those who live in 'the margins of home' (p 227), at different scales of home: domestic, private, global and local. Experiences of unhome, or those at the margins of home, are not positive or warm; they are devoid of authority and control and they are often racialised (Nethercote, 2022). Indeed, acknowledging negative emotions associated with power and home, when intersected with racial inequalities, encapsulates and pinpoints the recent discussions about capitalism, racism and home (Baxter and Brickell, 2014; Nethercote, 2022).

Although acknowledging that there is a dark side to home, Boccagni (2017), like others (Kearns et al, 2000), in defining home, attributes positive characteristics to home: security, safety and control (p 9). Taking into account the way that home can be positioned as a concept laid across a spectrum that evokes negative and positive feelings (rather than positioned at the border of a binary differentiation), one needs to find out what is enabling us to balance between 'private and public, domestic and civic, alienation and belonging, local and global, material and imaginative and so on' (Setten, 2008, pp 558–559). While home can be a place offering safety, control, protection and warmth, and evoke feelings of belonging, it can also turn into a space where exclusion and oppression are experienced, connoting a place to flee from (Wardhaugh, 1999; Blomley, 2006), and these feelings are evoked more in the public space. This leads me to the last section of this theoretical discussion, which considers negative feelings in migration and gender dynamics.

Negative emotions about home

Negative attributions of home for migrants are often linked to heteronormative gender roles. Studying emotion in migrants' experiences of home can open a new door to experiencing geographies of home and the importance of people, relations, politics and movements. As the process of migration involves displacement, dislocation and separation, one may argue that there are already negative emotions attached to home in migration. Several edited collections and special issues of journals (Svašek, 2008, 2010; Mai and King, 2009; Boccagni and Baldassar, 2015) argue the importance of emotions in migration processes. However, further focus on emotions in migration experiences can open up this line of enquiry into how one connects the self to the surroundings (spatial) and to different time frames (temporal). The consensus in the limited scholarship on emotions in migration is that further attention to emotions in the migrants' experiences from different angles can link their experiences of the everyday to bodies within different social realms.

The negative emotions about home in migration are not limited to the emotional impact of separation, loss and displacement. In public spaces, emotions can be harder to detect and recognise, as public spaces are fleeting and do not leave much room for emotional attachments or reflections to surface on a daily basis.

As I show in my research with young refugees and international students, emotional narratives that are expressed about public spaces in Cork are a valuable source for understanding emotions in migration. Secondly, exploring narratives of home in the public space can teach us a lot about transnational geographies such as routes of migration – an important aspect of migration trajectory that is often missed even in migration research. Migrants talking about the similarities and differences between spaces and localities in the public space can tease out these translocal connections (connecting a place in Cork to a place in Greece, and before that to a place in Turkey). By doing this, one can highlight how emotions develop throughout the trajectory of migration and, in relation to different scales, create a 'networked geography of home in migration', which I will address in the discussion section of this chapter. Before I move on to the findings section, I will briefly present the methodological tools used in this study.

Methodology

Youth Home, a study of the concept of home among young male migrants in Cork, Ireland (2019–2020) focused on two groups of male refugees and international students aged between 18 and 36 – a total of 20 participants. The project was aimed at younger migrants (18–25) but, throughout the sampling stage, I realised that such a group is hard to reach, particularly in the refugee group. The age group was thus extended to 18–36. The title of the project, 'Youth Home', was not changed due to funding restraints. The older participants belonged to the refugee group, as the asylum process in Ireland, similar to other European countries, may take a few years. Thus, participants in the refugee group (in their 30s) were, on average, older than the students (in their 20s). The main criterion for inclusion was being a migrant who has passed the hurdles of claiming asylum in Ireland or acquired a student visa. International students were included in the study because they would offer a valuable and different perspective from that of refugees in relation to homemaking, as usually they enjoy a status that is mostly seen as 'privileged' among migrant groups: they are mobile, enjoy high degrees of human capital and usually have wealthier families in their home countries on whom they can rely.

Data collection for this research was through a multi-stage ethnography based on a series of walking interviews in Cork city, combined with photography of places that migrants called 'home'. This method entailed long episodes of the researcher and the participant walking in the city of Cork, lasting between two and five hours. The walking method also included eating at a place that reminded participants of home. The participants were then invited for a second interview to discuss photos that they had to produce from their domestic spaces. This chapter is based on the data drawn from those walking interviews and associated photography.

As part of the project intended to investigate domestic spaces, it was important for participants to produce data from their places of living. There were differences between the housing situation of the two groups. All the students lived in shared accommodation and two in student halls of residence, while the refugees were all, except one, privately renting and living alone with no flat share. This difference in housing style was mainly due to a significant factor that one participant from the refugee group explained to me. Ranit, originally from Afghanistan, explained that asylum seekers in Ireland have to live in Direct Provision (DP) centres for years, sharing their rooms with other people whom they cannot select. This causes much anxiety, distress and dispute among residents. DP centres are temporary accommodation for asylum seekers, while they wait for the decision on their application. However, this temporary and communal accommodation has turned into long-term accommodation due to the lengthy time frame for processing applications. Once they leave DP centres, they prefer to live alone than share with others, although it is more difficult to secure accommodation in the tight housing market in Ireland and is much more costly for them. One refugee who, indeed, shared a house with others, did not agree to do the photography exercise in the domestic space, as he did not want to risk losing his accommodation.

Data analysis here is based on visual and narrative analysis of interviews and images following Rose (2016). I used images to understand how 'remaking' of home takes place through the choice of locations, angles and the justifications of objects and places within the photos. Due to the expansion of smart phones and photography as an everyday practice, our lives are filled with the ubiquitous presence of images (Banks, 2013). I used photography in these interviews as a collaborative method (this was not a photography project), a tool that connected me to the participants and to the process of walking and being in the city, experiencing participants' trails of meaning making of home in the urban space. In this context, images help an understanding of the dynamics of marginalisation, power relations and belonging in migration from both visual and social aspects (Pink, 2012; Fink and Lomax, 2014; Lomax, 2015; Rose, 2016). Although images produced by humans are in the context of and in response to a social action, Banks (2013) argues that they are also representations of things and demonstrate agency and the power to select, leave out and narrate from a particular standpoint. This is particularly useful for finding out why participants have some emotional attachments to certain places or objects displayed in a public place, and therefore why they want to walk with the researcher in that direction. This collaborative reconstructive method of homemaking in the public space was extremely important to their sense of being active in the research, rather than a simple participant. In this methodology, I reflect on my own experience in co-constructionist narrative analysis (Esin et al, 2013) and gendered identity as a woman conducting research with male participants. Being a migrant woman, I could relate to many experiences that they referred to as migrants, but, of course, experienced gendered differences. I have argued elsewhere (Torbati and Fathi, forthcoming) that there are specific issues related to cross-gender research that need honest and further explorations in feminist research.

Emotions about home in the public space

In this part, I discuss three dominant ways in which young male migrants experience their feelings in relation to home in migration.

Emotions and translocalism: ambiguous feelings

Emotional attachments are fluid and non-binary in migrants' lives. As Al-Ali and Koser (2002) argue, migrants develop 'multiple allegiances' to their home countries, and countries and places of residence, and perhaps to other places where they have lived or plan to live. Emotions and affective ties to seen and unseen places can fluctuate in relation to temporality, historical events and where migrants find themselves positioned in between these geographies and power relations. One of the important in-between positions is that between the place of living (country or place of residence) and the home country (country of birth and/or growing up). These two locations are significant in the personal histories of migrants. By focusing on this, I do not undermine the importance of other places. However, in the narratives of young migrants, these two locations are repeatedly compared to each other to emphasise the status of each in their formation of the sense of belonging and attachment.

The examples in this section show how these young men used descriptions of their emotions and feelings about places to make a physical connection between the two places. This physical description of these places stirs their emotions, as the scenes evoke a sense of familiarity from the past, thus connecting the places lived in the past and experienced in the present. The events in the past might have taken place just a few months before, when a sense of familiarity to the place was not shaped, such as related in this quotation from Madhav, a young international student from India, who described the significance of a bench and a tree in Cork city centre:

'So I would like to take [a] picture of this tree because when we first came, I'm with my friend. ... So we sat here for hours. For the first time we came into the city centre ... and I also have a picture of my friend. I can share it with you. And I'll also show you some pictures in my phone, which I collect during my initial days, [and] sent back to my family. I recorded a video as well ... because that is the original feeling when I came. This is something [that] is scripted.' (Madhav, interview, October 2019)

What Madhav was referring to here was his anxiety and sense of being lost as he arrived in an unknown place, the sense of anticipation combined with the fear of the unknown. His friend, who had been in Cork for longer, had promised to pick him up but was delayed. Waiting for him in the city centre, for Madhav on this first day, was juxtaposed with his present sense of familiarity, which he reflected on. He experienced two contrasting positions: being new in this context that belonged to a recent past, and his later sense of satisfaction with the familiarity of the place. It was evident from the extract and from his interview that he was becoming grounded in Cork, and he constantly compared his knowledge of the public space of Cork at the present time to the first few days when he knew 'nothing'. What can be gleaned here is that the notion of home for Madhav represented by the concrete bench referred to a passing time, a short episode in his life that was characterised by anxiety. This is an example of in-betweenness. In-between positions usually cause emotional turmoil and unfamiliar feelings about a place, as the physical presence is tied to unknown periods of stay. Cork and, particularly, this bench for Madhav represented an in-between home, which was temporary and did not represent a sense of security but, at the same time, his departure from such a fragile position in those initial days gave him a sense of security.

In-between places and emotions around them can be translocal: emotions about the proximity of immediate images and surroundings, differently or similarly compared to images of other places (Brickell and Datta, 2011. However, despite Madhav's underlying comparison, he was focusing on his emotions and how they changed over time. So, for Madhav, the focus was not spaces, but time and emotions.

Translocal comparisons were more vivid for Faraz, a refugee man in his early twenties, who compared Cork's hills to Afghanistan:

Mastoureh: What do you feel about Cork?
Faraz: It's nice. The areas around, like the mountains and things, they remind me of my country ... like, you see, like the hills and things.

Although there is not much description here of the hills and the exact definition of 'things' in Cork that resemble Afghanistan, the comparison between the two places gave him a sense of comfort and familiarity. Although Faraz lived in Iran for a long time during his childhood, with his family as refugees, his references to hills and to Afghanistan, which are combined by some sense of attachment to the place that cannot be visited, are reminiscent of an in-between home. Afghanistan, for Faraz, was manifested through Cork, two places that do not have much resemblance on the surface, but were connected through his emotions about the two places. Emotions, as Ahmed et al (2003) argue, are the bridges that connect us to different spaces and past homes as we uproot and reground through movement. Here, Faraz showed such uprooting and regrounding through comparing two places that do not have much similarity with each other, but to him had significant meanings.

Cork's hills and scenery were reflected in other participants' narratives, such as that of Ariq, a student from Indonesia from a strict family whom he tries to avoid as much as possible:

'So, if you ask me about the home, I can't say my home is a building. I would say my home is a place where I feel it's home. Especially in the no-pressure part. And you know what? Every time my parents call me here in Ireland, in Cork, and, with them, they call me and they discuss ... a pressure thing for me, I will go outside, especially to the park or maybe to the hill or maybe to the bridge. I will go there to take some air, like looking for some air, and, like, just sit down, hear some music, and it feels like relax, man, relax. No pressure at all. You need to be calm, something like that. Something like that.'

Ariq gained a sense of tranquillity from the sceneries of Cork. He did not compare Cork to other places, but the scenes offered him a sense of in-between calmness that lifted the pressure he suffered from when his parents stressed him out. Additionally, he used self-talk to calm himself in nature and, by doing this, he used his feelings to bridge his past and family members in his home country to his current surroundings and, as a result, to feel a sense of belonging to Cork.

These feelings about Cork could be about specific places, as well as about countries. For example, Mahmoud, a PhD student from Egypt, argued:

Mastoureh: Do you belong here?
Mahmoud: To the city or to the country or to the place?
Mastoureh: Tell me about all of it.
Mahmoud: To the place, yes. To the city, kind of. To the country, no.
Mastoureh: What do you mean by place?
Mahmoud: Place is the university, the research, the people that I've met, the surroundings. The city is the city, like, you know, the places where I go and where I visit and spend time and stuff like this, you know. As a country I haven't been through the whole country. I went to Dublin once. I find it very nice, but at the same time crowded. It reminds me of Cairo.

As we see from Mahmoud's words, the presence of home countries was important in making sense of Cork as home. Remembering places in other countries and making connections between the present location and a specific location in other places is what 'translocalism' refers to (Brickell and Datta, 2011). These connections between past and present are embedded within the feelings associated with places: they are ambiguous and are temporarily made. Feelings associated with these connections between past homes and present homes act as bridges. Feelings about places (Cork, Afghanistan, parks, university) carry elements of belonging across time, space and people to present homes, which are not fixed. These act as in-between spaces and evoke ambiguous feelings.

Emotions and future homes: hope

The second characteristic of young migrants' feelings of home is encapsulated in a sense of excitement about the possibilities that their future lives might bring. The 'unknown' element of not knowing what future life will be like, for young migrants, is expressed with an aura of positivity in relation to homemaking. Some of the participants were hopeful and aspirational, and their narratives were focused on comparing the present to the future. Negassi, a young student from a refugee family who arrived in Ireland from Ethiopia, spent much of his walking interview in silence. Negassi was determined to make a successful career for himself to be able to look after his siblings financially in the near future. His spatial belonging was very much framed in relation to financial security:

Mastoureh: If you were to choose a city in Ireland to build your future life, where would it be?
Negassi: I would say Dublin.
Mastoureh: Dublin? Why is that?
Negassi: One, there's big opportunities there and there are a lot of big companies there I could work for. And, I don't know, I love like crowded cities, I would say, yeah. The bigger the city, I think the bigger the opportunity I get. So I would love to move to Dublin.

Building a home for a young migrant like Negassi is tied to fulfilling and aspiring towards a brighter future that accompanies larger networks of people, corporations and structures. Negassi was young and aspiring and, for him, home was translated into a successful career that could offer him some stability. This sense of security that he could get through working for 'big companies' in Dublin, a neoliberal dream, was presenting itself as a motivator in the hard time he was currently experiencing. He was living in one room with another person who was hostile towards Negassi. He was feeling lonely in Cork but had to finish his degree in engineering and was hoping to stay in Ireland and look after his younger brother. His sense of responsibility was combined with his excitement about job opportunities that could arise after he graduated. His emotions about Dublin and the possible job 'opportunities' were directly linked to how he hoped his future home would be.

Other participants referred to such opportunities that came with the choice of spaces too. Sometimes the importance of opportunities was described in relation to spatial factors, such as the size of the place and the density of population in that area or the level of affordability, but at other times they were about their emotions about the place. Oorjit, a student from India, said:

'Now I've been in Cork for so many months, what I've heard, I would like to work in Cork. Dublin is very expensive for housing. So I would like to live in a very urban place or a busy place. But for me I wouldn't – I think that's the place for me.' (Oorjit, interview transcripts, December 2019)

In this interview, Oorjit referred to future possibilities in life and evaluated different places, such as Dublin and Cork's viability for starting a family of his own: "[I]f I want to just live, I would like to live in a quiet place … to form a family. … Besides, where I grew up it's like not a very big town. So Cork is still big for me compared to my town." What was important for Oorjit and others who mentioned different cities was also the time that is spent in a location that could lead to making family life in that place, which could at times be encapsulated in relation to patriarchal norms and meaning-makings, such as marrying in order to make a family home (Pease, 2009). As such, future homes as described here are about evaluating what the future may entail in relation to spaces but also people who would occupy these spaces. Others similarly expressed how places are evaluated in relation to their suitability for family formation. Ranit, a very young refugee from Afghanistan, said:

> 'I want to go to Manchester. Me and my brother we want to set up a business. Like I worked here for a few years in a mobile phone shop. I'm good with technical stuff, like computers and he [his brother] said, "If you come there, we might open up a shop." Plus, he said, "I could find you a wife here!"' (Ranit, interview transcripts, March 2020)

Ranit's excitement about the possibilities of making a life in another country (UK) was expressed directly. Similar to some other refugee participants, his experiences of public spaces were very much hampered by the stark racism he experienced within mainstream society. Therefore, much focus was diverted towards the possibilities of expanding domestic life and investing in it both financially and emotionally. As can be seen, some of these young migrant men viewed their futures filled with opportunities and the possibilities of making new homes. These new homes could be about job opportunities, living in a larger city, setting up a family. The excitement that accompanied these opportunities and possibilities was made possible by virtue of them either having high human capital (such as an internationally recognised degree) in the case of international students, or Irish citizenship in the case of refugees, which would allow them to be mobile. In any case, as we can see, feeling positively about making a home in a future time is a characteristic of their age as well as their immigration status (becoming Irish citizens after having their refugee status confirmed) or switching to a work visa (in the case of students), which facilitated the 'idea of moving' to a different place in search of a home.

Emotions and current homes: alienation and little comforts

This final section is about how public places can offer alienation, but this sense of alienation is reduced by some everyday rituals. The focus is on the everyday practice of home and finding little pockets in the city where migrants viewed certain practices as familiar and desirable.

Mahmoud, one of the participants whom I referred to earlier, discussed two important places in Cork: a place where he could find halal food and a mosque that he frequently visited to pray.

> 'This place has, like, the shops where I buy my [groceries] and stuff like that. So you see an old Lidl and Tesco just here. So I buy my [groceries] from here. ... And if you walk all this way, we will see the river. Once you cross the river you will find the mosque, so the Masjid where I meet, like, some of my friends and pray. And in front of this, like, some halal food where I can buy my food and stuff like that.' (Mahmoud, interview transcripts, November 2019)

He explained with excitement how the mosque has two doors, one for men (black door) and one for women (red door). Going into detail about the particularities and rituals of the mosque's operation, the gendered divisions and the logics behind every aspect of this location, he elaborated on how this particular mosque is situated within the Muslim communities in Cork. When I asked him why he came to this one, although there are other bigger mosques in the city, he said:

> 'It's a community thing. So this is where the Egyptian and the Arabic-speaking people come. The other mosques you're just – you know ... sometimes I go to the other mosques, but the other mosque you will see, like, there is another mosque this way. Pakistanian [*sic*] people go there. So I meet a lot of Pakistanian [*sic*] and Indian and stuff like that. So this is the mosque, if you wanted me to take a picture?' (Mahmoud, interview transcripts, November 2019)

The intimacy of this small mosque as well as the location being popular with Arab migrants in Cork made it a preferred social place to other mosques. Here Mahmoud referred to the importance of praying as well as the bond he shared with other people. These feelings of intimacy that he experienced came from sharing some similar characteristics (for example, speaking Arabic, praying at the same time, knowing the passcode for the door). The community members trusted each other to a point that everyone knew the passcode that opened the door without a caretaker being present: "Well, it has certain times where you can just go inside. But it has a lock with a password [passcode] on the door. So if I want to just go inside now, I can just put the password, this password shared between the people who comes to prayer. So I know the password." The present everyday life based on routine practices can give a sense of familiarity and security to these migrant men. Ranit, a young refugee from Afghanistan, talked about how he took long walks in the park to forget about the alienation he felt at work and in society.

Boccagni (2017) characterises three elements that are vital in calling a place home. These are the senses of familiarity, security and control. As was seen in the interview extracts, in all the different emotions expressed about home in the public space, most revolve around these three elements (or lack thereof). Although many of these participants' experiences were filled with adventures and feelings of loss and separation (from other people, from other spaces and other times), there was still a sense of excitement that accompanied these narratives. The excitement, in my view, is strongly linked to their age. Young migrants invest much on their future plans through emotionally connecting with an 'idea of home' (Fathi and Ní Laoire, 2021). Through moving from one country to another, their emotions about home become entangled with the current homes, but the idea of a 'real' home is mostly postponed until the future. In other words, what they experience currently is not about making a home at the present time, but one that can be invested in and actualised in a future time.

Conclusion

This chapter focused on the importance of emotions about constructing a home in the public space, narrated by a group of young migrant men who live in the city of Cork, Ireland. The two groups of migrants (international students and refugees) show similarities in terms of what they think of home in migration. Through conducting visual and narrative analysis of their stories and by focusing on the role of emotions in how they construct migrant homes, I presented three different categories of emotional responses to the public home.

The first focused on the feelings about particular locations in Cork in the current time and its resemblance to other places and other times. Some participants in this study focused on the similarities between Cork and other lived locations. I argue that such comparisons made the emotions about home ambiguous and, as a result, temporary. Emotions about these translocal connections are used to bridge between these locations while, at the same time, they are reminiscent of departures and losses experienced through displacement.

The second category of emotions are of hope, which is connected to possible future homes. The sense of hope that accompanies thinking about future homes is encapsulated through speaking of personal and career plans. Hope and aspiration are characteristic of young migrants' narratives of home. These are usually focused on the formation of a family (all were in heterosexual relationships) and achievement of home through such endeavour.

Finally, I discussed emotions that accompany narratives of present time, a sense of alienation from everyday experiences and the little comforts that migrants gain from rituals and practices.

This chapter claims that construction of home and experiencing spatial belonging in the public space are postponed to the future and that is a characteristic of young migrants' experiences. Although emotions, age and gender in the study of homemaking are a thriving area in understanding young people's experiences of home, there needs to be further research in this area.

Acknowledgements
Youth Home was a Marie Skłodowska-Curie Individual fellowship, funded by the H2020 scheme. Grant number 843333.

References
Ahmed, S. (1999) 'Home and away: narratives of migration and estrangement', *International Journal of Cultural Studies*, 2(3): 329–347.

Ahmed, S., Castaneda, C., Fortier, A.M. and Sheller, M. (2003) *Uprootings/Regroundings: Questions of Home and Migration*, Oxford: Berg.

Al-Ali, N. and Koser, K. (eds) (2002) *New Approaches to Migration? Transnational Communities and the Transformation of Home*, London: Routledge.

Banks, M. (2013) 'Analysing images', in U. Flick (ed) *The SAGE Handbook of Qualitative Data Analysis*, London: SAGE.

Basu, P. (2004) 'My own island home: the Orkney homecoming', *Journal of Material Culture*, 9(1): 27–42.

Baxter, R. and Brickell, K. (2014) 'For home unmaking', *Home Cultures*, 11(2): 133–143.

Blomley, N. (2006) 'Uncritical critical geography?', *Progress in Human Geography*, 30(1): 87–94.

Blunt, A. and Dowling, R. (2006) *Home*, London: Routledge.

Boccagni, P. (2017) *Migration and the Search for Home: Mapping Domestic Space in Migrants' Everyday Lives*, New York: Palgrave Macmillan.

Boccagni, P. and Baldassar, L. (2015) 'Emotions on the move: mapping the emergent field of emotion and migration', *Emotion, Space and Society*, 16: 73–80.

Bondi, L., Davidson, J. and Smith, M. (2007) 'Introduction: Geography's "emotional turn"', in J. Davidson, L. Bondi and M. Smith (eds) *Emotional Geographies*, Aldershot: Ashgate.

Brickell, K. (2011) '"Mapping" and "doing" critical geographies of home', *Progress in Human Geography*, 36(2): 225–244.

Brickell, K. (2014) '"Plates in a basket will rattle": marital dissolution and home "unmaking" in contemporary Cambodia', *Geoforum*, 51(1): 262–272.

Brickell, K. and Datta, A. (2011) *Translocal Geographies: Spaces, Places and Connections*, Farnham: Ashgate.

Brooks, A. and Simpson, R. (2012) *Emotions in Transmigration Transformation, Movement and Identity*, Basingstoke: Palgrave Macmillan.

Esin, C., Fathi, M. and Squire, C. (2013) 'Narrative analysis: the constructionist approach', in U. Flick (ed) *SAGE Handbook of Analysing Qualitative Data*, London: SAGE, pp 203–216.

Fathi, M. (2021) '"My life is on hold": examining home, belonging and temporality among migrant men in Ireland', *Journal of Gender, Place and Culture*. DOI: 10.1080/0966369X.2021.1916445

Fathi, M. and Ní Laoire, C. (2021) 'Urban home: young male migrants constructing home in the city', *Journal of Ethnic and Migration Studies*. DOI: 10.1080/1369183X.2021.1965471

Fathi, M. and Soleimani, T. (2021) 'Stay at unhome: asylum seekers' struggles in domestic spaces of heim(s) in Germany', *The Sociological Observer*, Special Issue: Black Lives Matter, 2(1): 37–44.

Fink, J. and Lomax, H. (2014) 'Challenging images? Dominant, residual and emergent meanings in on-line media representations of child poverty', *Journal for the Study of British Cultures*, 1(21): 79–95.

Flynn, M. (2007) 'Reconstructing "home/lands" in the Russian Federation: migrant-centred perspectives of displacement and resettlement', *Journal of Ethnic and Migration Studies*, 33(3): 461–481.

Fortier, A.M. (2000) *Migrant Belongings: Memory, Space, Identity*, Oxford: Berg.

Geurts, N., Davids, T. and Spierings, N. (2021) 'The lived experience of an integration paradox: why high-skilled migrants from Turkey experience little national belonging in the Netherlands', *Journal of Ethnic and Migration Studies*, 47(1): 69–87.

Ghorashi, H. (2003) *Ways to Survive, Battles to Win: Iranian Women Exiles in the Netherlands and United States*, New York: Nova Science Publishers.

Jupp, E. (2013). '"I feel more at home here than in my own community": approaching the emotional geographies of neighbourhood policy', *Critical Social Policy*, 33(3), 532–553.

Kearns, A. Rosemary H., Ellaway, A. and MaCintyre, S. (2000) '"Beyond four walls": the psycho-social benefits of home: Evidence from west central Scotland', *Housing Studies*, 15(3), 387–410.

Kochan, D. (2016) 'Home is where I lay down my hat? The complexities and functions of home for internal migrants in contemporary China', *Geoforum*, 71: 21–32.

Korac, M. (2009) *Remaking Home: Experiences of Reconstructing Life, Place and Identities in Rome and Amsterdam*, Oxford: Berghahn Books.

Lloyd, J. (2017) 'At home in public: the work of mobility and anti-racist mobile witnessing practices', in J. Lloyd and E. Vasta (eds) *Reimagining Home in the 21st Century*, Cheltenham: Edward Elgar, pp 121–134.

Lomax, H. (2015) 'Seen and heard? Ethics and agency in participatory visual research with children, young people and families', *Families, Relationships and Societies*, 4(3): 493–502.

Mai, N. and King, R. (2009) 'Love, sexuality and migration: mapping the issue(s)', *Mobilities*, 4(3), 295–307.

Mallett, S. (2004) 'Understanding home: a critical review of the literature', *The Sociological Review*, 52(1): 62–89.

Nethercote, M. (2022) 'Racialized geographies of home: property, unhoming and other possible futures', *Progress in Human Geography*. https://doi.org/10.1177/03091325221104480

Pink, S. (2004) *Home Truths: Gender, Domestic Objects and Everyday Life*, Oxford: Berg.

Pink, S. (2012) 'Domestic time in the sensory home: the textures and rhythms of knowing, practice, memory and imagination', in E. Keighley (ed) *Time, Media and Modernity*, New York: Palgrave, pp 184–200.

Raffaetá, R. and Duff, C. (2013) 'Putting belonging into place: place experience and sense of belonging among Ecuadorian migrants in an Italian Alpine region', *City & Society*, 25(3): 328–347.

Rose, G. (2016) *Visual Methodologies: An Introduction to Researching with Visual Materials*, Thousand Oaks, CA: SAGE.

Ryan, L. (2008) 'Navigating the emotional terrain of families "here" and "there": women, migration and the management of emotions', *Journal of Intercultural Studies*, 29: 299–313.

Sandu, A. (2013) 'Transnational homemaking practices: identity, belonging and informal learning', *Journal of Contemporary European Studies*, 21(4): 496–512.

Savaş, Ö. (2010) 'The collective Turkish home in Vienna: aesthetic narratives of migration and belonging', *Home Cultures*, 7(3): 313–340.

Schröder, N. (2006) *Spaces and Places in Motion: Spatial Concepts in Contemporary American Literature*, Tübingen: Gunter Narr Verlag Tübingen.

Setten, G. (2008) 'Blunt and Dowling, Home, 2006: review 1', *Social and Cultural Geography*, 9(5): 558–559.

Skrbiš, Z. (2008) 'Transnational families: theorising migration, emotions and belonging', *Journal of Intercultural Studies*, 29(3): 231–246.

Smith, M., Davidson, J., Cameron, L. and Bondi, L. (eds) (2009) *Emotion, Place and Culture*, Farnham: Ashgate.

Svašek, M. (2008) 'Who care? families and feeling in movement', *Journal of Intercultural Studies*, 29(3): 213–230.

Svašek, M. (2010) 'On the move: emotions and human mobility', *Journal of Ethnic and Migration Studies*, 36(6): 865–880.

Valentine, G. (2008) 'Living with difference: reflections on geographies of encounter', *Progress in Human Geography*, 32(3): 323–337.

van Liempt I. (2011) '"And then one day they all moved to Leicester": Somalis' relocation from the Netherlands to the United Kingdom', *Population, Space and Place*, 17: 254–266.

Vanni Accarigi, I. (2017) 'Transcultural objects, transcultural homes', in J. Lloyd and E. Vasta (eds) *Reimagining Home in the 21st Century*, Cheltenham: Edgar Elgar, pp 192–206.

Walsh, K. (2011) 'Migrant masculinities and domestic space: British home-making practices in Dubai', *Transactions of the Institute of British Geographers*, 36(4): 516–529.

Walsh, K. (2012) 'Emotion and migration: British transnationals in Dubai', *Environment and Planning D: Society and Space*, 30(1): 43–59.

Wardhaugh, D. (1999) 'The unaccommodated woman: home, homelessness and identity', *Sociological Review*, 47(1): 91–109.

Werbner, P. (2000) 'Divided loyalties, empowered citizenship? Muslims in Britain', *Citizenship Studies*, 4(3): 307–324.

Williamson, R. (2016) 'Vernacular cosmopolitanisms in suburban peripheries: a case study in multicultural Sydney', *Sites: A Journal of Social Anthropology and Cultural Studies*, 13(1), 111–133.

Yuval-Davis, N. (2006) 'Belonging and the politics of belonging', *Patterns of Prejudice*, 40(3): 197–214.

13

Homemaking through Music in Urban Africa: Creating Opportunities as a Refugee and a Migrant in Kinshasa and Dar es Salaam

Catherina Wilson

Introduction

Esatis (25) is a self-taught and engaged slam poet. Nathan-2K (30) is a gospel music guitarist. Esatis and Nathan-2K are artist names. Esatis fled the Central African Republic (CAR) in the aftermath of the 2013 *coup d'état* that plunged his country into a period of uncertainty and found refuge in Kinshasa (Democratic Republic of the Congo). Nathan-2K grew up in war-torn Eastern Congo. In 2017 he moved to Dar es Salaam where he was offered a job in a church choir. The two artists do not know each other. Yet their life trajectories, which meet in this chapter, share similarities: both were born in the 1990s and grew up in a context of 'neither war nor peace' (Larmer et al, 2013); and both left their home city and made their way to an African megapolis.

Based on these two trajectories, the purpose of this chapter is threefold. First, by concentrating on trajectories within Africa, it problematises South–North migration narratives. Second, by placing the biographical trajectory of one 'migrant' next to that of one 'refugee', it questions the artificial migrant–refugee divide. Third, by focusing on personal success, rather than on vulnerability, the chapter challenges, or at least complements, images of the vulnerable refugee or migrant. The accent comes to lie on self-affirmation and dignity instead.

Even if the lives of two individuals cannot contain all the diversity and complexities of youth in Africa, a biographical approach, nevertheless, sheds light on the context of critical decision moments in these young men's life trajectories. It is by exploring these moments that a deeper understanding of how lives unfold in a constant interplay of structure and agency is brought to life. In this chapter, moreover, agency, as it shapes the personal geographies of Esatis and Nathan-2K, is understood through music. It is through music that both artists constructed a niche for themselves in Kinshasa and Dar es Salaam respectively, turning these two cities into their homes. Throughout, the chapter alludes to meaningful spaces to which Esatis and Nathan-2K contribute musically. Woven together, these spaces (which include music recording studios, cultural podia, university classrooms, churches and the digital sphere) constitute some of many layers in urban African soundscapes.

The chapter is divided as follows. After a theoretical section that touches on migration, urban youth and space, I will briefly describe the approach and methods employed during the data collection period, paying particular attention to the changing roles of the artists and the researcher. The four empirical sections that follow deal chronologically with Esatis' and Nathan-2K's childhoods, their migration journeys to a city in a foreign country and, finally, with their emancipation through music.

Theoretical framework

The focus in migration and refugee studies on people leaving conflict-inflicted countries in the so-called Global South to 'the more stable' countries in the Global North is misleading. In Africa, migration between and within countries on the continent by far surpasses intercontinental migration. Eighty-six per cent of the world's refugees find refuge in the Global South.[1] In fact, only one-quarter of the international migrants south of the Sahara leave the continent (Landau and Bakewell, 2018). Additionally, there is a tendency to de-historicise refugee mobility and migration; in fact Africans have been on the move long before the refugee crises of the last decades, both for reasons related and unrelated to the crises (Whitehouse, 2012; Landau and Bakewell, 2018; Wilson, 2019).

By juxtaposing the trajectory of a migrant with that of a refugee, I also question the distinction made between these two groups. In legal terms, the difference appears concrete. Western media and public discourse equally make a stark difference between refugees and (economic) migrants, which is consequently linked to a politically inspired degree of deservingness. While the former are allowed in (if they can prove their vulnerability), the latter are unforgivingly forced out. In practice, the enactment of the refugee–migrant distinction is more messy (Zetter et al, 2020). The vital conjunctures (Johnson-Hanks, 2002) or decision-making moments (De

Bruijn and Lalaye, 2016), with which Esatis and Nathan-2K are confronted, do not necessarily differ diametrically. Both 'categories' can coexist in the life story of one individual.

Studies of urban refugees (and migrants) describe their journeys, livelihood strategies, modes of integration, sentiments of belonging, and their personal geographies in new and changing urban environments. Herein, Vigh's reviewed concept of navigation, as 'motion within motion', remains highly relevant (Vigh, 2009). That is the navigation of migrants who try to disentangle themselves from the confining structures of an environment that is undergoing constant change itself. But navigation alone, also understood as a mode of improvising, does not do justice to Esatis' and Nathan-2K's active making of strategic choices to create opportunities for themselves (see also Ungruhe, 2021).

In this chapter, I want to focus on hope and aspirations – in addition to constraints – as drivers of mobility (Bal and Willems, 2014; Wilson Janssens, 2018; Schapendonk and Belloni, 2020). Even if Esatis and Nathan-2K have left belligerent environments, their decision to move out was equally informed by the 'hope for a better future' (Turner, 2015) as much as it was coloured by the confining structures they left behind. Without overemphasising agency or resilience, this chapter aims to contribute to a growing literature that moves beyond frameworks of mere victimisation. Through the victimisation lens, refugees are turned into *vulnerables*, people who are acted upon (Clark-Kazak, 2011). Frustrated, Esatis pleads for the opposite: "Refugees should be seen as any other person. They should be treated with respect. They should not be considered from the outset as vulnerable people to be spat upon, people about whom others talk nonsense" (Interview, Esatis, WhatsApp audio call, 7 January 2021). Thus, admitting that structures continue to confine migrants' trajectories, it needs to be acknowledged that the latter are equally shaped by their moments of decision-making. Nathan-2K and Esatis are as actors of their own lives; they make decisions and through them they build opportunities for themselves and for those around them. In both trajectories, music informed their decisions and gave meaning to their lives. Thanks to their musical skills, Esatis and Nathan-2K have turned their refuge and migration into an asset (Turner, 2015). To do so, both artists do not sit still but roam the city on their way from choir practice to the recording studio, or in search for other artists to collaborate with. They frequent different spaces where people meet: the university, the church, artistic podia and cultural venues – not to forget the packed buses stuck in traffic, which they use to travel between spaces. In their meanders, they become inspired. Music shapes their mobility. At the same time, music creates spaces where they can emplace themselves as dignified individuals in the world.

Russell, who carried out research among Congolese refugees in Uganda, writes that there is a great value in music making and music sharing, because they create a sense of home away from home (Russell, 2011, p 309). The spaces where music is played are not always clearly delineated, nor do they fall under dyadic notions dividing the public from private (De Backer, 2016). Sound travels through walls and becomes part of the urban soundscape. When played within the premises of a church, choir repetitions are heard on sidewalks inviting the curious passers-by to peek inside. Equally, music made in recording studios does not stay within the confinements of these studios. Conversely, it is impossible to lock oneself out of what is being played on the pavement outdoors. Music transgresses established (social) boundaries from the public into the private and vice versa. It does not only travel sonically but also digitally on social media, for instance through YouTube videos or WhatsApp statuses. In addition to the physical spaces enumerated earlier, this chapter views the digital space as an urban space used by Esatis and Nathan-2K to promote their work. Music mingles public and private spaces, but also online and offline ones (Lane, 2016).

When describing non-citizens, however, there is the need to nuance public spaces. Contrary to what Simpson suggests, public spaces are not automatically accessible without permission to all (Simpson, 2011). Migrants and refugees often feel the need to comply to specific social norms in order not to appear foreign in the eyes of others, which ultimately reduces their freedom of mobility. Here I would like to go back to Russell, who, by pointing at the value of music in shaping spaces, also underlines the feelings of home it recreates. When discussing youth, however, the future is equally relevant to the past. The ways in which Esatis and Nathan-2K create music in public space is a central component in understanding emergent public spaces and citizenship practices in Africa's present and future (Dolby, 2006). Popular culture has important implications for the public spaces of a society, including the way in which youth conceptualise and enact their roles as citizens and contribute to their host society (Dolby, 2006). In the following sections, we turn to how Esatis and Nathan-2K make use of urban space and enact their roles as foreign citizens in their new country of residence, but first a note on method is due.

Methods and trajectories

In an attempt to define trajectories, scholars have moved beyond the journey from home to host country to include onward movements, periods of emplacement, detours, transit statuses, waiting, entrapment, serial decision-making and continuous navigation (Schapendonk et al, 2018). Trajectories are equally informed by aspirations and future perspectives. When collecting life stories of young people, one should keep in mind that the future is an important protagonist in their stories, at times more so than the past. As journeys are never complete, the term 'trajectory', with its outlook on the future, leans itself to the biographical narratives of youth. This does not mean that the past does not play a role in shaping their trajectories. As Schapendonk and Belloni underline, trajectories are closely linked to people's biographies (Pascual-de-Sans in Schapendonk and Belloni, 2020). 'Biographical trajectories', then, stretch out to meet past and future narratives in an individual's life. As biographies would do, biographical trajectories focus on and temporalise mobility. Is not life a trip after all?

Basing a chapter on two individuals runs the risk of being an idiosyncrasy. Can the lives and decision moments of two individuals stand for a generation across two countries? Certainly not. Are they representative? I believe they are. By taking a close look at Esatis' and Nathan-2K's biographical trajectories, this chapter focuses on decisive moments in their lives and the role of music therein. Their stories open up the possibility to explore these crucial moments not in a vacuum, but in connection to the sociopolitical context too; they form biographies in context (De Bruijn et al, 2017). If properly contextualised, the biographical trajectories allow for an exploration of the interaction between agency and structure and provide insights into community broader dynamics (Cole and Knowles, 2001). It is precisely this interconnectedness that is relevant for a broader analysis as it provides a basis for new understandings and details that pass otherwise unnoticed (Maynes et al, 2012). Understanding one, or in this case two, stories contributes to understanding the complexities of lives in communities (Kwaks, 2018), also in a context of urban displacement.

The stories of Esatis and Nathan-2K are two out of a greater number of biographical trajectories. The data on which they are based were collected in two different periods and in two different locations: in Kinshasa between 2013 and 2015 and in Dar es Salaam in 2019. The methods included a combination of interviews, informal conversations, participant observation and walks. Considering, as we saw above, that offline and online spaces mix, digital ethnography and social media conversations and interviews were part of the methods too. We have kept in contact with Esatis and Nathan-2K through Facebook and WhatsApp. One of the interviews was held through WhatsApp voice messages in January 2021. Even if both artists gave me their consent to write this chapter (and we have been communicating throughout the writing process), it remains a challenge to do justice to their stories and their voices. As a female Western-schooled researcher working on the Global South, the relationship with Esatis and Nathan-2K is imbued in power differences: it is easier for me to travel and meet them in Africa than the other way around. Esatis and I met on one occasion during the Ndjam s'enflamme en Slam festival that took place in Chad in 2017.[2] Some aspects of our positionality are ascribed (Holmes, 2020), such as gender, race, class and cultural background. Nevertheless, we should not essentialise these aspects, as they can be context-dependent and fluid too. Dual-heritage people, for instance, can be viewed as belonging to one or the other, depending on who the observer is. Others, though, are in constant flux (Rowe, 2014): locations in time and space are not fixed, and personal views evolve. While some aspects of our positionality are visible, others are invisible (Reyes, 2020). My own migration background has doubtlessly coloured my view on mobility (as being the norm, rather than the exception) and made me empathise with migrants, as decision-makers and not as *vulnerables*.

Even if I have juxtaposed Nathan-2K's story with that of Esatis, the nature of the exchanges with Nathan-2K differs from those with Esatis. I received Nathan-2K's phone number through a common friend, contacted him through WhatsApp and met him in person in July 2019. Although I have followed him to different places in the city and met some members of his family, our relationship is short-lived, less intense and less profound than my relationship with Esatis, whom I have known since 2014. With the passing of time, I have observed how Esatis, despite living in a foreign country, turned into an artist and an engaged citizen. My approach to his trajectory is longitudinal, yet equally incomplete, as his trajectory has not come to an end, and one can never know every detail. While our relationship started off as one between a researcher and an informant, it changed throughout the years and has grown into a friendship of mutual respect, and, at times, a joint endeavour towards a common goal. The process has been humbling. I reflect on this change in terms of the changing role of the 'researcher'; from somebody who collected data and pretended to be a 'voice of the voiceless', to a facilitator of projects, not my own, but Esatis'. Through our exchanges, I am continuously reminded that writing *with* someone is more enriching than writing *about* someone (Ingold, 2017).

Leaving a conflict-afflicted home

Leaving Butembo

Nathan-2K was born in 1991 in a small village in the province of North Kivu (Eastern Congo), the ninth child in a family of ten. When he was still a small boy, his parents decided to move to Butembo in order to offer their children a better education. There they worked as evangelists and merchants. Nathan-2K grew up surrounded by hymns and gospel music. From a young age, he loved music and eagerly went to church in order to see and hear people play different instruments. Nathan-2K soon joined the church choir and dreamed of being a musician one day. As there were no music schools in Butembo, his first music teacher was one of his older brothers who taught him to play the guitar. Nathan-2K looks back at this period of his life with a smile. He loved living in Butembo and spending time with his friends. Nathan-2K's description of an idyllic childhood stands in stark contrast to the way the international media has portrayed the Kivus in the past three decades, a mineral-rich, rebel-plagued zone within a violent fragile state: "Life in Butembo was wonderful, I think, because I had good friends. It was also with these good friends that I managed to achieve my dreams, what I wanted to become, it was with my friends" (Interview, Nathan-2K, Dar es Salaam, 30 July 2019).

As he grew older, Nathan-2K joined bigger and more famous church choirs and religious youth orchestras in Butembo. These choirs and orchestras recorded their songs on DVDs, which became highly popular. Nathan-2K's choir was invited to sing in different locations, and they started travelling around the region, performing in Goma and even across the border in Rwanda. Tanzanian church ministries travelled and performed in a similar fashion; the different choirs met one another during religious gatherings. The choir's DVDs also reached Tanzania and, according to Nathan-2K, Tanzanians fell in love with their music. It was they who got in touch with Nathan-2K's *mjomba* (paternal uncle in Swahili; in contrast to Western traditions, *mjomba* is considered as a father), Moises, who was a musician, a composer and a music teacher. Moises had not only studied music informally in Butembo, but, having spent time in Kenya and Kinshasa to broaden his knowledge, he was a qualified and respected musician. Nathan-2K's *mjomba* was invited to Dar es Salaam to teach music and lead the choir. With time, and taking into account that he performed live during church services, Moises brought his own musicians (and extended family members) to join him in Dar es Salaam. They included a drummer, a pianist and a second guitarist. Nathan-2K decided to join his *mjomba* in Dar es Salaam to continue playing music in the church where Moises was working. He left Congo in his mid-twenties: "I left Butembo for Goma. After that, I entered Rwanda and then Tanzania. At that time, we came with my aunt, who came to meet her husband, my paternal uncle. ... I travelled by bus. ... It took me three days. There are many [Congolese] who travel this route" (Interview, Nathan-2K, Dar es Salaam, 30 July 2019).

In her article, 'Refugees' journeys of trust', Lyytinen associates refugees' (mis)trust with reasons of flight, travel and arrival. She argues that this association is essential for understanding refugees' experiences of protection and search for durable solutions in exile (Lyytinen, 2017, p 506). Trust was certainly at play when Nathan-2K took the decision to leave Butembo. It took Nathan-2K three days by bus (or rather buses) to travel from Butembo to Dar es Salaam. His journey is embedded in particularised social (interpersonal) trust (Lyytinen, 2017, p 496). He did not need to travel alone and he knew his uncle would host him in Dar es Salaam on arrival.

Knowing this facilitated making the decision to leave. Nathan-2K's road seemed to have been paved for him.

Leaving Bangui

In 1995, around the time Nathan-2K left his village to Butembo, Esatis took his first breath of life in Bangui. He was born into a household of many children. His father worked as a photographer for the former president Kolingba. His mother was a gifted trader. Esatis grew up in Ouango, a neighbourhood known to be dominantly inhabited by the Yakoma, the ethnic group to which both his parents, Kolingba and a majority of the army staff in the late 1990s belonged. In 2001, after years of mutinies, repression, uncertainty and failed coups, the Yakoma were one of the groups that came to be targeted, and many decided to flee persecution by crossing the border into Congo. Esatis spent two years of his childhood in a refugee camp 35 kilometres across the border from his home city. He has bad memories of this time and remembers the lack of food, the lack of opportunities, the insalubrious environment and especially the difficulty in studying: "We didn't study well. Even though they offered primary education, we didn't study well because diseases prevented us from doing so. ... We were thwarted in our education" (Interview, Esatis, Kinshasa, 26 August 2014).

After two years, a *coup d'état* brought about a new regime, and Esatis and his family returned to Bangui. A sense of normality descended upon the city, even though there were worrisome signs of new rebellions in the northern part of the country. Esatis would divide his time between school, friends and the church. Just like Nathan-2K, Esatis, too, has joyful memories of growing up in Bangui, of eating sweet mangoes and of playing at the beach on the river's sandbanks during the dry season. Even though he was not gifted in singing, he joined the church choir, where he learned to rap. Sexion d'Assaut, a Parisian hip hop band composed mainly of children of African migrants, was equally an inspiration to him.

As he was about to finish school, Esatis envisaged becoming a writer. Unfortunately for him and so many other pupils and students, the Seleka rebel coalition marched towards Bangui and staged a *coup d'état* in March 2013. The city fell prey to chaos and plundering; thousands fled. At first, Esatis was firm in his decision to stay put, never to leave Bangui again. He did not want to endure a life in the camp again. Past experiences of conflict and the internalisation of experienced violence colour the decisions of individuals (De Bruijn and Both, 2018). But, after their house had been raided, Esatis' mother handed her son a significant sum of money and convinced him to cross the river into Congo again. Having the means, Esatis did not set foot in a refugee camp but sought a route to Kinshasa, where he hoped to continue his studies.

The mega-city as a site for opportunities
Slam poetry festivals in Kinshasa

After crossing the border by canoe, travelling by truck and motor bike, staying at a friend's house in Gemena (the provincial capital of the northern Sud-Ubangi province) while waiting to take a plane, Esatis arrived in Kinshasa. Unlike the journey of Nathan-2K, Esatis' journey was not always embedded in particularised interpersonal trust (Lyytinen, 2017). On the contrary, on his route, Esatis was forced to trust strangers and institutions (such as the United Nations High Commissioner for Refugees [UNHCR]). Arriving from CAR, Kinshasa was nothing short of overwhelming. Population-wise, Kinshasa alone is more than twice the size of the whole of CAR. To get by, Esatis had to learn a new language and adapted to a new code of behaviour. Soon enough, he managed to enrol at school and graduated in 2016. The next year he registered for journalism at university. The political atmosphere around the highly contested presidential elections at the time, with its recurrent manifestations and strikes on campus, as well as more personal financial challenges forced Esatis to put his studying ambitions on hold. But as the political climate calmed down and Esatis was awarded a DAFI (Albert Einstein German Academic Refugee Initiative) education scholarship, he picked up his studies and graduated successfully in 2022. The DAFI scholarship programme offers qualified refugee and returnee students the possibility to earn an undergraduate degree in their country of asylum or home country.[3]

Throughout, Esatis focused on art. Inspired by the music scene in the city, Esatis gave a twist to his writing aspirations and returned to his old friend, rap. He soon became interested in the more literary slam poetry and delved further into this art. Slam poetry originated in the early 1980s in Chicago, became popular in France in the mid-1990s and, a decade later, spread throughout the Francophone world, including West and Central Africa (De Bruijn and Oudenhuijsen, 2021). Today, through the work of African artists, slam has become an established art form with festivals in different African countries, including Congo, CAR and Tanzania. A slam poet, or poetess, situates him or herself between a poet and a rapper. Slammers master the spoken word, which they 'clamour' (or sing) with minor musical accompaniment. Just like hip hop, slam can be considered as part of the African orality register, turning slammers into 'modern *griots*'; in a way, slam has taken over hip hop's function of being a protest song against the wrongdoings of politicians (De Bruijn and Oudenhuijsen, 2021). Here, too, the online plays an important role: slammers' performance is built on the coexistence of orality, writing and visibility in digital media (Aterianus-Owanga, 2015).

Since 2015, Esatis has written dozens of songs and performed on different occasions in formal and informal spaces. These include the UNCHR and CAR embassy premises during the festivities of World Refugee Day or Independence Day respectively, podia in hotels and other cultural centres (both downtown as well as in the suburban popular neighbourhoods), the university campus, small recording studios, bars and private compounds when visiting friends. Esatis, who comes over as a calm, composed and thoughtful young man, metamorphoses on stage to become an engaged and passionate activist. In his poetry, Esatis proclaims his love for his country, speaks of the joys and pains of exile, the recent conflict in CAR, and African politics and poverty. At times, he pleads for help at the doorstep of international organisations; at other times, he reinforces pan-Africanism. Esatis' target audience is the African youth, about whom he constantly worries:

> 'What worries me more is the youth's future. … Because today, with the new CPC rebellion [Coalition des patriotes pour le changement (CPC) is a rebel coalition in the CAR that was created in the run-up to the 2020 elections] how many children have had to stop their studies? How many children were born in the bush? Tttt [regrets] how many children don't even have birth certificates? … When I think about my country, I have no memories of the past, I have only regrets about the future: Children who could not grow up like all children around the world, who did not spend time in libraries, did not play like all children around the world or had the privilege to grow up with their parents in a clean environment. This is what worries me, very much.'
> (Interview, Esatis, WhatsApp audio call, 7 January 2021)

Writing and performing songs are only one part of Esatis' musical endeavour. In the last couple of years, Esatis has combined his own musical career with entrepreneurship, turning himself into a cultural manager who, by organising music festivals and small cultural events, creates a platform for others to sing. By doing so, Esatis opens the dialogue between the refugee community and the local artist community, actively enacting his role as a citizen. Up to the time of writing, Esatis has thought out, raised funds for, and organised three festivals; others are in the making. In the past few years, he has grown more visible and audible in the cultural public sphere, both physically and digitally. Artists approach him to collaborate, and he has slowly built a name for himself. His refugee experience has taught him to capitalise on networks, which include, in addition to artists, contacts in humanitarian circles. While not depending solely on it, Esatis keeps close ties with the UNHCR. These networks can be of use when looking for funding for festivals, even though, often, promises are not kept. During the COVID-19 pandemic, he was quick to write a song on this topic. The song, partly in French, partly in

Sango (next to French, the official language in CAR), was soon picked up by the UNHCR, which used it in awareness-raising campaigns, earning Esatis more visibility. Just like the digitally connected youth Iwilade describes in Nigeria, Esatis turns crisis into opportunity (Iwilade, 2013). His ideas concretise in the social media space first, through which he can communicate and promote them. After that, they materialise in the offline world, while they continue to be mediated through social media. By organising festivals that bring together artists from Congo and the CAR, Esatis not only acts as a bridge between the two communities, but, as a musician, he has a goal while recreating a dignified home for himself.

Music ministry and music engineering in Dar es Salaam

In contrast to Esatis, Nathan-2K is not a refugee and does not consider himself as one. He did not flee home as a last resort but moved to Dar es Salaam to explore opportunities. Of course, one could argue that in a conflict-afflicted area and in a city (Butembo) that suffers from deficient infrastructure (Geenen, 2017) there were not many opportunities for him. Nevertheless, when asked about this, Nathan-2K was stern: No, he did not come to Tanzania fleeing war! Comparing Dar es Salaam to Butembo, Nathan-2K recounted war:

> 'Yes! It was severe. All types of gunfire could be heard from morning until evening. You're inside the house, you can't go outside and you hide under the bed. [He then switches to Lingala for emphasis:] You hide from gunfire under the bed, so that it doesn't hit you! But here [in Dar es Salaam] it's difficult to find a child who has lived through war, even someone my age. There are people who are older than me and who have never experienced anything like it.' (Interview, Nathan-2K, Dar es Salaam, 30 July 2019)

Even though Nathan-2K had been outside Congo before, he considered Tanzania as his first real experience of living abroad. Similarly to Esatis, Nathan-2K felt overwhelmed by the new city. Even though Butembo and Goma are big cities, Dar es Salaam felt like a real capital to him. He was particularly impressed by Dar's security – petty crime and gang formation were not what Nathan-2K was used to. He also found himself in an advantageous position: the church that took care of his trip attended to Nathan-2K's paperwork that was necessary for him to live and work legally in Dar es Salaam. According to Tanzanian law, non-citizens employed or engaged in approved religious organisations pay a reduced fee for a work permit (Wilson et al, 2021). In Tanzania, several Pentecostal churches work with Congolese band members in their choirs (see Sanga, 2010; Quigley,

2018). Nathan-2K's situation stood in stark contrast with that of many Congolese migrants living in Dar es Salaam without an official status or work permit. Unlike Nathan-2K, many of these vulnerable migrants in refugee-like situations are forced to seek a living in the informal sector, while being unable to move freely and living in constant fear of being recognised and stigmatised as refugees (Bwami, 2012). In this context, churches play an important role as a semi-public safe space of comfort (Wilson et al, 2021) and help urban refugees and migrants to find their way into a new society (see Chapter 1 in this volume).

Aside from the church where Nathan-2K leads and accompanies choir rehearsals twice a week, plays the guitar and the keyboard during Sunday mass services, and prepares and participates in manifestations and special prayer sessions, Nathan-2K is a sound producer, a profession he learned back in Congo when he was 19 years old. In Dar es Salaam, Nathan-2K capitalised on this knowledge and found work as a music engineer in a religious music studio, where he was brought by a friend. Impressed by the quality of the equipment and the religious devotion of the studio's manager, Nathan-2K decided to work for them on a freelance basis. He is paid for the number of songs he (co-)produces, which varies each week. Nathan-2K produces sound for individual singers as well as for choirs (*kwaya*) or bands that make their own (instrumental) music. While the nature of the music is religious, its style is eclectic. The price per song varies from 200,000 TZS to 400,000 TZS, depending on the number of people and the instruments employed (from €70 to €140, respectively). Capitalising on his network from church, Nathan-2K has expanded his services to other studios and TV stations, where he has been involved in sound production for commercial spots – proof that he is thirsty to learn and willing to embrace new challenges and partnerships. Similarly to Esatis, Nathan-2K developed entrepreneurial skills in music that are highly valued by the local Tanzanian market. By training Tanzanian choir members and being an active music engineer for local gospel singers, Nathan-2K enacts his role as a citizen, and through the safe space of the church has managed to create a new home for himself.

Conclusion

Esatis sings in Sango and Nathan-2K plays guitar solos inspired on *seben*; crying guitars typical of Congolese music. The seben is an instrumental interlude played towards the end of a song, inviting the audience to dance and loosen up. Through music, Esatis and Nathan-2K both keep memories of their home country alive – and create and recreate a new home for themselves in Kinshasa and Dar es Salaam. Despite the challenges, both cities have proven to be fertile ground for their ambitions. In addition to navigating continuously changing environments in their day-to-day lives, however, Esatis and Nathan-2K also imagine futures for themselves by actively making strategic choices and creating new opportunities. In this way, they capitalise on their network and musical skills. Esatis has turned himself into an engaged musician and cultural entrepreneur, who has taken part in awareness-raising campaigns and organised festivals. Nathan-2K has evolved in the growing gospel music sector, where he puts his musical and entrepreneurial skills to use. He does not shy away from learning to play new instruments and engaging himself in new businesses. The canvas on which Esatis and Nathan-2K make these choices consists of (semi-)public, offline and online, urban spaces and the expanding social networks that flow out of them, in which both artists enact urban citizenships and contribute to the creation of safe spaces of encounter and musical articulation. This is not to say that their horizons stop in these cities. Whether their home is in Bangui, Butembo, Kinshasa, Dar es Salaam or elsewhere, the location is secondary to the fact that it is created through Esatis' and Nathan-2K's own efforts.

By recounting Esatis' and Nathan-2K's trajectories, their successes as well as their moments of distress, the purpose of this chapter has been to challenge one-directional narratives in migration studies; to question the migrant–refugee divide; and finally, to problematise stereotypical images of displaced, vulnerable youth. This chapter counters the discourse of an African youth as being in a state of constant crisis. By combining the two trajectories with a biographical approach, the focus further shifts to the choices that shape the personal geographies of people on the move. Without neglecting suffering, this shift can help scholars to understand, not who *can* or *must* move, but who *wants* to move and why. By shaping their own biographical trajectories, Esatis and Nathan-2K actively create new spaces and layers of urbanity. Theirs is a musical mobile story of success *in* Africa.

Acknowledgements

This chapter is based on information collected during two projects: 'Connecting in Times of Duress: Understanding Communication and Conflict in Middle Africa's Mobile Margins', funded by the Dutch NOW (W 01.70.600.001) and 'Transnational Figurations of Displacement', funded by the European Union's Horizon 2020 research and innovation programme (grant no 822453). I am first and foremost indebted to Esatis and Nathan-2K for sharing their stories. I would also like to thank the editors for their patience, in particular Ilse van Liempt, Peter Hopkins and Elisabeth Kirndörfer for their constructive comments and motivation.

Notes

[1] For an up-to-date overview consult www.unhcr.org/refugee-statistics
[2] To view one of Esatis' performances: https://vimeo.com/242830206

[3] The scholarship is financed by donations from, among others, the governments of Germany, Denmark and the Czech Republic. See www.unhcr.org/dafi-scholarships

References

Aterianus-Owanga, A. (2015) '"Orality is my reality": the identity stakes of the "oral" creation in Libreville hip-hop practices', *Journal of African Cultural Studies*, 27(2): 146–158.

Bal, E. and Willems, R. (2014) 'Introduction: aspiring migrants, local crises and the imagination of futures "away from home"', *Identities*, 21(3): 249–258.

Bwami, N.N. (2012) 'It takes courage to be a refugee', *Realizing Rights* (blog), July, Wordpress, available from: https://realizingrights.wordpress.com/2012/07/06/it-takes-courage-to-be-a-refugee/

Clark-Kazak, C.R. (2011) *Recounting Migration: Political Narratives of Congolese Young People in Uganda*, Montreal: McGill-Queen's Press.

Cole, A.L. and Knowles. J.G. (2001) *Lives in Context: The Art of Life History Research*, Lanham, MD: Rowman Altamira.

De Backer, M. (2016) 'The publicness paradox: young people and the production of parochial places', *Environnement Urbain/Urban Environment*, 10, 1–19.

De Bruijn, M. and Both, J. (2018) 'Introduction: understanding experiences and decisions in situations of enduring hardship in Africa', *Conflict and Society,* 4(1): 186–198.

De Bruijn, M. and Lalaye, D. (2016) 'An engaged Chadian artist's digital itinerary towards political and civic success: pitfalls of oppression', in B. Mutsvairo (ed) *Digital Activism in the Social Media Era*, Cham: Springer International Publishing, pp 141–157.

De Bruijn, M. and Oudenhuijsen, L. (2021) 'Female slam poets of Francophone Africa: spirited words for social change', *Africa*, 91(5): 742–767.

De Bruijn, M., Sijsma, S., Ragazzi, L. and Lalaye, D. (2017) 'Nomadic minds – Croquemort: a biographical journey in the context of Chad', *Bridging Humanities (Brill).* doi:10.1163/25425099-00101001

Dolby, N. (2006) 'Popular culture and public space in Africa: the possibilities of cultural citizenship', *African Studies Review*, 49(3): 31–47.

Geenen, K. (2017) 'Light, dark and the powers that be: a hydroelectric project in Butembo', *Canadian Journal of African Studies/Revue Canadienne Des Études Africaines*, 51(1): 43–59.

Holmes, A. (2020) 'Researcher positionality: a consideration of its influence and place in qualitative research – a new researcher guide', *Shanlax International Journal of Education*, 8: 1–10.

Ingold, T. (2017) 'Anthropology contra ethnography', *HAU: Journal of Ethnographic Theory*, 7(1): 21–26.

Iwilade, A. (2013) 'Crisis as opportunity: youth, social media and the renegotiation of power in Africa', *Journal of Youth Studies*, 16(8): 1054–1068.

Johnson-Hanks, J. (2002) 'On the limits of life stages in ethnography: toward a theory of vital conjunctures', *American Anthropologist*, 104(3): 865–880.

Kwaks, J. (2018) 'Living with the legacy of displacement: an exploration of non-return and the long-term effects of displacement on social life in Pabo, Northern Uganda', Master's thesis, Universiteit Leiden.

Landau, L.B. and Bakewell, O. (2018) 'Introduction: forging African communities: mobility, integration and belonging', in O. Bakewell and L.B. Landau (eds) *Forging African Communities: Mobility, Integration and Belonging*, London: Palgrave Macmillan, pp 1–24.

Lane, J. (2016) 'The digital street: an ethnographic study of networked street life in Harlem', *American Behavioral Scientist*, 60(1): 43–58.

Larmer, M., Laudati, A. and Clark, J.F. (2013) 'Neither war nor peace in the Democratic Republic of Congo (DRC): profiting and coping amid violence and disorder', *Review of African Political Economy*, 40(135): 1–12.

Lyytinen, E. (2017) 'Refugees' "journeys of trust": creating an analytical framework to examine refugees' exilic journeys with a focus on trust', *Journal of Refugee Studies*, 30(4): 489–510.

Maynes, M.J., Pierce, J.L. and Laslett, B. (2012) *Telling Stories: The Use of Personal Narratives in the Social Sciences and History*, Ithaca, NY: Cornell University Press.

Quigley, C.L. (2018) 'A peripatetic search for the rumba of my imagined anthropology on the shores of Lake Tanganyika', presented at the American Anthropological Association Annual Conference, San Jose, CA.

Reyes, V. (2020) 'Ethnographic toolkit: strategic positionality and researchers' visible and invisible tools in field research', *Ethnography*, 21(2): 220–240.

Rowe, W.E. (2014) 'Positionality', in D. Coghlan and M. Brydon-Miller (ed) *The SAGE Encyclopedia of Action Research*, Thousand Oaks, CA: SAGE, pp 627–628.

Russell, A. (2011) 'Home, music and memory for the Congolese in Kampala', *Journal of Eastern African Studies*, 5(2): 294–312.

Sanga, I. (2010) 'The practice and politics of hybrid soundscapes in Muziki Wa Injili in Dar Es Salaam, Tanzania', *Journal of African Cultural Studies*, 22(2): 145–156.

Schapendonk, J. and Belloni, M. (2020) 'Constraints and transgressions in journeys of displacement', in P. Adey, J.C. Bowstead, K. Brickell, V. Desai, M. Dolton, A. Pinkerton and A. Siddiqi (eds) *The Handbook of Displacement*, Cham: Springer International Publishing, pp 297–311.

Schapendonk, J., van Liempt, I., Schwarz, I. and Steel, G. (2018) 'Re-routing migration geographies: migrants, trajectories and mobility regimes', *Geoforum*, 116: 211–216.

Simpson, P. (2011) 'Street performance and the city: public space, sociality, and intervening in the everyday', *Space and Culture*, 14(4): 415–430.

Turner, S. (2015) '"We wait for miracles": ideas of hope and future among clandestine Burundian Refugees in Nairobi', in E. Cooper and D. Pratten (eds) *Ethnographies of Uncertainty in Africa*, Basingstoke: Palgrave Macmillan, pp 173–191.

Ungruhe, C. (2021) 'Youth crisism: reflections on the persisting victimization of young people in Africa', panel at a conference presented at the VAD Africa Challenges, Goethe Universität, 10 June, available from: https://vad-africachallenges.de/panel/p-05-lifeworlds-in-crisis-challenging-notions-of-difference/

Vigh, H. (2009) 'Motion squared a second look at the concept of social navigation', *Anthropological Theory*, 9(4): 419–438.

Whitehouse, B. (2012) *Migrants and Strangers in an African City: Exile, Dignity, Belonging*, Bloomington, IN: Indiana University Press.

Wilson, C. (2019) 'Conflict (im)mobiles: biographies of mobility along the Ubangi River in Central Africa', Doctoral thesis, Universiteit Leiden, available from: https://openaccess.leidenuniv.nl/handle/1887/77742

Wilson, C., Msallam, B., Kabyemela, J., Demirdirek, M., Sanga, J. and Ruhundwa, J. (2021) 'Figurations of displacement in and beyond Tanzania: reflections on protracted displacement and translocal connections of Congolese and Burundian Refugees in Dar Es Salaam', working paper 8, TRAFIG working paper, Bonn: BICC, available from: https://trafig.eu/output/working-papers/trafig-working-paper-no-8

Wilson Janssens, M.C. (2018) '"Our future is already in jeopardy": duress and the palimpsest of violence of two CAR student refugees in the DRC', *Conflict and Society*, 4(1): 214–230.

Zetter, R., Crawley, H. and Schmalz, D. (2020) 'About the non/sense of distinguishing between migrants and refugees', online panel debate, Institute for Migration Research and Intercultural Studies, Osnabrück University, 1 October, available from: www.youtube.com/watch?v=YwUYVSreHGs&feature=youtu.be

14

Planetary Listening

Les Back

In the public imagination, refugees and migrants *appear* rather than speak. A stock range of visual clichés are evidence of the looming threat of human movement and migration. The news coverage unthinkingly recycles a whole repertoire of all-too-predictable images from boats crowded to sinking point, young faces trapped behind barbed wire fences or dead bodies of children tragically washed up on beaches. These pitiable portraits of abject displacement stand in the place of the important task of what I would call hospitable attention and listening. Martin Luther King Jr argued that pity is distancing. He wrote: 'Pity is feeling sorry for someone; empathy is feeling sorry with someone. Empathy is fellow feeling' (1968, p 119). What *Refugee Youth: Migration, Justice and Urban Space* offers is the opportunity to develop a different relationship to these young lives documented within it, based on 'fellow feeling', to offer an unspectacular human portrayal of young people seeking freer lives.

The completion of this collection has coincided with Russia's invasion of Ukraine. The violence of war once provided the impetus for the young to run from it. What we have seen is that the kind of 'fellow feeling' that Martin Luther King Jr talked about is damaged and shaped by the legacy of racism that shapes empathy and familiarity. Writing in the British newspaper, *The Daily Telegraph*, on 26 February 2022, Daniel Hannan commented: 'They [the displaced Ukrainians] seem so like us. That is what makes it so shocking. Ukraine is a European country. Its people … watch Netflix and have Instagram accounts, vote in free elections and read uncensored newspapers. War is no longer something visited upon impoverished and remote populations.' Being like 'us' – that is white Europeans in this context – is viewed as a natural empathy. This is not a product of nature but the result of the long history of European racism that conveys a greater value on some human beings than on others.

Nadine White, commenting in the British newspaper, *The Independent*, on 1 March 2022, on the contrast between the coverage of the war in Ukraine and that of the conflicts in Syria and in Afghanistan, points out, 'From France to the UK and the US, much of the media coverage of the war in Ukraine has been saturated with racial bias.' A vigilant attention to the different histories of racism across the globe is necessary in order to understand how the contemporary discussion of migration and refugee experience is shaped in the media and politically.

We also need to think of more hospitable ways in which the voices of young migrations are heard in our time. One of the things that unites many of the contributors to this book is their use of creative collaborative research methods, which includes photography, music, image making and narrative storytelling. As a result, we are able to inhabit the view of young refugees and learn about their perceptions of the work from the Brazilian municipality of Igarassu to the city of Leipzig, Germany. Putting these refugee stories at the centre shows how they make sense of the new places of arrival, recording their enchantments as well as their frustrations. The authors 'call out' the routine experiences of racism that shape the lives of young refugees, while at the same time they describe how young people resist racism. *Refugee Youth* offers an alternative to more traditional academic studies of integration by opening up a space for these voices to be represented and heard on their own terms.

This concern was also at the heart of the study conducted, from 2008 to 2018, by Shamser Sinha and the author, called *Migrant City* (2018). It is the story of London told from the vantage point of young migrants living in the capital through the torrid anti-immigrant decades of the early 21st century. The book took so long partly as a reaction to that. It transformed into an experiment that involved carrying out research in a sociable, ongoing way that valued migrants and refugees as young people with insights, feelings and their own stories to tell.

As the experiment unfolded, we realised that this required a new type of authorship. Some participants were becoming authors too – not in the way we were but in a new way that we were creating together. Doing this required loosening our grip on the research process and opening it up to the young migrants we were working with. Some participants became authors and commentators who were acknowledged and credited explicitly. Others could not for fear of being revealed and scrutinised by the immigration system that, for some, might lead ultimately to deportation. It took us a decade to finish partly because of our deep commitment to working *with* rather than *on* young migrants. The stories of these young lives just kept unfolding, making it hard to portray what we had learned.

Writing *Migrant City* has brought the author-participants into the sociological conversation as active knowledge producers. Some, like Charlynne Bryan, whom you'll hear from shortly, have become published authors. Their lives were not merely used as evidence to be presented through sociological ventriloquism. Instead, the process of dialogue made them active readers, interpreters and contributors to theory construction too. We repeatedly circled back to them, arranging more meetings in cafes and informal urban spaces to pick up the conversation.

We wanted to hold to an analytical project at the same time as staying close to the emotional texture of lives being lived sometimes against the odds and in the face of real violence and danger. *Migrant City* is a sociology that tried to connect the heart and head. But, perhaps more than anything else, it is a sociology written from the heart, out of deep long-standing affiliations and intellectual friendships that are personal, sociological and political. I think this is an orientation to scholarship that we need to argue for with greater conviction. I see resonances with that orientation to scholarship throughout this volume too, like Catherina Wilson's extraordinary work with young African musicians and artists that has been conducted through long-standing and ongoing relationships (see Chapter 13).

It seems to me that documenting the human experience of young lives on the move requires us to undermine the categories – like 'refugee' or 'asylum seeker' – that are so often applied to them in reductive ways through their immigration status. They are more than the flag they were born under or the designation on their passport. The complexity of their experience is an insight into the kinds of human beings we have become in the midst of the global COVID-19 pandemic and threats of war and premature death.

I met Charlynne again in the summer of 2021 at Westfield Shopping Centre in East London, a regular place for us to catch up over coffee and cake. She came to London from Dominica where she was born, to study at the University of East London. Charlynne explained, "I've been here for 14 years now. I mean, that's, that's a long time to be in any place. And in a few years' time, it will, I would have lived in London longer than I've lived in the Caribbean, you know, in five years' time."

Through her father's French citizenship, Charlynne came to Britain as a citizen of the European Union. However, after the Brexit vote, she had to apply to the Home Office to secure her status.

> '[The UK] leaving the Eurozone was particularly important because I felt like I'm going to be sent back to where I came from, which is the term that sometimes comes with, with immigrants. And I wasn't sure what that would look like, because I was, like, where would I be sent back to? Would I be sent back to Dominica that I left ages ago and

have no ties to? Would I be sent back to France where I'm a national of, but I've never lived?' (Charlynne)

Charlynne applied for indefinite leave to remain in the UK through the 'Pilot Program of Settled Status in the UK'. She is a schoolteacher in permanent employment. However, there were two years that the Home Office queried and asked her to provide documentary evidence that she lived in London during that time. It was unsettling, but she found documentation to prove her residency and she forwarded the proof. She was granted settled status. Charlynne reflected on the impact of the COVID-19 global pandemic on the migrant city:

> 'I always start with the fact that this country is built on the back of migrants. And during this pandemic, you saw that more, so that lots of the people who are National Health Service workers, lots of the people who are teachers, lots of the people, you know, who are the frontline workers are people who are migrants in this country.' (Charlynne)

It was not just the public services either. As the restaurants closed, migrant labourers delivered food via Uber Eats and the like to keep Londoners fed. Thousands of small supermarkets staffed by those with migrant heritages stayed stocked and open, which meant that food was available within walking distance throughout the capital.

London's migrant workers have been exposed to extreme physical and emotional pressure during the pandemic. Yasmin Gunaratnam pointed out in her article, 'When doctors die', that healthcare professionals of migrant background risked and lost their lives providing care. In March 2020, Adil El Tayar, Habib Zaidi and El-Hawrani were the first National Health Service doctors to die from COVID-19. All three had migrant backgrounds. A recent article in *The British Medical Journal* showed that, on almost all health measures, what they termed ethnic minority groups have the worst outcomes. This was especially true for Black and South Asian people. The mortality rates for some minority communities are identified as three or four times higher than those experienced by White Britons (Razai et al, 2021, p 372). Charlynne explained that social isolation and 'the lockdown' are more intensely experienced in migrant and refugee communities.

Dr Siema Iqbal, who is a general practitioner, summed it up like this, in September 2020: 'Migrants and people of colour kept this country alive during the pandemic, and still do. Let's address the structural and institutional racism and inequalities that exist in our country and hold those that allow it to flourish to account. What bigger wake-up call do we need?' For Charlynne, one of the deep lessons of the pandemic is how to live in the face of possible infection and premature death. She explained:

'And everybody knew that they could die from it. And that's all they focused on, the death. ... COVID kind of brought that to the forefront of our mind that we're not going to live forever, that there is an end. And we don't know when that end is; it could be any minute.' (Charlynne)

I think her words also resonate in the context of wars within the Ukraine and elsewhere that force young people to see freedom in the shadow of death. This, for Charlynne, poses moral or philosophical question about how to live in the face of this. For many, these threats bring out the worst fears and phobias about others. She explained, "And so the reaction wasn't a reaction of 'Oh my goodness, I'm going to do my best and live the best life that I can'."

For Charlynne, there is another impulse. That is to live a better, more open-hearted life. Charlynne wrote poems as part of her contribution to the 2008–2018 research, which were published in *Migrant City*. She published a collection of poems during the pandemic entitled *Letters to My Soul*. Throughout the pandemic, Charlynne continued with her poetry group that is based in East London.

'And so, my poetry group moved online and so all of the Colombian people, and you know the Jamaican people and the Trinidadian people, all of us were coming together and the Bangladeshi people as well and sharing our poetry and talking about what COVID did to us and how we were affected by it.' (Charlynne)

In the face of death during the pandemic, Charlynne points to how to refuse isolation and fear and choose connection and community as a better way to live.

Living in the migrant city through this pandemic has left Charlynne with a deep sense of pride:

'I generally don't like to generalise, but when I think of my people, and ... I'm using "my people" as a general term to talk about migrants, be it migrants from the Caribbean, or migrants from Europe or migrants from Africa. And my people know how to make things work when things aren't working. And that's one of the things that's always struck me about migrant communities is that they ... you put them in a situation where they have nothing, and they will magic something out of nothing, you put them in a situation where they're illegal, and they can't work to get money, but they will find some way to make it work for their family, you put them in a situation where it's hard, and there's a pandemic, and they will find a way to make something out of that so that it doesn't become something that destroys them. You know, and this pandemic has definitely proven that – that even though as migrants we are ostracised in so many ways, that we're needed in so many ways, that we can make it in so many ways. And that's been the beautiful thing for me. ... I'm kind of proud of my people, you know, really proud of my people for that.' (Charlynne)

Listening to voices of refugees and young migrants and creating sociable forms of hearing offers one way to foster 'fellow feeling' in the face of war, global threats and hateful exclusions. I call this 'planetary listening', in which each individual life contains the traces of a global human story. Rather than caring only for those who seem to look like us, this kind of attention opens us to the experience of displaced young people in a way that invites a more inclusive planetary consciousness. Achille Mbembe calls this 'a radical openness of and to the world, a deep breathing for the world as opposed to insulation'. A 'deep breathing for the world'. What an extraordinary and urgent idea. This taking in of the world is precisely what is at stake as we sit and talk and listen to each other.

References

Back, L. and Sinha, S. (2018) *Migrant City*, London: Routledge.

Hannan, D. (2022) 'Vladimir Putin's monstrous invasion is an attack on civilisation itself', *The Daily Telegraph*, 26 February, available from: www.telegraph.co.uk/news/2022/02/26/vladimir-putins-monstrous-invasion-attack-civilisation/

Iqbal, S. (2020) 'COVID-19: how infectious disease exposes the racism within our healthcare system', British Society for Antimocrobial Chemotherapy, 15 September, available from: https://bsac.org.uk/covid-19-how-infectious-disease-exposes-the-deadly-racism-at-the-heart-of-our-healthcare/

King, M.L. (1968) *Where Do We Go from Here: Chaos or Community*, Toronto: Bantam Books.

Razai, M.S., Kankam, H.K.N., Majeed, A., Esmail, A. and Williams, D.R. (2021) 'Mitigating ethnic disparities in COVID-19 and beyond', *British Medical Journal*: 372, available from: www.bmj.com/content/372/bmj.m4921

White, N. (2022) 'The racial bias in western media's Ukraine coverage is shameful', *The Independent*, 1 March, available from: www.independent.co.uk/voices/ukraine-refugees-racial-bias-western-media-b2024864.html

15

Refugee Youth: Politics, Publicness and Visibility

Mattias De Backer, Peter Hopkins and Ilse van Liempt

All the contributions to this collection draw on qualitative research with refugee youth, and many use participatory research and creative methods to trace the personal geographies, politics and emotions associated with migration, justice and urban spaces. Interesting theoretical discussions have emerged across the chapters, especially around the notions of politics, publicness and visibility, and we expand on these in this conclusion.

Politics

Asylum seekers and refugees often arrive in a hostile political context with very clear demarcation lines around who belongs and who does not belong. In this collection, among others, in Chapter 8 by Anne Grent and Ajay Bailey, and in Chapter 3 by Malene Jacobsen, the politics of belonging is prominently present. The former leans conceptually on Antonsich (2010), who identifies the politics of belonging as a discursive resource that constructs, claims, justifies or resists forms of socio-spatial inclusion or exclusion (p 1). The latter describes how migrant boys are framed as a security risk in public space and engage in counter-politics, by reclaiming spaces, identities and ways of being, via artistic performances characterised by a self-conscious politics of refusal, which reconfigures the relationship of domination and subordination altogether.

This also resonates with the Lefebvrian call for the right to the city echoed in several chapters (Lefebvre, 1996; Mitchell, 2003). In Chapter 7, Rana Aytug connects this with the notion of inclusive city planning. The right to the city signifies the right for all city inhabitants 'to appear on all the networks and circuits of communication, information and exchange'

(Lefebvre, 1996, pp 194–195). The urban environment is a fertile ground for emerging forms of civic engagement in response to challenges like an imbalance of power among urban stakeholders. Examining justice in the city through the lens of inclusive planning, Aytug argues, has the potential to generate new possibilities and raise a greater sense of political consciousness.

This politics- and rights-based analysis surfaces also in Chapter 4 by Camila da Silva Lucena and Fabiele Stockmans De Nardi, which emphasises mothers' access to education, basic services and cultural expression, and in Chapter 6 by Mohd Al Adib Samuri and Peter Hopkins, which details the ways in which female Rohingya refugees in Malaysia are denied access to education, where community-based schools lack the resources, transportation, teaching equipment and basic facilities necessary to teach refugee children. Without a doubt, there is something explicitly (micro-)political about the restriction from acquiring knowledge (De Backer et al, 2019).

The complexity of political issues and the hostile political contexts in which refugee youth often find themselves are a key issue for ongoing research in this field. So too are the creative and engaging ways in which young refugees engage in, resist, challenge and rework political issues in different spaces and times. Several chapters in this volume reflect on how art production can be a form of political expression. In Chapter 2, Elisabeth Kirndörfer, for instance, shows how participatory theatre and more particularly the act of not-speaking in that context are a political act; it is a statement about and enactment of citizenship. The theatre group in the focal point of the chapter criticises storytelling as a colonial dynamic where non-White people are telling their stories for their White peers. In contrast, Yuval-Davis (2010) as cited by Luke Macauley in Chapter 10 conceptualises identity as a narrative: 'stories that people tell themselves about who they are, who they are not, as well as who and how they would like to/should be' (p 266). As, indeed, Macauley emphasises, the act of storytelling may also be empowering for young refugees. In Chapter 13, Catherina Wilson considers popular culture and music as important for the public spaces of a society, including the ways in which youth conceptualise and enact their roles as citizens and contribute to their host society.

Publicness

The notion of 'publicness', that is, the analyses in each chapter of the social scenes in myriad possible settings, along the continuum of private, semi-public, quasi-public, public, hidden, discursive, segregated and non-spaces, is an important issue for refugee youth. This includes reflections on what constitutes the public nature of such spaces. In Chapter 10, Luke Macauley considers public space as occupiable space that exists outside the private sphere and, at the same time, is differentiated from occupiable institutional fields that have organisational mandates and that individuals need approval to enter.

Chapters focus on the role of theatre organisations (Chapter 2), cultural festivals (Chapter 4), community centres (Chapter 5) and hair salons (Chapter 11) as semi-public spaces, which offer important opportunities to experience safety, belonging and conviviality for newcomers (Rovisco, 2020). They allow refugees to talk about themselves, in their language, based on what they want others to know about their culture, giving them the opportunity to build an open space for dialogue on their own terms.

Some of these spaces can offer other opportunities for young refugees. Some other spaces are also hidden spaces for informal work, enabling opportunities to informally earn a living while ensuring that refugees stay below the radar and hidden from police, immigration officers and other potentially threatening state actors. Public spaces can be spaces of artistic expression, as with the performance artists discussed in Chapter 3 by Malene Jacobsen, who reclaim belonging on their own terms, reclaiming their right to public spaces while redressing ongoing racialised dispossession of their identities, cultures and ways of life through performances characterised by a self-conscious politics of refusal. According to Camila da Silva Lucena and Fabiele Stockmans De Nardi in Chapter 4, belonging and identity are also constructed in discursive public and semi-public spaces, observing that interventions in and interdiction of native languages mould behaviour and interfere with the individual identify construction, rendering native languages and cultures as 'non-place' (Augé, 1995).

Several chapters reflect on the potential of fleeting moments of encounter in public space, which may turn into public familiarity when they repeat themselves. For refugees, the recognition of language or visual appearance might create quick bonds in public space with people whom they assume share their cultural heritage, as Ilse van Liempt and Mieke Kox explore in Chapter 5. Occasional everyday encounters in public spaces are brought into dialogue with the notion of social capital and are deemed not sufficient to enhance a sense of connectedness to others, as Anne Grent and Ajay Bailey demonstrate in Chapter 8. In Chapter 9, Seyma Karamese stresses urban space as a 'negotiated reality', where encounters are not fixed but open to surprise (Ahmed, 2000), unpredictable but potentially having a transformative capacity (Wilson, 2017).

Public spaces are also places where refugees are judged, excluded and stigmatised because of the language they speak or the garments they wear, as Mastoureh Fathi, for example, considers in Chapter 12. Respondents in several chapters talked about frequent and long looks, which resonate feelings such as being judged or unwelcomed, and about the strategies they apply to feel more comfortable to navigate public space. Here, one theme resonating across several chapters is the observation that public spaces are often highly gendered, for instance in the purdah culture of Rohingya in Malaysia explored in Chapter 6 by Mohd Al Adib Samuri and Peter Hopkins, and in the way Syrian refugees navigate public spaces in Turkey, discussed in Chapter 12 by Mastoureh Fathi. Due to their publicness, these spaces of 'unhome' can be intimidating to refugees and filled with potential micro-aggressions. Yet, as Seyma Karamese argues in Chapter 9, both public and private spaces can be exclusionary. These tensions between spaces marked as public and as private, and the complex negotiations of publicness, are important issues for further consideration in research with refugee youth.

Visibility

The third concept seeping through various analyses in this volume is the one of visibility, foregrounded by Brighenti (2007) as a new category for the social sciences. Visibility is a key characteristic of publicness: 'the visibility (as in disclosure or opening) of norms and political power to scrutiny by all affected persons, persons granted the freedom to form and make visible (as in express and publish) their opinions through participation in rational public debate' (Dahlberg, 2018, p 35). The political world can be seen as the space of appearances, where we appear to others and they appear to us (Brambilla and Pötzsch, 2019, p 71). Public visibility is key, oscillating between an empowering pole (visibility as recognition) and a disempowering pole (visibility as control) (Brighenti, 2007; De Backer, 2018). The essential difference between privateness and publicness lies in the fact that there are elements of the former that need to be hidden, while elements of the latter need to be shown in order for them to be either private or public (Arendt, 1998). Visibility is what brings an analysis of behaviour in public space together with that of the public and political debate.

Authors in this volume present theatre (see Elisabeth Kirndörfer's reflections in Chapter 2), music (as Catherina Wilson explores in Chapter 13), inclusive place-making (as Rana Aytug considers in Chapter 7) and performance art (as Malene Jacobsen critically reflects on in Chapter 3) as ways to make visible, to give recognition, or to claim citizenship and belonging. In Chapter 5, Ilse van Liempt and Mieke Kox describe how newcomers are engaged in remaking everyday life in a new context after migration: processes that are not only taking place in their own neighbourhoods but also in the dynamic space of the city where there is a wide range of opportunities to make connections with others. Yet, precisely due to the visibility of the city's spaces, it is not that straightforward for all refugees to immediately exploit the potential of public spaces in the city after arrival. Arrival should be conceptualised as a process that evolves step by step, is highly dependent on previous and personal preferences and takes time. It is definitely not a static event.

Moreover, young refugees are 'visibly different' (as Luke Macauley points out in Chapter 10) from socially and politically constructed contextual identity norms, which can disrupt their overall sense of belonging to the new place and result in marginalisation within public spaces. Migrant boys are, for example, often framed as a security risk (as Malene Jacobsen outlines in Chapter 3) because of their enhanced visibility in public spaces, rendering them a prominent topic in the public debate and in Danish politics of casting out *'indvandrerdrenge'* ('immigrant boys'). As a result, young refugees engage in tactics to strike a balance between being visible enough to gain a footing in the city and being invisible enough to elude persecution and harassment (as Rebecca Walker and Glynis Clacherty consider in Chapter 11).

In Chapter 6, Moh Al Adib Samuri and Peter Hopkins describe the heavily gendered nature of public and private spaces in the purdah culture of the Rohingya, which invites husbands to keep their spouses indoors, while also stressing how the presence of (male and female) Rohingya refugees in public spaces makes them vulnerable to harassment and discrimination by authorities and members of the local community. The private space of the home is alternately a space of belonging (as Catherina Wilson notes in Chapter 13), a space of violence and incarceration (as made clear in Chapter 6 by Mohd Al Abid Samuri and Peter Hopkins) and an ambiguous site composed of the simultaneous interconnection of protective and limiting characteristics (as Mastoureh Fathi notes in Chapter 12).

In Chapter 8, Anne Grent and Ajay Bailey analyse the multiple variations in translocal attachments among Tibetan refugees in India, caught between visible and invisible boundaries that exist between Tibetan and anti-Tibetan views, and oscillating between the imagined motherland, everyday cultural practices and the attractions of Western culture.

The challenge for refugees and asylum seekers, as well as for researchers working with them, is to negotiate a balanced visibility. Dahlberg (2018, p 38), for instance, insists that '[c]ontrol over visibility, and not just having visibility, is important for democracy as a social actor might be made a subject of visibility without having a say over this visibility' (see also Brighenti, 2010). When a group is visible and the observer is not, we can no longer speak of being recognised but of being exposed. To be too exposed as an object of suffering renders one inert, passive and existing *only* out of suffering. Refugees and asylum seekers, therefore, are actively managing a 'balanced visibility of suffering' (Smets et al, 2019, p 190) instead of undergoing the dominant images of the victim-refugee or the freeloader-refugee in media representations. The real objective is, according to Smets et al, to be visible *and* receive positive affirmation from the broader society. Considering the political importance of doing research and that doing research always brings topics and participants into the public realm, an ongoing reflection on the role, effects and importance of visibility is important in future work.

Indeed, the relative invisibility of girls and women in migration research, as highlighted by Rebecca Walker and Glynis Clacherty in Chapter 11, is an invitation to think with them about the desired degree of their visibility, between privacy and intimacy on the one hand, and issue ownership and political expression on the other, against the background of the 'triple anomaly' that young women migrants pose to hegemonic social orders.

References

Ahmed, S. (2000) *Strange Encounters: Embodied Others in Postcoloniality*, London: Routledge.

Antonsich, M. (2010) 'Searching for belonging: an analytical framework', *Geography Compass*, 4(6): 644–659.

Arendt, H. (1998) *The Human Condition* (2nd edn), Chicago, IL: University of Chicago Press.

Augé, M. (1995) *Non-Places: Introduction to an Anthropology of Supermodernity*, London: Verso Books.

Brambilla, C. and Pötzsch, H. (2019) 'In/visibility', in J. Schimanski and S.F. Wolfe (eds) *Border Aesthetics: Concepts and Intersections*, Oxford: Bergahn Books, pp 68–89.

Brighenti, A.M. (2007) 'Visibility: a category for the social sciences', *Current Sociology*, 55(3): 323–342.

Brighenti, A.M. (2010) *The Publicness of Public Space: On the Public Domain*, Quaderno 49, Trento: Università di Trento.

Dahlberg, L. (2018) 'Visibility and the public sphere: a normative conceptualisation', *Javnost – The Public*, 25(1–2): 35–42.

De Backer, M. (2018) 'Regimes of visibility: hanging out in Brussels' public spaces', *Space and Culture*, 22(3): 308–320.

De Backer, M., Dijkema, C. and Hörschelmann, K. (2019) 'Preface: the everyday politics of public space', *Space and Culture*, 22(3): 240–249.

Lefebvre, H. (1996) *Writings on Cities*, translated by E. ven Kofman and E. Lebas, Cambridge, MA: Wiley-Blackwell.

Mitchell, D. (2003) *The Right to the City: Social justice and the Fight for Public Space*, New York: Guilford Press.

Rovisco, M. (2020) 'Artistic conviviality', in J. Tacchi and T. Tufte (eds) *Communicating for Change: Concepts to Think With*, Cham: Springer International Publishing, pp 135–144.

Smets, K., Mazzochetti, J., Gerstmans, L. and Mostmans, L. (2019) 'Beyond victimhood: reflecting on migrant-victim representations with Afghan, Iraqi, and Syrian asylum seekers and refugees in Belgium', in L. van d'Haenens, W. Joris and F. Heinderyckx (eds) *Images of Immigrants and Refugees in Western Europe: Media Representations, Public Opinion and Refugees' Experiences*, Leuven: Leuven University Press, pp 177–198.

Wilson, H.F. (2017) 'On geography and encounter: bodies, borders, and difference', *Progress in Human Geography*, 41(4): 451–471.

Yuval-Davis, N. (2010) 'Theorizing identity: beyond the "us" and "them" dichotomy', *Patterns of Prejudice*, 44(3): 261–280.

Index

References to endnotes show both the page number and the note number (78n1).

A
accommodation 196
ActionAid Denmark 40
Afghanistan 1
Africa, migration within 210
African gangs' 160, 161
Afro Danish Collective 40
age 121
agency 30, 101, 109, 172, 197, 210, 213
Ahmed, S. 66, 71, 199
Al-Ali, N. 197
Aldeias Infantis SOS 48
alienation 202–204
Altinget (newspaper) 40
Amin, A. 144, 181, 191
Amman
 inclusive urban planning
  research findings 106–112
  research methodology 104–106
Amman 2025 110
Amsterdam
 (semi-)public spaces 65–78
  building connections through 66–67
  encounters in 75–77
  participatory research methods 67–69
  reluctance to navigate 70–72
  strategies to navigate 72
  use of 72–75
Antonsich, M. 119–120, 121, 231
Arnstein, S.R. 111
arrival infrastructures 5–7
Arshad, M. 93
arts-based research 177–178
 see also participatory theatre
Asadullah, M.N. 86
aspirations 211
asylum cases 2
asylum seekers
 definitions 4, 78n1
 Denmark 36
 Ireland 196

Australia 33
 Sudanese and South Sudanese
  Youths 153–165
  experiences in public spaces 157–163
  research methods 155–157
 Tibetan refugees 132
Australian identity 154
auto rickshaws 126–127

B
Baak, M. 162
Bangladesh 87
Bangui, CAR 216
Banks, M. 197
Bartlett, L. 53–54, 57, 59, 60
Beazley, H. 172, 175–176, 181
belonging
 and emotion 192
 and identity 109, 233
 in participatory theatre 16–18
 politics of 231
 Sudanese and South Sudanese Youths 163
 Tibetan refugees, India 119–122, 125–133, 134, 135–136
  economic integration 127–129
  exposure to host society 130–133
  host society's receptivity 129–130
  social capital 126–127
 and urban planning 101
 see also integration
Benier, K. 160
Bhabha, H. 134–135
Bhabha, J. 55
Bhandar, B. 34, 35
Bhutan 118, 119
Bianisa, N. 176
bilingual education 59
biographical strangers 66, 70
biographical trajectories 209–210, 212–214
Black others 154, 158
Blackness 155

INDEX

Blunt, A. 194
Boccagni, P. 194, 204
bonding social networks 120, 126
Bourdieu, P. 148, 149
Braun, V. 125
Brazil
  refugee law 53
  support systems 181
  Venezuelan immigrants 48–49
    context of arrival 51–54
    integration into public education 53–54, 57–62
    research methodology 49–51
    numbers 62n1
    right to education 54–57
Brexit 227–228
Brickell, K. 194
bridging social networks 120, 126
Brighenti, A.M. 161, 234
British Medical Journal 228
British Muslims 144
Brooks, A. 192
burden of care 179–180
Butembo, Estern Congo 214–215
Butterwick, S. 15, 16, 18, 23
Bylakuppe settlement 122–123
  research project
    data analysis 125–133
    observation and interviews 124–125
    participant recruitment 123–124

C

Cahill, C. 34
Candau, V. 55–56
care
  burden of 179–180
  space of 191
  see also childcare
Central African Republic (CAR) 209, 218
  see also Bangui, CAR
Central Tibetan Administration (CTA) 117, 118
charity 148
Chen, S.T. 122
Cherem, M. 4
child marriage 82, 83, 86, 87–89
  confinement after 89–91
  effect on education 91–93
  effect on healthcare access 93–95
child migration 55
childcare 181
children 6, 35–36, 49, 53, 91, 170
  see also refugee youth
China 5, 119, 132
Chinese People's Liberation Army 117, 119
cities 100–101, 113
  inclusive 101, 102–104, 106–112
  just city 8, 102–104
  right to the city 8, 103, 109, 231
  see also inclusive urban planning; urban space
citizenship
  Australia 164
  and belonging 121
  and Brexit 227–228
  Ireland 202
  in participatory theatre 15, 16–18
  Syrian migrants, Turkey 141
  Syrian refugees, Jordan 109
  Tibetan refugees, India 117, 134
civic integration programmes 35
civil inattention 76
civil inattention 67
class 22, 24
collaborative research 226
collective voice 160–161
Colombia 1
colonialism 35
comfort zones 143–144, 151
coming out 23
community centres 65–66, 67–68, 73, 77
contraception 94, 95
control 157, 161, 162
conviviality 67, 77–78
cooperational space 147–149, 151
Cork, Ireland
  migrant men's emotional geographies 190–205
  emotions about home 197–204
  research methodology 195–197
  theoretical framework 190–195
counter-politics 231
COVID-19 1, 72, 74, 75, 77, 227, 228–229
critical geographies of home 194
cultural homogenisation 55–56
cultural influences 131, 133
cultural strangers 66, 70, 71
culture 56, 60, 61, 62

D

Dahlberg, L. 235
Daily Telegraph 225
Dalai Lama 117, 118, 136
Dar el Salam 209, 215, 219–220
De Backer, M. 157–158
de Certeau, M. 183
Denmark
  invandrerdrenge (immigrant boys)
    discourse 32–34, 37–39, 235
    reactions to 40–42
  politics of dispossession 35–37, 39, 43
  search-and-seize orders 8
diaspora studies 191
Direct Privision (DP) centres 196
discrimination 103–104, 121, 129–130, 146
displacement 1–2, 34
  Tibetan refugees 118–119

239

dispossession 33, 34–37, 39, 43
documentation 53, 170, 173, 228
Dublin claim 68
Dutch language 72

E

Eastern Congo 209, 214–215
economic integration 121, 127–129
education
  Rohingya refugees, Malaysia 91–93
  scholarships 217
  Syrian students, Istanbul 141, 149
  Venezuelan immigrants, Brazil
    integration 53–54, 57–62
    research methodology 49–51
    right to 54–57
  see also schools
educational integration 127
educational sociology 56
Elias, N. 139, 143
emotional attachments 193, 197
emotional dislocation 192
emotional geographies of home 190–205
  emotions about home 197–205
  research methodology 195–197
  theoretical framework 190–195
empathy 225
employment 107, 173, 228
  see also occupational integration; work
encounters 66–67, 75–77, 140, 191–192, 233
Erel, U. 16
ethnic minority groups 228
ethnography 50
Europe 132
exclusion 34–35, 103–104, 108, 192
  see also discrimination; integration
exclusion spaces 150
experience-centred approach to data analysis 178–179
exposure to host society 121, 130–133

F

Fainstein, S. 8
familiar strangers 67
family planning 94–95
Farris, S. 35
fear, spaces of 173–174
feelings see emotions
fellow feeling 225, 230
fluid encounters 66–67
food 131, 180, 203, 228
forced migration 34
foreigners 4
France 35, 38
Frederiksen, M. 32, 37, 40
Freire, P. 56, 57
future homes 200–202

G

gatekeepers 123
gender 165, 169
gender segregation see purdah culture
geographies of resistance 181
Germany
  as host country 1
  participatory theatre project 18–30
    empirical analysis 20–27
    methodological approach 18–20
    researcher presence 27–29
Giddens, A. 158
Gilligan, C. 156
Gilroy, P. 73
girls 170
  see also child marriage; South Africa: young migrant women in
Global Trends report (UNHCR) 1
Goffman, E. 74, 146
gospel music 209, 214–215, 219–220, 221
Greater Amman Municipality (GAM) 110, 111
Greenland 36
Griffiths, M.B.E. 82
group identity 160–161
Guglielmi, S. 90
Gunaratnam, Y. 228
Gyatso, Tenzin see Dalai Lama

H

habitus 140, 148
Hækkerup, N. 37
hair salons 170
  research in 175–184
    research approach 177–179
    research findings 179–183
Hannan, D. 225
Healey, P. 113
healthcare 93–95, 180–181
  see also hospitals
healthcare professionals 228
Hénaff, M. 154
Hennink, M. 124
hidden spaces 171–173, 174, 181, 233
hijab 87
Hindi 130
Hochschild, A. 193
home 182
  emotional geographies of 190–205
    emotions about home 197–205
    research methodology 195–197
    theoretical framework 190–195
  future homes 200–202
  see also private spaces
homemaking through music 209–221
  biographical trajectories 212–214
  leaving a conflict-afflicted home 214–216
  mega-cities as sites of opportunities 217–220
  theoretical framework 210–212

INDEX

hope 144, 171, 183, 200–202, 204, 211
Hopkins, P.E. 109
hospitable attention and listening 225, 226
hospitals 176
host countries 1
host society
  exposure to 121, 130–133
  receptivity 121, 129–130
Hou, F. 120–121
housing 196
Huang, S. 183
human rights law 4
Human Rights Watch 180

I

identity/identities
  Australian 154
  and belonging 109, 233
  and home 194
  immigrant boys, Denmark 42
  as narrative 232
  Sudanese and South Sudanese Youths, Australia 158–161, 162–163, 164
  Syrian students, Istanbul 139–140, 142–149
  Tibetan refugees, India 128, 134–135
  see also positionality
Igarassu 48, 57, 60
illegal immigrants 173
immigrant boys *see invandrerdrenge* (immigrant boys) discourse; migrant boys
immigrants
  social climate towards 121, 129
  'western' v. 'non-western' 33, 38
  see also migration
Immigration Restriction Act 1901, Australia 154
in-betweenness 198–199
in-depth interviews 124, 141–142
inclusion spaces 150–151
inclusive cities 101, 102–104, 106–112
inclusive urban planning 101–114, 231–232
  intercultural, inclusive and just cities 102–104
  research findings 106–112
  research methodology 104–106
Independent 226
India
  Tibetan refugees 117–136, 235
    belonging 119–122, 125–133, 134, 135–136
    Bylakuppe settlement 122–123
    migration towards India 118–119
    research project
      data analysis 125–133
      observation and interviews 124–125
      participant recruitment 123–124
Indigenous children 35–36
Indigenous land ownership 154

Indonesia 172, 175–176, 181
infrastructural perspective 6–7
injustice 8
Instituto Unibanco 55
integration 49, 52, 59
  economic 121, 127–129
  educational 127 (*see also* Venezuelan immigrants, Brazil: integration into public education)
  see also belonging; civic integration programmes; exclusion
intercultural cities 102–104
intercultural place-making 103, 109, 112
interculturality 62
internalisation project, Brazil 52–53
internally displaced people 1, 2, 4
international displacement 1
international human rights law 4
international students 195, 196, 198, 200–201
intersectional story-work 29
interviews 124, 141–142
invandrerdrenge (immigrant boys)
  discourse 32–34, 37–39, 235
  reactions to 40–42
invisibility 172, 175
invisible spaces 179–181
Iqbal, S. 228
Ireland
  migrant men's emotional geographies 190–205
    emotions about home 197–204
    research methodology 195–197
    theoretical framework 190–195
Irish migrant nurses 193
Islamic law 83
Istanbul, Syrian students in 139–151
  identities and spaces 139–140, 142–149
  research methodology 141–142
  social functions of spaces 149–151
  socioeconomic backgrounds 140–141

J

Jacobs, J. 113
Jewellery Bill, Denmark 36
Johannesburg 171
Jordan
  inclusive urban planning
    research findings 106–112
    research methodology 104–106
judicial spaces 145–146, 150
just city 8, 102–104
justice 7–9
Justice and the Politics of Difference (Young) 8

K

Kihato, C.W. 172, 176, 182
King, M. L., Jr 225
Kinshasa 209, 216, 217–219

L

language 57, 58, 59, 61, 233
language proficiency 121, 130
language skills 72
Lefebvre, H. 8, 103, 231
legal status 35, 54, 121
  see also illegal immigrants
Leibzig, Germany
  participatory theatre project 18–30
    empirical analysis 20–27
    methodological approach 18–20
    researcher presence 27–29
Libya 4
Lofland, L. 66, 67, 70, 76
London 226, 227–228
Lyytinen, E. 215

M

Maalouf, A. 112–113
Majavu, M. 155
Malaysia
  Islamic law 83
  Rohingya refugee women 10, 81–96, 235
    background 83–85
    education 91–93
    marriage 87–89
      confinement after 89–91
    public health facilities 93–95
    purdah culture 85–87
    research study 82–83
male migrants
  emotional geographies 190–205
    emotions about home 197–204
    research methodology 195–197
    theoretical framework 190–195
  see also invandrerdrenge (immigrant boys)
    discourse; migrant boys
Mallett, S. 191, 193
Mann, G. 182
Mapedzahama, V. 154, 163
marriage *see* child marriage
Marshall, L.W. 3
Massey, D. 108, 140, 192
master status 158
Mbembe, A. 230
media coverage 225–226
medical facilities *see* healthcare; hospitals
mental health 155
Mexican migration 54
migrant boys 182–183, 231
  see also invandrerdrenge (immigrant
    boys) discourse
Migrant City (Back and Sinha) 226–227
migrant-refugee distinction 210–211
migrant workers 228
migration 5–7
  within Africa 210
  South Africa 174

Tibetan refugees 118–119
  see also immigrants
Milgram, S. 67
Minh-ha, T.T. 17
Mino Danmark 41–42
mixed groups 15, 17, 18
monasteries 122–123
mortality rates 228
mosques 87, 143, 203
motherhood 179–181
Mozambican migrants, South
  Africa 169–184
  motherhood 179–181
  research approach 177–179
  research project 175–177
  securitised migration and spaces of
    fear 173–174
  support systems 181–183
  urban context and hidden spaces 171–173
music 133, 232
  homemaking through 209–221
    biographical trajectories 212–214
    leaving a conflict-afflicted home 214–216
    mega-cities as sites of
      opportunities 217–220
    theoretical framework 210–212
music engineering 220
music ministry 219–220
Muslims 33, 35, 38, 71, 144
  see also purdah culture

N

navigation 211
negotiated reality 139, 233
Nepal 118
Netherlands 35
  see also Amsterdam; Dutch language
newcomers 139, 143
non-governmental organisations (NGOs) 147–148
non-refoulement principle 4
'non-western' immigrants 33, 38

O

occupational integration 127–128
Oliveira, G. 54
open spaces 149, 151
Organisation of African Unity 4

P

Pakistan 1
Palestine refugees 1, 2, 5
participant observation 50, 124, 141–142
participatory theatre 14–15, 232
  citizenship and belonging 16–18
  research project 18–30
    empirical analysis 20–27
    methodological approach 18–20
    researcher presence 27–29
people smugglers 87–89

INDEX

People's Republic of China *see* China
Pernamnuco, Brazil 53
Phillips, D. 144
piece jobs 181
pity 225
place-making, intercultural 103, 109, 112
planetary listening 230
poetry 229
 see also pronoun poems; slam poetry
police 162–163
political community 109
politics 231–232
 of belonging 231
 of dispossession 34–37
 of refusal 36–37, 42
Politiken (newspaper) 40
popular culture 212, 232
 see also music
Portuguese language 58, 59
positionality 28, 29, 142, 213–214
power differences 213
power relations
 geographies of home 194
 and interview locations 106
 and storytelling 17
 Syrian students, Istanbul 139, 140, 143, 145
 Tibetan refugees, India 135
Prakash, L.O. 119
pregnancy 94–95
Pritchard, P. 10
private-public spaces 170, 175–177, 182
 see also (semi-)public spaces
private spaces 146–147, 150
 see also home
privateness 234
privilege 28
pronoun poems 156–157, 158–159, 160–161, 162–163
public education, Brazil
 integration of Venezuelan immigrants 53–54, 57–62
 research methodology 49–51
 refugee/migrant youth's right to 54–57
public health facilities 93–95
public insecurity 32, 37–38, 42
public space(s) 3, 9, 103, 146, 154, 232–234
 Denmark 32, 33, 38, 39, 41, 42, 43
 Germany 18, 19, 20
 and home 191–193
  emotions about 195, 197–204
 and music 212
 Sudanese and South Sudanese Youths, Australia 157–163
 Syrian students, Istanbul 147, 150
 see also (semi-)public spaces; private-public spaces
public transport 145, 146
publicness 232–234
purdah culture 81–82, 85–87, 93, 96, 235

Q

Quick Urban Diagnosis 50, 53

R

racial identity 158–160, 162–163
racial profiling 161–163
racialisation 39
 see also invandrerdrenge (immigrant boys) discourse
racialised dispossession 33, 34–37
racialised exclusion 34–35
racism 27, 71, 164, 202, 225–226
Rajiman, R. 135
Razack, S. 17, 26
Rea, A. 4
reception 52
receptivity of host society 121, 129–130
recognition 3, 157, 164–165
refugee children 6, 49, 53, 91
 see also refugee youth
Refugee Convention 1951 (UNHCR) 3, 5
refugee law, Brazil 53
refugee-migrant distinction 210–211
refugee youth 2–3
 non-refoulement principle 4
 research on 5, 6, 10
 and urban space 9
 see also unaccompanied minors
refugees
 definitions 3–5, 78n1
 Global South 210
 Jordan 104
 Malaysia 84
 numbers 1, 2
refusal, politics of 36–37, 42
relationships 182
religious neighbourhoods 142–143
reproductive health 94–95
resident permits 121, 141
resistance 183
 geographies of 181
 see also recognition
Revuz, C. 59
right to the city 8, 103, 109, 231
risk-taking 23, 29
Ritzau (newsagency) 40
Rockwell, E. 50
Rohingya refugee women, Malaysia 10, 81–96, 235
 background 83–85
 education 91–93
 marriage 87–89
  confinement after 89–91
 public health facilities 93–95
 purdah culture 85–87
 research study 82–83
Russell, A. 211–212
Russian invasion of Ukraine 1, 225
Ryan, L. 193

S

Sanchez, A. 23
Sassen, S. 9
Save the Children 169–170, 172, 179, 183–184
Schapendonk, J. 213
Schensul, S.L. 124
schools 123, 126
  see also education
search-and-seize orders 8
segregated spaces 142–143, 144, 150
  see also Bylakuppe settlement; self-segregation
segregation by gender *see* purdah culture
self-assertion 26
self-segregation 145
(semi-)public spaces 65–78
  building connections through 66–67
  encounters in 75–77
  participatory research methods 67–69
  reluctance to navigate 70–72
  strategies to navigate 72
  use of 72–75
  see also private-public spaces
Sera monastery 122–123, 124
sexualised violence 21
Shaker Ardekani, R. 71
silence
  as articulation 24–27, 28
  as disarticulation 20–24
  right to 17
Simpson, A. 36
Sinha, S. 226
slam poetry 209, 217–219
Smets, K. 235
social capital 120, 126–127, 149, 233
social climate towards immigrants 121, 129
social interactions 75–76, 91, 112
  see also encounters
social locations 120
social media 40, 41, 212, 213
social networks 120–121, 126, 180
  see also support systems
society's receptivity 121, 129–130
sociology of education 56
Soja, E. 7–8, 135
solidarity 181–182
Sonn, C. 18
South Africa
  young migrant women in 169–184, 235
    motherhood 179–181
    research approach 177–179
    research project 175–177
    securitised migration and spaces of fear 173–174
    support systems 181–183
    urban context and hidden spaces 171–173
South Sudan 1, 153
South Sudanese Youths, Australia 153–165
  experiences in public spaces 157–163
  research method 155–157

space 140
third space theory 134–135
spaces
  of care 191
  cooperational 147–149, 151
  of fear 173–174
  hidden 171–173, 174, 181, 233
  invisible 179–181
  judicial 145–146, 150
  open 149, 151
  private 146–147, 150 (*see also* home)
  private-public 170, 175–177, 182 (*see also* (semi-)public spaces)
  segregated 142–143, 144, 150
  social functions 149–151
  urban 9–10, 103–104, 139
  see also comfort zones; public space(s)
Spanish language 57, 58, 59, 61
spatial justice 7–9
sports 74–75
Stam, V. 16
statelessness 117
Statistics Denmark 32–33
stories/storying 15, 16–18, 232
  intersectional story-work 29
  return of stories 24–27
  withdrawal of stories 20–24
stranger danger 66, 71
strangers
  biographical 66, 70
  cultural 66, 70, 71
  familiar 67
Street, A. 176
stress 74–75
Sudanese Youths, Australia 153–165
  experiences in public spaces 157–163
  research method 155–157
support systems 181–183
  see also social networks
symbolic interactionism 140
Syria 1
Syrian migrants 139
Syrian society 86
Syrian students, Istanbul 139–151
  identities and spaces 139–140, 142–149
  research methodology 141–142
  social functions of spaces 149–151
  socioeconomic backgrounds 140–141

T

Tanzania 215, 219–220
Tashi Lhunpo monastery 123
thematic data analysis 125
Thembisa 171
third space theory 134–135
Thrift, N. 144
Tibetan refugees, India 117–136, 235
  belonging 119–122, 125–133, 134, 135–136
  Bylakuppe settlement 122–123

migration towards India 118–119
research project
  data analysis 125–133
  observation and interviews 124–125
  participant recruitment 123–124
translocalism 7, 197–200, 204
Trump, D. 38
trust 23, 71, 91, 105, 163, 175, 203, 215, 217
Turkey
  as host country 1
  refugee law 5
  Syrian students 139–151
    identities and spaces 139–140, 142–149
    research methodology 141–142
    social functions of spaces 149–151
    socioeconomic backgrounds 140–141

U

Uganda 1
Ukrainian refugees 1, 225
unaccompanied minors 6
United Nations Children's Fund (UNICEF) 49, 52, 82
United Nations High Commissioner for Refugees (UNHCR) 1, 2
  financial support from 107
  Refugee Convention 1951 3, 5
  Rohingya refugees, Malaysia 83
  UNHCR cards 84–85, 93, 94, 95
  support for artists 218–219
  Venezuelan immigrants, Brazil 52, 53
United Nations Refugee Agency support centres 112
United Nations Relief and Works Agency (UNRWA) 1, 2, 5
United States 33, 54, 61, 132, 155
universities 141
urban planning, inclusive 101–114, 231–232
  intercultural, inclusive and just cities 102–104
  research findings 106–112
  research methodology 104–106
urban space 9–10, 103–104, 139
  see also public space

V

Valentine, G. 146
Venezuela 1
Venezuelan immigrants, Brazil 48–49
  context of arrival 51–54
  integration into public education 53–54, 57–62
  research methodology 49–51
  numbers 62n1
  right to education 54–57
Vigh, H. 211
visibility 157–158, 162, 163, 234–236
  see also invisibility
visible difference 158, 160–161

voice-centred relational methodology (VCRM) 156, 164
volunteering 148

W

Wahab, A.A. 87
Walker, R. 179–180, 183
Western culture 133
'western' immigrants 33
White, N. 226
Whiteness/whiteness 23, 24, 29, 154, 158, 163
Wise, A. 71, 73
women
  Rohingya refugee women, Malaysia 10, 81–96, 235
    background 83–85
    education 91–93
    marriage 87–89
      confinement after 89–91
    public health facilities 93–95
    purdah culture 85–87
    research study 82–83
  Tibetan refugees, India 124
  Venezuelan immigrants, Brazil 53
  young migrant women, South Africa 169–184, 235
    motherhood 179–181
    research approach 177–179
    research project 175–177
    securitised migration and spaces of fear 173–174
    support systems 181–183
    urban context and hidden spaces 171–173
Wood, P. 111
work
  Rohingya refugees, Malaysia 85, 86, 90, 95
  Tibetan refugees, India 121
  young migrant women, South Africa 172, 174, 181
  see also employment; occupational integration

X

xenophobia 180
xenophobic violence 171, 173, 192

Y

Young, I.M. 8
young people *see* refugee youth; women: young migrant women, South Africa
youth 104–105
Youth Home study 195–204
  findings 197–204
  research methodology 195–197
Yuval-Davis, N. 158, 192, 232

Z

Zamani, N. 40

www.ingramcontent.com/pod-product-compliance
Lightning Source LLC
Chambersburg PA
CBHW070042040426
42333CB00041B/1959